Frommer's®

P O R T A B L E

Venice

7th Edition

by Darwin Porter & Danforth Prince

Here's what critics say about Frommer's:

"Amazingly easy to use. Very portable, very complete."

—*Booklist*

"Detailed, accurate, and easy-to-read information for all price ranges."

—*Glamour Magazine*

WILEY

Wiley Publishing, Inc.

Published by:

WILEY PUBLISHING, INC.

111 River St.
Hoboken, NJ 07030-5774

ISBN 978-0-470-39904-0

Editor: Stephen Bassman
Production Editor: Jana M. Stefanciosa
Cartographer: Andrew Murphy
Photo Editor: Richard Fox
Production by Wiley Indianapolis Composition Services

For information on our other products and services or to obtain technical support, please contact our Customer Care Department within the U.S. at 800/762-2974, outside the U.S. at 317/572-3993 or fax 317/572-4002.

Wiley also publishes its books in a variety of electronic formats. Some content that appears in print may not be available in electronic formats.

Manufactured in the United States of America

5   4   3   2   1

Contents

List of Maps

ABOUT THE AUTHORS

As a team of veteran travel writers, **Darwin Porter** and **Danforth Prince** have produced titles for Frommer's including guides to Italy, France, the Caribbean, England, and Germany. A film critic, columnist, and broadcaster, Porter is also a Hollywood biographer and author of *Brando Unzipped*, documenting the private life of Marlon Brando, and *Jacko: His Rise and Fall*, a biography of the tumultuous life of Michael Jackson. Prince was formerly employed by the Paris bureau of the *New York Times* and is currently the president of Blood Moon Productions and other media-related firms. Porter and Prince's latest non-travel-related venture, jointly co-authored and published in 2008 by Blood Moon, is *Hollywood Babylon—It's Back!*, which one critic described as "the hottest compilation of inter-generational scandal in the history of Hollywood."

AN INVITATION TO THE READER

In researching this book, we discovered many wonderful places—hotels, restaurants, shops, and more. We're sure you'll find others. Please tell us about them, so we can share the information with your fellow travelers in upcoming editions. If you were disappointed with a recommendation, we'd love to know that, too. Please write to:

Frommer's Portable Venice, 7th Edition
Wiley Publishing, Inc. • 111 River St. • Hoboken, NJ 07030-5774

AN ADDITIONAL NOTE

Please be advised that travel information is subject to change at any time—and this is especially true of prices. We therefore suggest that you write or call ahead for confirmation when making your travel plans. The authors, editors, and publisher cannot be held responsible for the experiences of readers while traveling. Your safety is important to us, however, so we encourage you to stay alert and be aware of your surroundings. Keep a close eye on cameras, purses, and wallets, all favorite targets of thieves and pickpockets.

FROMMER'S STAR RATINGS, ICONS & ABBREVIATIONS

Every hotel, restaurant, and attraction listing in this guide has been ranked for quality, value, service, amenities, and special features using a **star-rating system.** In country, state, and regional guides, we also rate towns and regions to help you narrow down your choices and budget your time accordingly. Hotels and restaurants are rated on a scale of zero (recommended) to three stars (exceptional). Attractions, shopping, nightlife, towns, and regions are rated according to the following scale: zero stars (recommended), one star (highly recommended), two stars (very highly recommended), and three stars (must-see).

In addition to the star-rating system, we also use **seven feature icons** that point you to the great deals, in-the-know advice, and unique experiences that separate travelers from tourists. Throughout the book, look for:

Finds	Special finds—those places only insiders know about
Fun Fact	Fun facts—details that make travelers more informed and their trips more fun
Kids	Best bets for kids and advice for the whole family
Moments	Special moments—those experiences that memories are made of
Overrated	Places or experiences not worth your time or money
Tips	Insider tips—great ways to save time and money
Value	Great values—where to get the best deals

The following **abbreviations** are used for credit cards:

AE	American Express	DISC	Discover	V	Visa
DC	Diners Club	MC	MasterCard		

FROMMERS.COM

Now that you have this guidebook to help you plan a great trip, visit our website at **www.frommers.com** for additional travel information on more than 4,000 destinations. We update features regularly to give you instant access to the most current trip-planning information available. At Frommers.com, you'll find scoops on the best airfares, lodging rates, and car rental bargains. You can even book your travel online through our reliable travel booking partners. Other popular features include:

- Online updates of our most popular guidebooks
- Vacation sweepstakes and contest giveaways
- Newsletters highlighting the hottest travel trends
- Podcasts, interactive maps, and up-to-the-minute events listings
- Opinionated blog entries by Arthur Frommer himself
- Online travel message boards with featured travel discussions

The Best of Venice

You don't exactly have to jump on the next plane to see Venice while it's still around, but scientists are warning that only a miracle—or more advanced engineering than exists today—can save one of the world's most fabled cities of art and architecture, especially in view of global warming and the possibilities of ocean levels rising 6m (20 ft.).

Reports indicate that Venice is sinking faster than had been anticipated. The gloomiest forecast is that the encroaching waters of the Adriatic Sea could devastate Venice within this century, especially if global warming causes waters to rise even faster.

What a catastrophe that would be. Surely there is no more preposterous monument to the folly of humankind than *La Serenissima,* the Serene Republic of Venice, a fantasy city on the sea.

Once you arrive and are stunned by all the architectural wonders and riches of Venice, its vivid colors of sienna, Roman gold, and ruby peach, you may think that reports of tide damage are overblown. Once you experience your first flood and see for yourself how close the sea is to sweeping over Venice, you'll most likely change your mind.

Pollution, uncontrolled tides, and just plain old creaky age are eating away daily at the treasures of this cherished city of art. As the debate rages about how to save Venice, with no real solution in sight, the waters just keep rising.

Why did those "insane" Venetians build on such swampy islands and not on dry land, of which there was plenty centuries ago?

In an effort to flee the barbarians, Venetians left dry dock and drifted out to a flotilla of "uninhabitable" islands in the lagoon. For a long time, Venice did elude foreign armies intent on burning, looting, and plundering. Eventually, Napoleon and his forces arrived; however, the Corsican's intent was never to destroy Venice.

Foreign visitors have conquered Venice in ways most barbarian armies did not. Millions of people visit Venice every year. Since Venice is known as an expensive city and has only a limited number of accommodations, there are countless day-trippers invading every day, all summer long. Few Venetians desire the presence of so many day-trippers, as they tend to spend little money. Some Venetian officials, to counter the presence of these nonspenders, have advocated that the city institute an admission charge.

Those who spend the night and dine in the restaurants are received with a much warmer embrace by the merchants, hoteliers, and restaurateurs. But even these big spenders are viewed with a certain disdain by Venetians, who'd rather have their city to themselves. However, high prices have forced out many locals, who've fled across the lagoon to dreary Mestre, an industrial complex launched to help boost the regional economy and make it far less dependent on tourism. Mestre, with its factories, helps keep Venice relatively industry-free, though it spews pollution across the city—hardly what the art of Venice needs.

The capital of the Veneto, Venice encompasses some 466 sq. km (180 sq. miles), if Mestre, Marghera, and the islands of the lagoon are counted. Of these square kilometers, about 260 (100 sq. miles) are water. The city is built around some 117 islands or, as is often the case, "islets." Venice is bisected by 177 canals, including its showcase artery, the *palazzo-* (palace-) flanked Grand Canal. The islands are joined together by 400 small concrete-and-iron bridges, the most important of which are the Accademia, the Degli Scalzi, and the Rialto, all spanning the Grand Canal. Venice itself is connected to the mainland by a 5km (3-mile) bridge that crosses the Venetian lagoon to Mestre.

What will you find in Venice? Unendurable crowds; dank, dark canals and even danker, claustrophobic alleys; outrageous prices; and a certain sinister quality in the decay. But you'll also find one of the most spectacular cities ever conceived.

1 Frommer's Favorite Venice Experiences

- **Riding the Grand Canal in a Gondola:** Just before sunset, order some delectable sandwiches from Harry's Bar and a bottle of chilled *prosecco* (a type of sparkling wine), then take someone you love on a gondola ride along the Grand Canal for the boat trip of a lifetime.
- **Sipping Cappuccino on Piazza San Marco:** Select a choice spot on one of the world's most famous squares, order a cappuccino, listen to the classical music, and absorb the special atmosphere of Venice.
- **Sunning on the Lido:** The world has seen better beaches, but few sights equal the parade of flesh and humanity on this fashionable beach on a hot summer day.

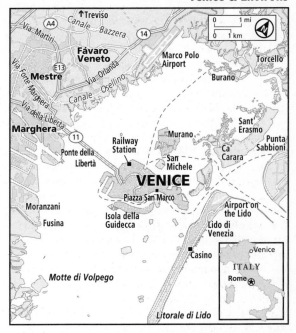

- **Contemplating Giorgione's *Tempest:*** If you have time to see only one painting, make it this one at the Accademia. The artist's haunting sense of oncoming menace superimposed over a bucolic setting will stay with you long after you leave Venice.
- **Trailing Titian to the High Renaissance:** Known for his technical skill, use of brilliant color, and robust style, Titian was a master of the High Renaissance. In Venice you can see some of this great painter's major works (the ones Napoleon didn't haul off to Paris) in the Accademia, Santa Maria Gloriosa dei Frari, and Santa Maria della Salute.
- **Spending a Day on Torcello:** Of all the islands in the lagoon, our favorite is Torcello, the single best day trip from Piazza San Marco. Visit to see Santa Maria Assunta, the first cathedral of Venice and home to splendid 11th- and 12th-century mosaics. But also come to explore the island, wandering around at leisure in a place time seems to have forgotten. Follow your discoveries with a lunch of cannelloni at Locanda Cipriani, and the day is yours.

- **Making a Pub-Crawl in Search of *Cicchetti:*** There's no better way to escape the tourists and mingle with locals than wandering Venice's back streets in search of local color, drink, and *cicchetti* (the local version of tapas). By the time you've made the rounds, you'll have had a great time and a full meal—everything from deep-fried mozzarella and artichoke hearts to mixed fish fries and pizza. Finish, of course, with an ice cream at a gelateria. A good place to start a pub-crawl is Campo San Bartolomeo near the Rialto Bridge—one of Venice's authentic neighborhoods.

- **Paying a Visit to the World's Greatest Outdoor Market:** When you tire of Gothic glory and High Renaissance masterpieces, head for the **Il Mercato di Rialto (Rialto Market,** p. 91). Here you can sample local life and see what the Venetians are going to have for dinner. Barges, or *mototopi,* arrive throughout the day loaded with the rich produce of the Veneto area. Somehow, blood-red oranges are bloodier here, fresh peas more tender and greener than elsewhere, and red radicchios redder. Of course, you'll get to meet all the sea creatures from the lagoon as well. Sample a pastry fresh from a hot oven at some little hole in the wall, then cap your visit at the vendors' favorite place, the **Cantina do Mori,** Calle del Do Mori 429 (ⓒ **041-5225401,** p. 160), where you can belt down a glass of wine made from Tocai grapes. There's been a tavern at this site since 1462.

- **Wandering Around Dorsoduro:** Dorsoduro attracts everybody coming to see the Peggy Guggenheim Collection or the Accademia—but few stick around to explore the neighborhood in any depth. Susanna Agnelli, sister of Gianni Versace, keeps a place here, as do many wealthy industrialists who could afford to live anywhere. Yet parts are so seedy as to look haunted. The most intriguing promenade is the Zattere, running the length of the district along the Giudecca Canal.

- **Visiting the Island of the Dead:** For a Venetian, "the last gondola ride" is to **San Michele,** in a traditional funeral gondola decorated with golden angels. San Michele is a walled cemetery island shaded by massive cypresses, and there's no place quite like it. Celebrities are buried here, but so are ordinary Venetians. Time stands still in more ways than one at this cemetery. There's no more room here; today, Venice has to send its dead to the mainland for burial. But poet Ezra Pound, who lived in Venice from 1959 until his death in 1972, made it just in time. It's reached by *vaporetto* (public motorboat) no. 52, running from Piazza San Marco to Murano.

- **Seeing the Sun Rise on the Lagoon:** For us, there's no more enthralling experience than to get up before dawn and cross the lagoon to San Giorgio Maggiore. Architect Andrea Palladio knew exactly what he was doing when he created the church on this exact spot. The church faces Piazza San Marco and the entrance to the Grand Canal. While the tourist zillions are still asleep, waiting to overtake the city, you'll have Venice to yourself as the sun comes up. The architectural ensemble seen in the first glow of dawn, the panorama in all directions as the city awakens, ranks as one of the greatest man-made spectacles on earth.

- **Experiencing Venice at 2am:** You'll truly know the meaning of the word *spectacular* when sitting at 2am on an outdoor seat on *vaporetto* no. 1 as it circles Venice. Only the most die-hard night owls will be on board with you. With its twinkling lights and "Titian blue" skies, Venice at this time takes on an aura unique in Europe. It's very quiet at this hour (except for the sound of the *vaporetto's* motor). Perhaps a gondola will silently glide by. The buildings themselves take on a different mood and color, looking like ghostly mansions from another time. When you get back home, this experience may be the one that lingers longer in your memory than any other.

2 Best Bets for Accommodations

See chapter 4 for full reviews of hotels in all price ranges.

- **Best Historic Hotel:** Hemingway called it "my home in Venice," and the **Gritti Palace,** Campo Santa Maria del Giglio (© **041-794611**), still rules supreme for those lucky enough to afford its celestial price tags. The 15th-century *palazzo* of a former doge opens onto the Grand Canal in the heart of Venice. It's like living in a museum, but with all the grand comforts. See p. 41.

- **Best for Value:** In a tranquil part of Venice near the Doge's Palace, **Ca' Dei Dogi,** Corte Santa Scolastica (© **041-2413759**), combines luxury and value at the same time, a condition you'll almost never encounter in Venice. Each individually decorated bedroom is the epitome of comfort and style. See p. 45.

- **Best-Kept Secret:** Opening onto the Grand Canal, **Locanda Vivaldi,** Riva degli Schiavoni 4152 (© **041-27770477**), is one of the best examples of recycling in Venice: It was once the private home of composer Antonio Vivaldi (1678–1741).

Bedrooms are comfortably lush, and the hotel is appropriately adorned with baroque ornamentation. See p. 48.

- **Best Boutique Hotel:** Near the Accademia, **Ca' Pisani,** Dorsoduro 979A (℗ **041-2401411**), a hotel of charm and grace, was originally constructed at the end of the 16th century by a Venetian nobleman. With its wide variety of bedrooms, it's a stylish address that successfully combines modern technology with tradition. See p. 55.
- **Best for a Romantic Getaway:** A one-of-a-kind hotel, the oddly named **DD724,** Dorsoduro 724 (℗ **041-2770262**), near the Peggy Guggenheim Museum, is both luxurious and romantic, filled with modern art and elegant touches. It's perfect for a honeymoon, as no one will disturb you unless you need something—perhaps an intimate breakfast or a dinner reservation at an address where you'll never be found. See p. 55.
- **Best B&B:** The most patrician of the *pensioni* of Venice, **Pensione Accademia,** Fondamenta Bollani, Dorsoduro 1058 (℗ **041-5210188**), is an old-fashioned villa with Victorian-era furnishings and Gothic touches. This venerated choice has long endured as a favorite of the *Room with a View* crowd; it once served as the Russian embassy. See p. 56.

3 Best Bets for Dining

See chapter 5 for full reviews of restaurants in all price ranges.

- **Best for Romance:** Since 1907, **Taverna la Fenice,** Campiello de la Fenice, San Marco 1939 (℗ **041-5223856**), has stood near the opera house. It still lures with its old-fashioned, romantic atmosphere and its traditional, first-rate Venetian cuisine, specializing in fresh fish. See p. 66.
- **Best-Kept Secret:** Well off the beaten track, **Il Sole Sulla Vecia Cavana,** Rio Terrà SS. Apostoli, Cannaregio 4624 (℗ **041-5287106**), has existed in some form or other since the medieval era. Venetians regard it as a secret address, a place to go for authentic recipes, including fresh fish and shellfish. See p. 72.
- **Best Discovery of the Year:** Near Ponte di Rialto, **L'Osteria di Santa Marina,** Campo Santa Marina 5911 (℗ **041-5285239**), is rustic yet classic, serving a finely honed Venetian and traditional Italian cuisine in a cozy, warm setting. The team who runs this first-class restaurant is one of the most skilled in Venice, specializing only in deftly handled, market-fresh ingredients. See p. 73.

- **Best for Seafood:** In the San Polo district, **Osteria da Fiore,** Calle del Scaleter, San Polo 2202 (© **041-721308**), is the maritime restaurant supreme, known for serving the freshest and best-prepared fish in Venice. Here's your chance to dig into all those mysterious fish and shellfish you've been seeing in the open-air markets: tiny green crabs eaten shell and all, sweet Adriatic prawns, you name it—if it swims, it's here. See p. 75.

- **Best Old-Fashioned Inn:** Since World War II, this Dorsoduro legend, **Locanda Montin,** Fondamenta di Borgo, Dorsoduro 1147 (© **041-5227151**), has drawn diners as diverse as Brad Pitt and Jimmy Carter. Its take on international and Italian recipes, including fresh fish caught in the Adriatic, comes from time-tested recipes that have won repeat fans over the decades. See p. 77.

- **Best Dining in the Lagoon:** On the island of Torcello, reached by *vaporetto,* **Locanda Cipriani,** Piazza San Fosca 29 (© **041-730150**), is operated by the same folks who run the legendary Harry's Bar, the most famous restaurant in Venice. This old-fashioned and remote inn is far removed from the tourist bustle of Venice. Its location is romantic and elegant, and the Venetian cuisine—so beloved by Hemingway—is a time-tested favorite. Diners sit on the outdoor terrace in summer. See p. 80.

2

Venice in Depth

Venice no longer rules a huge part of the world, as it once did, and visitors today come to pay homage to its illustrious past when it reigned as "the Queen of the Adriatic." Through its port were shipped silk, spices, and coffee, which were hungrily received by parts of Europe. Its decline began when other ports moved in to capture the trade from the East.

Venice sank into a romantic decay, but the glory of its architecture and art remained to enchant future generations.

The beauty of Venice and its cultural eminence are just as powerful today as ever. Venice is unique, romantic, and magical. Before you arrive you may want to peruse this brief preview of what awaits you. You can learn something of its spectacular past and its art and architecture, and prepare to enjoy yourself at the Venetian table, consuming its superb food and wines from the neighboring Veneto.

1 Venice Today

With so many tourists thronging the streets, it's easy to believe that no locals live here. But they do, of course, sitting in their decaying palaces with rats in the basement and the floodwaters rising.

Vincente Rizzo, a local, told us, "I don't know which element will inundate us first—the hordes of tourists arriving daily at our doorstep or the rising waters of the Adriatic. We used to dominate that sea. Now it sweeps through St. Mark's Square every winter."

Another Italian, Vittorio Angeli, told us, "We're going, going, but far from gone. We fully expect to be around for at least another three generations. By then, we hope our great grandchildren will have developed the technology to save us from the unrelenting sea."

Cynics say Venice is overpriced, overcrowded, and overphotographed, and that may be true but **Le Serenissima,** as it is known, still holds the world in its thrall.

Venice today is often likened to an aging courtesan who simply applies another coat of heavy makeup to her face in a hopeless attempt to conceal her age. Of course, that belle of the ages has to raise her silk gown every now and then to keep it from getting wet.

Many Venetians since the 1950s have opted for the easier life, or at least the less expensive life, and have fled to the mainland. Thousands of others have decided to stay behind, refusing to leave this timeless seductress.

One of Peggy Guggenheim's young lovers once said, "I was born Venetian, and I plan to die Venetian. I will stay here for better or worse, because after experiencing the glories of Venice the rest of the world looks like a very dull place."

There are Venetians still left who dream of a great tomorrow, perhaps building an underground to unite Venice with the mainland. There are ideas to turn the city into various headquarters for international organizations, the way that Geneva has done.

There are opportunities opening that may make Venice a major port again with a thriving trade in the Mediterranean, not just the Adriatic. Other city planners want to turn Venice into "the cultural meeting place of the world."

Many who are genuinely concerned for the future of their city, and who desperately want it to be around to enchant generations in the 25th century and beyond, feel the *Serenissima* can find some real work to do, some real purpose, other than showing off past grandeur.

"So Venice lives in the past," said author John Berendt, who wrote *The City of Falling Angels,* "So what? At least Venice has a glorious past to live in."

2 Looking Back at Venice

THE EARLY SETTLERS   Fleeing Attila the Hun, "The Scourge of God," during the invasion of Italy by the barbarians, refugees fled in the wake of the advancing armies from the north. Unknown to them at the time, they would lay the foundation of the world's most beautiful city, but that would be centuries later.

The site they chose was a geographical disaster, a series of isolated islands in impregnable shallows and mud banks. Once here, these refugees discovered a small colony of hearty fishermen, who had been living in isolation, perhaps for centuries.

The major part of this mass evacuation from the mainland occurred around A.D. 452. A series of lagoon communities grew up governed by the Ostrogoths of Ravenna. However, this Ostrogoth kingdom, including the Venetian islands, was later conquered by the Byzantine general Belisarius, in A.D. 539.

The early Venetians not only had to worry about barbarian invasions from the mainland, but they also were attacked by pirates from the sea.

Venetians sided with the Byzantines in their overthrow of the Gothic capital of Ravenna. By doing so, the lagoon settlers of Venice found new allies in the East. The Byzantines granted them trading privileges, which led to the first wave of prosperity for Venice.

The Venetian ruler, the aptly named Narses the Eunuch, ordered that a church be built in Venice and dedicated to St. Theodore. That church was constructed over the present site of today's Basilica of St. Mark.

In A.D. 568 a massive invasion of northern Italy by more barbarians, the pillaging Lombards, led to more migration to the lagoons. The little towns of Grado, Malamocco, and Torcello were settled. By 639 the Bishop of Altino founded a cathedral on Torcello, an island that is a popular tourist attraction today.

From 568 to 810 the lagoon settlers were a thriving community, living in wood-and-thatch houses with fishing boats tied up at their front doors. Historians have said that the Venetians held up a candle against the ignorance of the Dark Ages.

The year of 697 marked a turning point in Venetian history, as citizens threw off at least part of the yoke of Byzantium and elected Paulo Lucio Anafesto as their first "Dux" or doge. Thus, began the long rule of Venice by a series of doges—some excellent, some good, some bad, and others a complete disaster. A dozen lagoon townships were formed, eventually emerging into the State of Venice.

THE QUEEN OF THE ADRIATIC   In its struggle for freedom from foreigners, a *Pax Nicephori* was reached between Charlemagne and the Byzantine emperor between the years 811 and 814. Under this new agreement Venice became a semi-independent province of Byzantium.

Around 828 an important theft took place. The body of St. Mark was stolen from his tomb in Alexandria by two Venetian merchants and shipped to Venice. The doge, Anelo Partecipazio, ruling from the newly established government at Rialto in Venice, ordered that St. Mark replace St. Theodore as patron saint of the city.

The first church of San Marco was constructed on the site, and this movement seemed to symbolize the creation of a united Venice. A new wave of imperialism and prosperity was about to dawn for the city.

By 1000 the seafaring people of Venice were in control of the coasts of Dalmatia and Croatia. The takeover of the Dalmatian coast was a direct result of pirates raiding Venetian ships and harassing their trade as well as making off with the cargo. The pirates were crushed in their stronghold at Lagosta, which came under Venetian control.

In a political shake-up in 1032, the doge, Domenico Flabanico, abolished the ducal privilege of nominating colleagues and successors. This led to democratic reforms, including the establishment of a privy council and a senate.

In 1109 Venice joined the Crusades. By the time of the Fourth Crusade, the port had blossomed into "the Queen of the Adriatic." Proclaimed at Soissons, the Fourth Crusade saw Venice becoming the chief agent for transporting soldiers, horses, knights, and provisions. Its rivalry with the western ports of Genoa and Pisa grew even more intense.

Venetians in 1204 made a decision to attack Constantinople, which fell to their invading forces. In the partition of the spoils, Venice won "a half and a quarter of Byzantium."

The sack of Byzantium had been ordered by the blind doge Enrico Dandolo. Many of the greatest artistic treasures of the East, including the four bronze horses that for centuries adorned the roof of the Basilica of St. Mark, were brought back to Venice as booty.

Venice now ruled the Adriatic and the Ionian Islands as well as the trade route between Constantinople and western Europe. The Venetians also acquired the strategic island of Crete.

The journey of the Venetian merchant Marco Polo from Venice to China is one of the great stories of the Middle Ages. His adventures from 1271 to 1295 and his meeting with Genghis Khan are told in such books as *Il Milione.* Marco Polo became the first European merchant to open what became known as "the Silk Road."

THE COUNCIL OF TEN RULES WITH AN IRON FIST   The draconian Council of Ten came into being in the early 14th century, eventually becoming a permanent body in 1335. One of its functions was to hunt down and hang any conspirators of the government, including the Baiamonte Tiepolo, a rich merchant who had attempted to seize the government back in 1310.

The Council had other duties as well. Usurping power formerly held by the doge, it also looked after foreign policy and even found time to police the morals of the Venetians.

It was amazing that Venice continued to expand its empire, even though the Black Death of 1348 had left two-thirds of the population dead. A Venetian ship in 1347 had brought the disease from the Crimea where it had ravaged the Mongol Golden Horde.

Between 1350 and 1381, Venice fought an intermittent war with the Genoese fleet. Although the Venetian sailors suffered defeats, they destroyed the Genoese navy at the Battle of Chioggia in 1380. That victory allowed them to retain their supremacy in the eastern sector of the Mediterranean and it was marked by a new wave of imperial expansion.

Riding high, Venetians turned not just to the sea but inland, moving into mainland Italy and extending its empire as far west as Bergamo and Crema and east through the Friuli and Istrian peninsula.

Venice basked in prestige in 1406 when Angelo Correr became the first Venetian patrician to be elected pope. He ruled the Vatican as Gregory XII.

On the eastern front, the Turks continued to harass Venetian interests, resulting in the Battle at Negropont in 1416 in which the Venetian fleet emerged victorious. But the victory was only temporary, as the Ottoman Empire continued to be a threat.

In 1423 when Francesco Foscari was elected doge, Venice was at the apex of its glory, basking in its reputation as the richest city in Europe. It may also have been the largest city—or was that Paris?—in spite of its precarious geography. Venice certainly had the largest fleet in Europe, now that the sea power of Genoa was yesterday.

But trouble lay ahead. In 1453 the Turks took back Constantinople. Venice lost its territorial and commercial rights in the Byzantine Empire but signed trade agreements with the Turkish sultan anyway.

A new challenge came in 1487 when Vasco da Gama rounded the Cape of Good Hope. By the year 1489 the Portuguese adventurer reached Calcutta by sea. This shattered the monopoly that La Serenissima, as Venice was called, had on the riches of the East. Yet in spite of this setback, Venice that same year (1489) conquered the island of Cyprus.

In 1501 Leonardo Loredan ascended the throne as the doge, little knowing how he'd be tested in his position as Venice entered one of the greatest trials in its history. In France an army was mounted to move against Venetian territories, and in 1510 Venice was crushingly defeated at the Battle of Agnadello. When mercenaries hired by Venice deserted and went home, La Serenissima, without an army, lost its empire on mainland Italy in this single blow, although Treviso and Udine chose to remain under the banner of St. Mark. Although Venice was to regain some of its mainland territories, its hold on its empire was doomed to eventual defeat.

A LONG, SLOW DECLINE   In the Turkish War of 1537 to 1540, Venice chose the wrong side, allying itself with Spain. The invaders from the West were defeated by the Turks at the Battle of Prevenza in 1538. Venice was forced to sign a humiliating treaty with Turkey in 1540, which meant that the supremacy of the sea had passed from Venice to Turkey.

Venice tried for a comeback in 1571, when it was allied with the pope and Spain as part of the Holy League. The Christians emerged victorious at the battle of Lepanto on October 7, 1571. Even so, Venice suffered the loss of Cyprus in 1573. At home, the population of Venice, had dwindled down to 125,000 souls by 1581. Thirteen percent of the female population was working as prostitutes at the time. Venice had entered a long, slow period of decline.

Events grew worse and worse for the Venetians. In 1606 Pope Paul V excommunicated the Venetian Republic. Then in 1630 Venice was hit with the worst plague in its history. Some 60,000 citizens died, including the great artist Titian. Trouble never stopped for Venice, as a fire the following year ravaged the Doge's Palace.

In another humiliation in 1699, Venice lost Crete to the Turks. This was the last major Venetian possession outside the Adriatic. The Venetian empire was virtually at an end. At the Congress of Passarowitz in 1718, Venice was forced to surrender the Peloponnese (Morea) to the Turks, marking the end of Venetian power in the Eastern Mediterranean.

In the 18th century, other ports such as the Habsburg-controlled Trieste and the papal town of Ancona rose to rob Venice of its trade from both the Levant and the West. Its decline continued.

After staging its last naval battles with the pirates of Tunis from 1784 to 1786, Venice virtually retired as mistress of the Adriatic. By 1792 its once-great merchant fleet had declined to only 310 men. Its ships numbered four, its galliots seven.

By 1796 Piedmont fell and the Austrians were defeated from Montenotte to Lodi, their armies in retreat. Napoleon's soldiers crossed the frontiers of neutral Venice in pursuit. The Venetian Republic fell to Napoleon in 1797, and the Veneto was placed under Austrian rule as the price of peace with the French. That same year the last doge, Lodovico Manin, was deposed.

By 1805 Napoleon had changed his mind and ordered that Venice be absorbed back into the State of Italy. But by 1815 Napoleon was having its own problems, and Venice was returned to Austrian control. A revolt by Daniele Manin (no relation to the late doge) flared in 1848, leading to war against the Austrians. An independent republic was declared, but it lasted for only 5 months. The Austrians returned and held onto Venice until 1866 when the Prussians defeated Austria. The city of Venice was handed over to the newly created Italian state.

THE GLORY OF YESTERDAY   In the decades to come Venice reverted to just a provincial capital, its glory long gone. What remained was a city of stunning architectural beauty that future generations would flock to, restoring an economy that had completely stalled. During the 19th century Venice virtually faded from the history books. It was no longer a world player.

An industrial expansion began on the edge of the lagoon in the 1920s, and this provided employment for the local population.

All artistic activities in Venice were suspended during World War II. Its art exhibitions ended in 1942 and did not resume until 1948. Fortunately Venice was not bombed by the allies or the retreating Nazi armies. Both warring factions seemed to respect the most gorgeous city on earth. In a move not carried out by his general, Hitler had ordered the burning of Paris. No such edict was issued for Venice. Even Hitler may not have wanted to have as his legacy the dubious role of being the commander who had ordered the destruction of Venice.

By the 1950s most of the population of Venice had moved to Mestre on the mainland. In those days after World War II, tourists virtually had Venice to themselves. The floodgates of visitors continued throughout the 20th century at such a rate that one can hardly walk around the city today because of overcrowding. All the old buildings were left intact and Venice experienced no industrial or commercial growth.

Venice truly became a relic of yesterday and only occasionally made world headlines. Such publicity came on November 4, 1966, as the city experienced its worst flood. This led to the setting up of international funds to aid in the restoration of its buildings and works of art.

As Venice moves deeper into the millennium, hordes of tourists arrive like the barbarians of old. The leaders of Venice are considering treating Venice like a Disney attraction, charging a high admission just to enter this beautiful city in the lagoons.

Dateline

- 452   Fleeing the barbarians, settlers from the mainland arrive in the lagoon.
- 568   More settlers escape from mainland to populate Venice.
- 697   Venetians escape Byzantium and elect first doge.
- 828   Body of St. Mark, stolen from Alexandria, arrives in Venice and becomes patron saint.
- 1000   Venetian fleet destroys Dalmatian pirates and takes control of Adriatic Sea routes.

- 1032   Doges forbidden to nominate their own successors.
- 1109–1204   Venice joins crusades; sacks Constantinople, acquires colonies in the East.
- 1271–95   Marco Polo opens "the Silk Road" to the Far East.
- 1335   The draconian Council of Ten rules Venice with iron fist.
- 1348   Black Death kills two-thirds of population.
- 1381   Venice ends long-running battles with Genoa to emerge victorious at Chioggia.
- 1300–1400s   Venice expands empire to Italian mainland.
- 1453   Turks take back Constantinople.
- 1489   Venice acquires the island of Cyprus.
- 1510   League of Cambrai defeats Venice at Agnadello.
- 1573   Venice loses Cyprus.
- 1630   Black Death strikes again.
- 1699   Venice loses Crete to the Turks.
- 1718   Venice forced to surrender Peloponnese (Morea) to the Turks.
- 1797   The Venetian Republic falls to Napoleon's troops, as Austria rules the Veneto.
- 1805   Venice made part of Napoleon's Kingdom of Italy.
- 1815   Venice becomes part of Austro-Hungarian empire.
- 1866   Venice annexed to the Kingdom of Italy.
- 1920s   Venice citizens find industrial jobs on neighboring mainland.
- 1940–45   Venice spared bombardment in World War II.
- 1950s   Residential expansion of nearby Mestre leads to depopulation of Venice.
- 1966   Venice hit by worst flood in its history as international funds pour in to restore its art.
- 1960s–present   Venice becomes world tourist mecca.

3 Venice's Art & Architecture

BYZANTINE VENICE   Because of its lonely position in the lagoons, and the absence of the strong classical tradition of Rome, art and architecture in the 12th and 13th centuries adhered to the tenets of the Byzantine world.

But long before art and architecture flourished in Venice, an isolated cathedral, Santa Maria Assunta, was founded in 639 and has become the oldest surviving building in Venice. Of course, it's been altered and remodeled over the centuries, especially in the 9th and 11th centuries.

The most enduring monument, attracting visitors from around the world, is the Basilica di San Marco, founded in 829. The original church that stood here was modeled on the Church of the Apostles in Constantinople. The building standing today dates primarily from 1042 to 1085. It was constructed to receive the body of St. Mark which was stolen from Alexandria. Facing the huge Piazza San Marco, it still remains the center of Venetian life and is resplendent with its eastern character. The original basilica plan was altered to the Byzantine concept with a Greek cross and two transepts. There is a central dome as well as a dome over each arm of the cross. The sculptures, marbles, mosaics, and alabasters from the 12th and 15th centuries create more of a palace than a church.

GOTHIC VENICE   Next door to San Marco stands the Doge's Palace, which was substantially rebuilt in the 14th century, but not completed until the 15th century. The Doge's Palace represents the highest achievement of architecture in Venice and is the classic symbol of the city's beauty.

Built in the Gothic style, the building has two equal facades—one on the canal, one opening on the main square. Two tiers of delicate arcades are surrounded by walls faced with rose-colored marble. The solid weight of this upper part, resting on hundreds of white "legs" of the arcading, is pierced by a few pointed-arch windows and topped with a lacy parapet.

In private homes, including mansions and palaces, the Gothic style prevailed. But it was so graceful and lighthearted that it was almost feminine when compared to the buildings of Florence. Balconies were much used in Venetian facades. Wrought iron and stone railings were major decorative and spatial features against the flat facades.

EARLY RENAISSANCE VENICE   The Gothic style gradually gave way to Renaissance forms. Mauro Codussi (1440–1504) became the first Venetian to execute the Tuscan Renaissance style, as evoked by his buildings of Santa Maria Formosa, San Michele in Isola, and San Zaccaria. He brilliantly converted the traditional Venetian Gothic facade in a Renaissance equivalent, as evoked by the Vendramin Calergi palace.

In painting, Jacopo Bellini (1400–70) was the founder of the most famous family of artists in Venice. He experimented with perspective and passed his knowledge on to his two also-famous sons, Gentile and Giovanni (see box in this section).

Vittore Carpaccio (1460–1523) was the successor to Gentile Bellini in his narrative commissions for Venetian *sculo* (schools). His brush was lighter than Gentile's, his settings grander. Carpaccio was essentially a storyteller and portrayed life in Venice as a fairy tale.

HIGH RENAISSANCE VENICE   The Renaissance still continued into the 16th century. Its first luminary, Giorgione (1477–1510) died as the style was taking hold. He popularized a new kind of picture, the easel painting, which was meant to be looked at for pleasure. His special achievement was in the handling of light, and his richness of color produced a glow from within. His pictures have a mystical and compelling charm—both brooding and tranquil as in "The Tempest."

Giorgione had a great influence on the divine Titian (see box in this section).

One of the pioneers of Mannerism was the great **Il Tintoretto** (see box), who borrowed from Michelangelo the violence of movement in large sculptural forms and the methods of distortion to increase the impression of power. The major work of his life was done for the Scuola di San Rocco.

Another great painter to emerge from the 16th century was Veronese (1528–88), who took his subjects from the Bible, from mythology, and from history (see box in this section).

Though it lasted for only 2 decades, the High Renaissance style remains known for its rich color and subtle variations in painting, its great technical mastery, and its overall grandeur.

THE BAROQUE ERA   When the more elaborate baroque era came to Venice, the citizens of the lagoon plunged into the new style with abandon. The freedom of line and frivolity of decor typical of the baroque was well suited to the decadent Venetian life style.

Buildings such as the Palazzo Balbi (1582–90) on the Grand Canal, the work of Alessandro Vittoria, showed the first signs of baroque opulence.

Baldassare Longhena in the 1620s created the church of Santa Maria della Salute, the greatest baroque building outside of Rome. It took half a century to complete.

Canaletto (1696–1768) specialized in painting scenes of life in his native city and he enjoyed popularity among the English. He moved from bold angle shots to detailed, dotted panoramas of Venice bathed in the Adriatic sun.

Francesco Guardi (1712–93) became an even greater painter of the *vedutisti* or views. He used swift brush strokes, skimming in lines and fleeting splashes of color to bring his perspectives alive. Pietro Longhi (1702–85), another Venetian artist, became known for his ironic paintings of the decadent Venetian nobility and their frivolous entertainment.

MODERN ARCHITECTURE   Venice may never be known as a center of modern architecture. In fact, anything really new in Venice has a certain shock value because it looks out of place.

Launched in 2002, the new Airport Terminal is called a high-tech interpretation of Venice's Arsenale. It was the creation of Giampaolo Mar, a Venetian architect of note.

Creating a pedestrian link between the bus and rail stations, the fourth bridge over the Grand Canal was the work of the Spanish-born Santiago Calatrava. Frank Gehry, famous as the architect of Bilbao's Guggenheim Museum, was selected to provide a twisty complex of avant-garde buildings near the airport and ferry terminals to house a hotel and convention center, among other buildings.

For cutting-edge architectural design, the **Biennale** showcases "designs for the future" by the world's leading architects, including those from the United States, Britain, Italy, and France, even Japan and China.

By the time of the conquest of Venice by Napoleon's troops, Venice had ceased to be a center of great artists. The focus of the art world was on Paris. Instead of being a great center of art as it was, Venice became a mecca for those who flock to see art and architecture from another era.

4 Venice in Popular Culture: Books, Film & Music
BOOKS

The Likeness of Venice: A Life of Doge Francesco Foscari by Dennis Romano is one of the best books ever penned about Venetian politics and its convoluted culture. The doge, who appears in works by Lord Byron, reigned from 1423 to 1457.

The name of this Venetian stands for romance, and his story is told in *History of My Life* by Giacomo Casanova. He is known for his womanizing, but his memoirs can also be read for their insiderish view of European life, especially Venetian life, in the 1700s. Both the sexual exploits and the noble backdrop of Venice make for a gripping read.

Othello by William Shakespeare remains an enduring classic. Othello is one of the Bard's most noble creatures, but readers often ask, "Is there any other character in all of literature as calculatingly evil as

Iago?" Many critics have claimed that Othello is Shakespeare's greatest hero, and therefore his downfall is the greatest tragedy by the writer. Of course, what would the play be without Desdemona? All this heavy drama takes place against a Venetian backdrop.

Shakespeare returns to Venice again for the setting of *The Merchant of Venice,* this time a comedy filled with romantic subplots. The value of gold and money is tested against friendship and loyalty. Shylock, the Jewish moneylender, is hardly a sympathetic character but his persecutors seem equally sordid. Shylock's conversion to Christianity near the end of the play is a bit hard to swallow.

Death in Venice is the world-famous masterpiece by Nobel laureate Thomas Mann. It was published on the eve of World War I and became the most celebrated novel ever written about Venice. It tells the story of Gustav von Aschenbach, an aging writer who becomes obsessed with a beautiful Polish boy, Tadzio. "It is the story of the voluptuousness of doom," Mann wrote. Critics noted that although the more literal interpretation of von Aschenbach's constant pursuit can be seen as wanton lust, the real undercurrent that Mann provides is the writer's self-validation as an artist.

A Stopover in Venice by Kathryn Walker is a novel that combines art and history with love, loss, and renewal in a sensually realized Venice. Full of mystery and discovery, the story of a modern-day marriage is also about self-discovery. The descriptions of Venice are quite wonderful.

Daughter of Venice by Donna Jo Napoli is a historical novel about a young woman experiencing the world back in 1592 Venice. The novel is rich and loaded with intriguing historical detail, and Napoli herself is the best of all female Venetian scholars. The novel is seen through the eyes of a teenage girl with big dreams for her uncertain future.

Although it jumps around Italy like a travelogue, *The Talented Mr. Ripley* by Patricia Highsmith is set partially in Venice. Matt Damon and Jude Law brought the narrative to life in a movie of the same name. The story tells of how the chameleon-like Tom Ripley is sent by a rich American to retrieve his dilettante son, Dickie Greenleaf, in Italy. In that Tom does not succeed. He kills Dickie and assumes his identity as the plot thickens.

Francesco's Venice: the Dramatic History of the World's Most Beautiful City by Francesco da Mosto sums it up nicely in its long title. Legends and lore fill this entertaining volume. Was Othello, the Moor of Venice, really a dark-skinned Sicilian? That question and others are answered in this intriguing volume. Beautifully illustrated, the tome makes great armchair reading if you can't visit the real thing. It's a history book that reads like a novel.

Across the Bridge of Sighs: More Venetian Stories by Jane Turner Rylands is a follow-up to the author's debut, *Venetian Stories,* first published in 2003. Everyone from workaday Venetians to fallen aristocrats makes an appearance in these tales. Thirteen interconnected stories appear in this volume, but actually the City of Venice itself is the main character of the book.

John Berendt put Savannah on the tourist map with his *Midnight in the Garden of Good and Evil,* which was made into the unsuccessful Clint Eastwood film. With his latest, *The City of Falling Angels,* he hardly puts Venice on the tourist map, a place it has occupied for centuries, but his *Falling Angels* does introduce us to an array of colorful characters, ranging from master glass blowers to surrealist painters. The plot centers around the arson of the Fenice Opera House, but that is mere gas to throw on the fire. Berendt exploits Venice as brilliantly as he did Savannah.

FILMS

The great Orson Welles brought a classic to the screen when he directed and starred in *The Tragedy of Othello: The Moor of Venice* in 1952. It remains an enduring fave among Welles fans. Cast as the evil Iago was Michael MacLiammoir, with Suzanne Cloutier as Desdemona. As one reviewer of the time put it, "Commenting on Shakespeare films is rather like admiring Easter eggs." *Othello* was shot over a period of 3 years, with production stopping whenever Welles ran out of money.

Director Michael Radford brought *The Merchant of Venice* to the screen in 2004, with Al Pacino playing Shylock and Lynn Collins cast as Portia. Even though the budget was tight, the costumes and scenery of Venice have their own enchantment. Trivia footnote to the film: Those bare-breasted prostitutes depicted in the film were not to make it salacious. It was a note of historical authenticity. To prevent homosexuals from dressing in drag and secretly servicing male clients, Venetian law called for all prostitutes to bare their breasts before clients. Those were the good old days before "she-males" could get breast enlargements by plastic surgeons, of course.

Summertime, directed by David Lean, brought a highly mannered Katharine Hepburn to the screen in 1955, with the Italian actor Rossano Brazzi playing her lover. It was based on Arthur Laurent's play, *The Time of the Cuckoo.* Hepburn plays a mousy secretary from Akron (a bit of a stretch for the grand diva) in the film, which is actually a valentine to Venice. It contains the famous scene where Hepburn falls into the water of a Venetian canal. She developed an eye infection that lasted until her death.

To be expected, some director was to bring Thomas Mann's *Death in Venice* to the screen, and Luchino Visconti did just that in his 1971 *Morte a Venezia*. Dirk Borgarde was cast as Gustav von Aschenbach, with Bjorn Andresen as the stunningly beautiful Tadzio, the poster boy of all pedophiles. In this visionary masterpiece, Venice at the turn of the 20th century is depicted in all its elegant decay. Borgarde delivers the performance of his career.

One of the most underrated James Bond films, *Moonraker* (1979), has many beautiful scenes set along the Venetian canals. Roger Moore, as Bond, investigates the disappearance of a U.S. space shuttle.

Woody Allen invaded Venice with his *Everyone Says I Love You*, a 1996 film that he both wrote and directed. Starring Edward Norton and Drew Barrymore, the film is a comedy/musical/romance. Not one of Woody's best, the movie is a romp through musical bliss and the heartache of romance, as it explores unfaithfulness and an ex-husband, ex-wife relationship.

Federico Fellini also brought the great lover to the screen with his *Casanova di Federico Fellini, II,* released in 1976 with Donald Sutherland playing Casanova. This was a beautiful and rather melancholic film which was originally to star Robert Redford. In the movie, *Casanova,* the eternal libertine parades around Venice, collecting seductive women and performing sexual feats.

3

Planning Your Trip to Venice

For more than 1,000 years, people have flocked to Venice because it is unlike any other destination in the world. This chapter will give you information about the city's layout, tips on how to get around, and facts that you'll need to know to settle yourself into this unique city, plus more.

1 Orientation

CITY LAYOUT

Venice lies 4km (2½ miles) from the Italian mainland (connected to Mestre by the Ponte della Libertà) and 2km (1¼ miles) from the open Adriatic. It's an archipelago of 118 islands. Most visitors, however, concern themselves only with **Piazza San Marco** and its vicinity. In fact, the entire city has only one *piazza,* which is San Marco (all the other squares are *campos*). Venice is divided into six quarters *(sestieri):* **San Marco, Santa Croce, San Polo, Castello, Cannaregio,** and **Dorsoduro.**

Many of Venice's so-called streets are actually *rios* (canals), somewhere around 150 in all, spanned by a total of 400 bridges. Venice's version of a main street is the **Grand Canal** (or Canal Grande), which snakes through the city like an inverted *S* and is spanned by three bridges: the white marble **Ponte di Rialto,** the wooden **Ponte Accademia,** and the stone **Ponte degli Scalzi.** The Grand Canal splits Venice into two unequal parts.

South of Dorsoduro, which is south of the Grand Canal, is the **Canale della Giudecca,** a major channel separating Dorsoduro from the large island of La Giudecca. At the point where Canale della Giudecca meets the **Canale di San Marco,** you'll spot the little **Isola di San Giorgio Maggiore,** with a church by Palladio. The most visited islands in the lagoon, aside from the **Lido,** are **Murano, Burano,** and **Torcello.**

If you really want to tour Venice and experience that hidden, romantic *trattoria* (less formal eatery) on a nearly forgotten street, don't even think about doing so unless you have a map that details

Venice Orientation

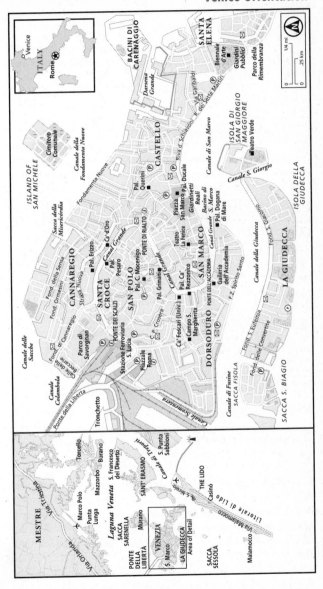

Tips **Finding an Address**

A maniac must have numbered Venice's buildings at least 6 centuries ago. Before you set out for a specific place, get detailed instructions and have someone mark the destination on your map. Don't depend on street numbers; instead, try to locate the nearest cross street. Because old signs and numbers have decayed over time, it's best to look for signs posted outside rather than for a house number.

Every building has a street address and a mailing address. For example, a business at Calle delle Botteghe 3150 (3150 Botteghe St.) will have a mailing address of San Marco 3150, since it's in the San Marco *sestiere* and all buildings in each district are numbered continuously from 1 to 6,000. (To confuse things, several districts have streets of the same name, so it's important to know the *sestiere*.) In this chapter, we give the street name first, followed by the mailing address.

---

every street and has an index in the back. The best of the lot is the **Falk map** of Venice, sold at many news kiosks and all bookstores.

A broad street running along a canal is a *fondamenta,* a narrower street running along a canal is a *calle,* and a paved road is a *salizzada, ruga,* or *calle larga.* A *rio terrà* is a filled canal channel now used as a walkway, and a *sotoportego* is a passage beneath buildings. When you come to an open-air area, you'll often encounter the word *campo*— that's a reference to the fact that such a place was once grassy, and in days of yore cattle grazed there.

NEIGHBORHOODS IN BRIEF

This section will give you some idea of where you may want to stay and where the major attractions are.

SAN MARCO   Welcome to the center of Venice. Napoleon called it "the drawing room of Europe," and it's one crowded drawing room today. It has been the heart of Venetian life for more than a thousand years. **Piazza San Marco (St. Mark's Square)** is dominated by **St. Mark's Basilica.** Just outside the basilica is the **campanile (bell tower),** a reconstruction of the one that collapsed in 1902. Around the corner is the **Palazzo Ducale (Doge's Palace),** with its **Bridge of Sighs.** Piazza San Marco is lined with some of the world's most overpriced cafes, including **Florian** (opened in 1720) and **Quadri** (opened in 1775). The most celebrated watering hole, however, is away from the square: **Harry's Bar,** founded by Giuseppe Cipriani but made famous by Hemingway. In and around the square are some of the most convenient hotels in Venice (though not necessarily the best) and an array of expensive tourist shops and *trattorie.*

CASTELLO The shape of Venice is often likened to that of a fish. If so, Castello is the tail. The largest and most varied of the six *sestieri,* Castello is home to many sights, such as the **Arsenale,** and some of the city's plushest hotels, such as the Danieli. One of the neighborhood's most notable attractions is the Gothic **Santa Giovanni e Paolo (Zanipolo),** the Pantheon of the Doges. Cutting through the *sestiere* is **Campo Santa Maria Formosa,** one of Venice's largest open squares. The most elegant street is **Riva degli Schiavoni,** which runs along the Grand Canal; it's lined with some of the finest hotels and restaurants and is one of the city's favorite promenades.

CANNAREGIO This is Venice's gateway, the first of the six *sestieri.* It lies away from the rail station at the northwest side of Venice and shelters about a third of the population, some 20,000 residents. At its heart is the **Santa Lucia Station** (1955). The area also embraces the old **Jewish Ghetto,** the first one on the Continent. Jews began to move here at the beginning of the 16th century, when they were segregated from the rest of the city. From here, the word *ghetto* later became a generic term used all over the world. Attractions in this area include the **Ca' d'Oro,** the finest example of the Venetian Gothic style; the **Madonna dell'Orto,** a 15th-century church known for its Tintorettos; and **Santa Maria dei Miracoli,** with a Madonna portrait supposedly able to raise the dead. Unless you're coming for one of these attractions, this area doesn't offer much else; its hotels and restaurants aren't the best. Some of the cheapest lodging is found along **Lista di Spagna,** to the left as you exit the train station.

SANTA CROCE This area generally follows the snakelike curve of the Grand Canal from Piazzale Roma to a point just short of the Ponte di Rialto. It's split into two rather different neighborhoods. The eastern part is in the typically Venetian style and is one of the least crowded parts of Venice, though it has some of the Grand Canal's loveliest *palazzi* (palaces). The western side is more industrialized and isn't very interesting to explore.

SAN POLO This is the heart of commercial Venice and the smallest of the six *sestieri.* It's reached by crossing the **Ponte di Rialto (Rialto Bridge),** which spans the Grand Canal. The shopping here is much more reasonable than that around Piazza San Marco. One of the major attractions is the **Erberia,** which Casanova wrote about in his 18th-century autobiography. Both wholesale and retail markets still pepper this ancient site. At its center is **San Giacomo di Rialto,** the city's oldest church. The district also encloses the **Scuola Grande di San Rocco,** a repository of the works of Tintoretto. **Campo San Polo** is one of the oldest and widest squares and one of the principal venues for Carnevale. San Polo is also filled with moderately priced hotels and a large number of *trattorie,* many specializing in seafood. In general, the hotels and restaurants are cheaper here than along San Marco, but not as inexpensive as those around the train station in Cannaregio.

DORSODURO   The least populated of the *sestieri,* this funky neighborhood is filled with old homes and half-forgotten churches. Dorsoduro is the southernmost section of the historic district, and its major sights are the **Accademia Gallery** and the **Peggy Guggenheim Foundation.** It's less trampled than the areas around the Rialto Bridge and Piazza San Marco. Its most famous church is **La Salute,** whose first stone was laid in 1631. The **Zattere,** a broad quay built after 1516, is one of Venice's favorite promenades. Cafes, *trattorie,* and *pensioni* (boardinghouses) abound in the area.

THE LAGOON ISLANDS

THE LIDO   This slim, sandy island 12km (7½ miles) long and about 1km (half a mile) wide, though reaching 4km (2½ miles) at its broadest point, cradles the Venetian lagoon, offering protection against the Adriatic. The Lido is a chic beach resort and site of the fabled **Venice Film Festival.** It was the setting for many famous books, including Thomas Mann's *Death in Venice* and Evelyn Waugh's *Brideshead Revisited.* Some of the most fashionable and expensive hotels are found along the Lido Promenade. The most famous is the Grand Hotel des Bains, but there are cheaper places as well. The best way to get around is by bike or tandem, which you can rent at Via Zara and Gran Viale.

TORCELLO   Lying 9km (5½ miles) northeast of Venice, Torcello is called "the mother of Venice," having been settled in the 9th century. It was once the most populous of the islands in the lagoon, but since the 18th century it has been nearly deserted. If you ever hope to find solitude in Venice, you'll find it here. It's visited today chiefly by those wishing to see the **Cattedrale di Torcello,** with its stunning Byzantine mosaics, and to lunch at the Locanda Cipriani restaurant.

BURANO   Perched 9km (5½ miles) northeast of Venice, Burano is the most populous of the lagoon islands. In the 16th century, it produced the finest lace in Europe. Lace is still made here, but it's nothing like the product of centuries past. Inhabited since Roman times, Burano is different from either Torcello or Murano. Forget lavish palaces: The houses are often simple and small and painted in deep blues, strong reds, and striking yellows. The island is still peopled by fishers, and one of the reasons to visit is to dine at one of its *trattorie,* where, naturally, the specialty is fish.

MURANO   This island, about 1.5km (less than a mile) northeast of Venice, has been famed for its glassmaking since 1291. Today, Murano is the most visited island in the lagoon, with tons of guided tours visiting the glass-blowing shops. You can also visit a glass museum, the **Museo Vetrario di Murano,** and see two of the island's notable churches, **San Pietro Martire** and **Sante Maria e Donato.** You'll likely be on the island for lunch, and there are a number of moderately priced *trattorie* to choose from.

2 Visitor Information

TOURIST OFFICES ABROAD

For information before you go, contact the **Italian National Tourist Board.**

In the United States: 630 Fifth Ave., Ste. 1565, New York, NY 10111 (✆ **212/245-5618;** fax 212/586-9249); 500 N. Michigan Ave., Chicago, IL 60611 (✆ **312/644-0996;** fax 312/644-3019); 12400 Wilshire Blvd., Ste. 550, Los Angeles, CA 90025 (✆ **310/820-1898;** fax 310/820-6357).

In Canada: 175 Bloor St. E., South Tower, Ste. 907, Toronto, ON M4W 3R8 (✆ **416/925-4882;** fax 416/925-4799).

In the United Kingdom: 1 Princes St., London W1B 2AY (✆ **020/ 7399-3562;** fax 020/7399-3567).

INFORMATION WITHIN VENICE

Visitor information is available at the **Azienda di Promozione Turistica,** Palazzetto Selva–Ex Giardini Reali (Molo S. Marco; ✆ **041-5298711**). Hours are daily from 10am to 6pm. Ask for a schedule of the month's special events and an updated list of museum and church hours, which can change erratically and often. There's also a tourist office at the train station, **Stazione Venezia–Santa Lucia** (✆ **041-892021**), open daily from 10am to 6pm.

Anyone between 16 and 29 is eligible for a **"Rolling Venice" pass,** offering discounts in museums, certain restaurants and stores, language courses, some hotels, and even some bars. Valid for a year, it costs 4€ ($6.40) and can be picked up at the special "Rolling Venice" office set up in the train station during summer; it can also be purchased at tourist offices. The card is valid until December 31 of the year it is purchased.

USEFUL WEBSITES

On the Web, the Italian National Tourist Board sponsors the sites **www.italiantourism.com** and **www.enit.it**. Other useful sites include:

www.carnivalofvenice.com   Experience the Carnevale celebration of Venice. Or explore past carnivals, dating back to the year 1268, in the historic section of this online guide to one of Italy's grandest annual events. Travelers can also find information about transportation, city services, and other Venice basics.

www.doge.it   Take virtual tours of the Doge's Palace and Piazza San Marco; skim through directories of hotels and travel agencies; find out when you can catch the Carnevale celebration or the Venice Film Festival; and more.

www.initaly.com   This extensive site lists all sorts of accommodations (including villas, apartments, and gay-friendly hotels) and tips on shopping, dining, driving, and viewing works of art. There are sections dedicated to each region of Italy, plus info on books and movies. Join the mailing list for monthly updates.

www.veniceworld.com   This site lists links to Venice's accommodations, centers for the arts, nightclubs, restaurants, sporting events, travel agencies, transportation, newspapers, and so forth.

MAPS

The best detailed street map of Venice is from the **MultiMap.com** site, closely followed by **Google Maps.** At **ombra.net** you'll find a locally produced interactive map. You can search for a street name by clicking "**searchmaps**" in the navigation column on the left and choosing "street guide."

The best map for getting around Venice is the **Illustrated Venice Map** sold at news kiosks, various hotels, and all bookstores. The map is illustrated with numerous line drawings of the major attractions. Hundreds of shops are also located as well as numerous restaurants, bars, and cafes, plus museums. Its main function is to guide you through the maze of narrow streets in this ancient city.

3 Entry Requirements

Citizens of the United States, Canada, Australia, New Zealand, and the Republic of Ireland, as well as British subjects, need only a **valid passport** to enter Italy. (For information on how to get a passport, go to the "Venice Fast Facts" section in the appendix.)

Under Italian law, all nonresidents are required to complete a *dichiarazione di presenza* (declaration of presence). Tourists arriving from Canada or the United States should obtain a stamp in their passport at the airport on the day of arrival. This stamp is considered the equivalent of the declaration of presence. It is important that applicants keep a copy of the receipt issued by the Italian authorities. Failure to complete a declaration of presence is punishable by expulsion from Italy. Additional information may be obtained (in Italian only) from the Portale Immigrazione at www.portaleimmigrazione.it and the Polizia di Stato at www.poliziadistato.it/pds/ps/immigrazione/soggiorno.htm.

Americans staying in Italy for more than 3 months are considered residents and must obtain a *permesso di soggiorno* (permit of stay). This includes Americans who will work or transact business and persons who want to simply live in Italy. An application "kit" for the *permesso di soggiorno* may be requested from one of the 14,000 national post offices (Poste Italiane). The kit must then be returned to one of 5,332 designated post office acceptance locations. It is important that applicants keep a copy of the receipt issued by the post office. Additional information may be obtained from an Italian immigration website via the Internet at www.portaleimmigrazione.it. Within 20 days of receiving the permit to stay in Italy, Americans must go to the local Vital Statistics Bureau (Anagrafe of the Comune) to apply for residency. It generally takes 1 to 2 months to receive the certificate of residence *(Certificato di Residenza).*

Although European Union regulations require that non-E.U. visitors obtain a stamp in their passports upon initial entry, many borders are not staffed with officers carrying out this function. If an American citizen wishes to ensure that his or her entry is properly documented, it may be necessary to request a stamp at an official point of entry. Under local law, travelers without a stamp in their passport may be questioned and asked to document the length of their stay at the time of departure or at any other point during their visit, and could face possible fines or other repercussions if unable to do so.

CUSTOMS
WHAT YOU CAN BRING INTO VENICE

Foreign visitors can bring along most items for personal use duty-free, including fishing tackle, a pair of skis, two tennis racquets, a baby carriage, two hand cameras with 10 rolls of film, and 400 cigarettes or a quantity of cigars or pipe tobacco not exceeding 500 grams (1.1 lb.). There are strict limits on importing alcoholic beverages. However, for alcohol bought tax-paid, limits are much more liberal than in other countries of the European Union.

WHAT YOU CAN TAKE HOME FROM VENICE

Returning **U.S. citizens** who have been away for at least 48 hours are allowed to bring back, once every 30 days, $800 worth of merchandise duty-free. You'll be charged a flat rate of duty on the next $1,000 worth of purchases. Any dollar amount beyond that is taxed at whatever rates apply. On mailed gifts, the duty-free limit is $200. Be sure to have your receipts or purchases handy to expedite the declaration process. *Note:* If you owe duty, you are required to pay on your arrival in the United States, either by cash, personal check, government or traveler's check, or money order (or, in some locations, Visa or MasterCard).

To avoid having to pay duty on foreign-made personal items you owned before you left on your trip, bring along a bill of sale, insurance policy, jeweler's appraisal, or receipt of purchase. Or you can register items that can be readily identified by a permanently affixed serial number or marking—think laptop computers, cameras, and CD players—with Customs before you leave. Take the items to the nearest Customs office or register them with Customs at the airport from which you're departing. You'll receive, at no cost, a Certificate of Registration, which allows duty-free entry for the life of the item.

With some exceptions, you cannot bring fresh fruits and vegetables into the United States. For specifics on what you can bring back, download the invaluable free pamphlet *Know Before You Go* online at **www.cbp.gov** (click on "Travel"; then click on "Know Before You Go! Online Brochure"). Or request the pamphlet from the **U.S. Customs & Border Protection,** 1300 Pennsylvania Ave. NW, Washington, DC 20229 (© **877/287-8667;** www.cbp.gov).

Citizens of **Canada** are allowed a C$750 exemption once a year and only after an absence of 7 days. You're allowed to bring back duty-free one carton of cigarettes, one can of tobacco, 40 imperial ounces of liquor, and 50 cigars. In addition, you're allowed to mail gifts to Canada valued at less than C$60 a day, provided they're unsolicited and don't contain alcohol or tobacco (write on the package "Unsolicited gift, under C$60 value"). All valuables should be declared on the Y-38 form before departure from Canada, including serial numbers of valuables you already own, such as expensive foreign cameras. Contact the **Canada Border Services Agency** (© 800/ 461-9999 in Canada, or 204/983-3500; www.cbsa-asfc.gc.ca) for the booklet *I Declare.*

Citizens of the **United Kingdom** can contact **HM Revenue & Customs** (© 0845/010-9000 in the U.K., or 02920/501-261 from outside the U.K.; www.hmrc.gov.uk). U.K. citizens who are returning from a European Union (E.U.) country will go through a separate Customs line especially for E.U. travelers. In essence, there is no limit on what you can bring back from an E.U. country, as long as the items are for personal use (this includes gifts) and you have already paid the necessary duty and tax. However, Customs law sets out guidance levels. If you bring in more than these levels, you may be asked to prove that the goods are for your own use. Guidance levels on goods bought in the E.U. for your own use are 3,200 cigarettes, 200 cigars, 400 cigarillos, 3 kilograms of smoking tobacco, 10 liters of spirits, 90 liters of wine, 20 liters of fortified wine (such as port or sherry), and 110 liters of beer.

The duty-free allowance in **Australia** is A$900 or, for those 17 and under, A$450. Citizens can bring in 250 cigarettes or 250 grams of loose tobacco, as well as 2.25 liters of alcohol. If you're returning with valuables you already own, such as foreign-made cameras, you should file form B263. A helpful brochure available from Australian consulates or Customs offices is *Know Before You Go.* For more information, call the **Australian Customs Service** (© 1300/363- 263; www.customs.gov.au).

The duty-free allowance for **New Zealand** is NZ$700. Citizens 17 or older can bring in 200 cigarettes, 50 cigars, or 250 grams of tobacco (or a mixture of all three if their combined weight doesn't exceed 250g); plus 4.5 liters of wine and beer, or 1.125 liters of liquor. Fill out a certificate of export, listing the valuables you are taking out of the country; that way, you can bring them back without paying duty. Most questions are answered in a free pamphlet available at New Zealand consulates and Customs offices: *New Zealand Customs Guide for Travellers, Notice no. 4.* For information, contact **New Zealand Customs** (© 04/473-6099 or 0800/428-786; www.customs.govt.nz).

4 When to Go

The best times to visit are April to June and September to October. Summers are hot and muggy (and the canals are smelly). Winters are gray and wet but not severe, because the natural barrier of the Lido protects central Venice from much of the fury of the Adriatic. Yet in spite of the weather, many savvy visitors prefer to visit Venice in winter, when the city is emptier (the tourist crowds in summer are practically unbearable).

If you're planning to be in Venice anytime from October to March, high boots can be useful. The canals flood frequently because of a combination of the tides and the winds. If a flood is expected, a warning siren will be sounded 1 hour before crest so people can get home. The city puts out *passarelle* (boardwalks) along major routes. The *acqua alta* (high water) lasts only about 2 or 3 hours at a time.

Venice's Average Daily Temperature (°F & °C) & Monthly Rainfall (in.)

	Jan	Feb	Mar	Apr	May	June	July	Aug	Sept	Oct	Nov	Dec
Temp. (°F)	43	48	53	60	67	72	77	74	68	60	54	44
Temp. (°C)	6	9	12	16	19	22	25	23	20	16	12	7
Rain (in.)	2.3	1.5	2.9	3.0	2.8	2.9	1.5	1.9	2.8	2.6	3.0	2.1

VENICE CALENDAR OF EVENTS

February

Carnevale. At this riotous time, theatrical presentations and masked balls take place throughout Venice and on the islands in the lagoon. The balls are by invitation only (except the Doge's Ball), but the street events and fireworks are open to everyone. For information, contact the Venice Tourist Office (✆ 041-5298711; www.turismovenezia.it or www.carnivalofvenice.com). The week before Ash Wednesday, the beginning of Lent.

May

La Sensa. Municipal authorities conduct a pale reenactment of the once-famed ritual of the Marriage of Venice to the Sea. On the same day, the vast **La Vogalonga ("Long Row")** is held. This is an exciting 32km (20-mile) race to Burano and back, open to all comers. Participants reach the San Marco basin between 11am and 3pm. The Sunday after Ascension Day.

June

Biennale d'Arte (International Exposition of Modern Art). One of the most famous art events in Europe takes place during alternate (odd-numbered) years in the public gardens. Call ✆ 041-5218711;

www.labiennale.org for more information. Between June and September.

July

Feast of Il Redentore (Feast of the Redeemer). This festival commemorates the end of the 1576 plague. Half of Venice picnics aboard boats and gondolas to watch the spectacular fireworks. A bridge of boats spans the Giudecca Canal and connects Dorso-duro to Palladio's Church of the Redentore on the island of Giudecca. Third Saturday and Sunday in July.

August

Venice International Film Festival. This festival brings together stars, directors, producers, and filmmakers from all over the world. Films are shown between 9am and 3am in various areas of the Palazzo del Cinema on the Lido. Though many of the seats are reserved for international jury members, the public can attend virtually whenever it wants, depending on seat availability. For ticket information, contact the Venice Film Festival, c/o the Biennale office, Ca' Giustinian, Calle del Ridotto 1364A, 30124 Venezia (© **041-5218711;** www.labiennale.org). Late August to early September.

September

Regata Storica. This is a maritime spectacular. Many gondolas participate in the Grand Canal procession and in the regatta itself. First Sunday in September.

November

Opera Season. During the wet and rainy season, the new opera season begins at La Fenice (© **041-2424;** www.teatrolafenice.it) and lasts until July.

Feast of the Madonna della Salute. For approximately 24 hours, a pontoon bridge spans the Grand Canal to the great baroque church of Santa Maria della Salute for a religious procession commemorating the deliverance of Venice from the plague of 1630 and 1631. November 21.

5 Getting There & Getting Around

GETTING THERE

All roads lead not necessarily to Rome but, in this case, to the docks on mainland Venice. The arrival scene at the unattractive Piazzale Roma is filled with nervous expectation; even the most veteran traveler can become confused. Whether arriving by train, bus, car, or airport limo, everyone walks to the nearby docks (less than a 5-min.

walk) to select a method of transport to his or her hotel. The cheapest way is by *vaporetto* (public motorboat), the more expensive by gondola or motor launch (see "Getting Around," below).

Warning: If your hotel is near one of the public *vaporetto* stops, you can sometimes struggle with your own luggage until you reach the hotel's reception area. In general, however, excess baggage is bad news, unless you're willing to pay dearly to have it carried for you to the docks. Porters can't accompany you and your baggage on the *vaporetti*. Pack light!

BY PLANE

High season on most airlines' routes to Italy is usually from June to the beginning of September. This is the most expensive and most crowded time to travel. **Shoulder season** is April through May, early September through October, and December 15 to December 24. **Low season** is November 1 to December 14 and December 25 to March 31.

FROM NORTH AMERICA   There are no direct flights from the United States to Venice; all flights go via Rome or Milan.

Flying time to Rome from New York, Newark, and Boston is 8 hours; from Chicago, 10 hours; and from Los Angeles, 12½ hours. Flying time to Milan from New York, Newark, and Boston is 8 hours; from Chicago, 9¼ hours; and from Los Angeles, 11½ hours.

American Airlines (© 800/433-7300; www.aa.com) offers daily nonstop flights to Rome from Chicago's O'Hare. **Delta** (© 800/221-1212; www.delta.com) also flies from New York's JFK to Milan, Rome, and Venice; separate flights depart every evening for both destinations. And **Continental** (© 800/231-0856; www.continental.com) flies five times a week to Rome from its hub in Newark.

Air Canada (© 888/247-2262; www.aircanada.ca) flies out of Toronto daily to both Milan and Rome.

British Airways (© 800/AIRWAYS [247-9297]; www.british airways.com), **Virgin Atlantic** (© 800/821-5438; www.virgin-atlantic.com), **Air France** (© 800/237-2747; www.airfrance.com), **Northwest/KLM** (© 800/225-2525; www.nwa.com), and **Lufthansa** (© 800/645-3880; www.lufthansa.com) offer some attractive deals for anyone interested in combining a trip to Italy with a stopover in, say, London, Paris, Amsterdam, or Germany.

Alitalia (© 800/223-5730 in the U.S. and Canada; www.alitalia.com) is the Italian national airline, with nonstop flights to Rome from different North American cities, including New York (JFK), Newark, Boston, Chicago, and Miami. Nonstop flights into

Milan are from New York (JFK) and Newark. From Milan or Rome, Alitalia can easily book connecting domestic flights if your final destination is elsewhere in Italy. Alitalia participates in the frequent-flier programs of other airlines, including Continental and US Airways.

FROM THE UNITED KINGDOM   Operated by the European Travel Network, **www.discount-tickets.com** is a great online source for regular and discounted airfares to destinations around the world.

British newspapers and magazines are always full of classified ads touting slashed fares to Italy. Try *Time Out* or London's *Evening Standard.* One well-recommended company that consolidates bulk ticket purchases and then passes the savings on to its consumers is **Trailfinders** (© **0845/050-5945;** www.trailfinders.com in London).

Both **British Airways** (© **0870/850-9850** in the U.K.; www.britishairways.com) and **Alitalia** (© **0871/424-2241;** www.alitalia.it) have frequent flights from London's Heathrow airport to Rome, Milan, Venice, Pisa (the gateway to Florence), and Naples. Flying time from London to these cities is from 2 to 3 hours. British Airways also has one direct flight a day from Manchester to Rome. **British Midland Airways** (© **0870/60-70-555;** www.flybmi.com) has one flight from London and one from Manchester to Venice daily.

ARRIVING AT THE VENICE AIRPORT

After landing in Rome, Milan, or another Italian gateway city, you can take a flight on **Alitalia** (see above) to Venice.

You'll land at Venice's **Aeroporto Marco Polo** (VCE; © **041-260-9260;** www.veniceairport.it) at Mestre.

The **Alilaguna** (© **041-541-6555;** www.alilaguna.it) operates a water-bus service from the airport, with several convenient drop-off locations in Venice. The cost of the trip is from 6€ to 30€ ($9.60–$48); it takes about 45 minutes to get to the center of town.

If you've got some extra euros to spend, you can arrange for a **private water taxi** by calling © 041-2406711. The cost to ride to the heart of Venice is 98€ ($157).

You can also get from the airport to the city by land. Traveling overland will get you to Piazzale Roma, which is immediately southwest of the train station. The cheapest way is to catch a blue city bus no. 5, which leaves the airport every 30 minutes. The trip will cost about 1.50€ ($2.40) and should take about 30 minutes. Blue shuttle buses that make the trip in 20 minutes or so cost about 3€ ($4.80).

BY TRAIN

Trains from all over Europe arrive at the **Stazione Venezia–Santa Lucia** (© **041-785-670;** www.veneziasantalucia.it). To get here, all trains must pass through (though not necessarily stop at) a station marked VENEZIA-MESTRE. Don't be confused: Mestre is a charmless industrial city and the last stop on the mainland. Occasionally trains end at Mestre, in which case you'll have to catch one of the frequent 10-minute shuttle trains connecting Mestre with Venice; when booking your ticket, confirm that the train's final destination is Stazione Santa Lucia.

Travel time from Rome is about 5¼ hours; from Milan, 3½ hours; from Florence, 4 hours; and from Bologna, 2 hours. The best and least expensive way to get from the station to the rest of town is to take a *vaporetto,* which you can catch near the main entrance to the station.

BY BUS

Buses from mainland Italy arrive in Venice at Piazzale Roma. For information about schedules, call the **ACTV office** at Piazzale Roma (© **041-27-2211;** www.actv.it). If you're coming from a distant city in Italy, it's better to take the train. But Venice does have good bus connections with nearby cities like Padua. A one-way fare between Padua and Venice costs 4€ ($6.40). The cheapest way to reach the heart of Venice from the bus station is by *vaporetto.*

BY CAR

Venice has *autostrada* (expressway) links with the rest of Italy, with direct routes from such cities as Trieste (driving time: 1½ hr.), Milan (3 hr.), and Bologna (2 hr.). Bologna is 150km (93 miles) southwest of Venice, Milan 264km (164 miles) west of Venice, and Trieste 115km (71 miles) east. Rome is 523km (325 miles) southwest.

If you arrive by car, there are several multi-tiered **parking areas** at the terminus where the roads end and the canals begin. One of the most visible is the **Garage San Marco,** Piazzale Roma (© **041-5232213;** www.garagesanmarco.it), near the *vaporetto,* gondola, and motor-launch docks. You'll be charged 28€ ($45) per day, maybe more, depending on the size of your car. From spring to fall, this municipal car park is nearly always filled. You're more likely to find parking on the **Isola del Tronchetto** (© **041-5207555;** www.veniceparking.it), which costs 20€ ($32) a day. From Tronchetto, take *vaporetto* no. 82 to Piazza San Marco. If you have heavy luggage, you'll need a water taxi. Parking is also available on the mainland at Mestre.

GETTING AROUND

Since you can't hail a taxi, at least not on land, get ready to walk and walk and walk. Of course, you can break up your walks with *vaporetto* or boat rides, which are great respites from dealing with the packed (and we mean *packed*) streets in summer.

However, note that in autumn the high tide *(acqua alta)* is a real menace. The squares often flood, beginning with Piazza San Marco, one of the city's lowest points. Many visitors and locals wear knee-high boots to navigate their way. In fact, some hotels maintain a storage room full of boots in all sizes for their guests.

With packed streets, more than 400 bridges, and difficult-to-board *vaporetti*, Venice isn't too user-friendly for those with disabilities. Nevertheless, some improvements have been made. The tourist office distributes a free map called *Veneziapertutti* ("Venice for All"), illustrating what parts of the city are accessible by the use of different color-coded references; it also outlines a list of accessible churches, monuments, gardens, public offices, hotels, and lavatories with facilities for travelers with disabilities.

Time and again while exploring, you'll think you know where you're going, only to wind up on a dead-end street or at the side of a canal with no bridge to get to the other side. Just remind yourself that Venice's physical complexity is an integral part of its charm—getting lost is part of the fun.

Fortunately, around the city are yellow signs whose arrows direct you toward one of five major landmarks: FERROVIA (the train station), PIAZZALE ROMA, the RIALTO (the main bridge), SAN MARCO (the *piazza*), and the ACCADEMIA (the only other Grand Canal bridge below the train station). You'll often find these signs grouped together, their arrows pointing off in different directions.

BY PUBLIC TRANSPORTATION

Much to the chagrin of the once-ubiquitous gondoliers, Venice's **vaporetti** (public motorboat buses) provide inexpensive and frequent, if not always fast, transportation in this canal city. The service is operated by **ACTV (Azienda del Consorzio Trasporti Veneziano),** Isola Nova del Tronchetto 32 (© **041-2424).** An *accelerato* is a vessel that makes every stop; a *diretto* makes only express stops. The average fare is 6.50€ ($10). They run daily, with frequent service from 7am to midnight, then hourly from midnight to 7am. Note that in summer, the *vaporetti* are often fiercely crowded. Pick up a map of the system at the tourist office.

Note: Visitors to Venice can buy a 1-day travel card for 16€ ($26) that's valid for 24 hours, or a 3-day travel card for 31€ ($50) that's valid for 72 hours.

The Grand Canal is long and snakelike and can be crossed via only three bridges, including the one at Rialto. If there's no bridge in sight, the trick in getting across is to use one of the *traghetti* **gondolas** strategically placed at key points. Look for them at the end of any passage called "Calle del Traghetto." Under government control, these charge a fare of only .60€ (95¢).

BY MOTOR LAUNCH (WATER TAXI)

Motor launches *(taxi acquei)* cost more than public *vaporetti*, but you won't be hassled as much when you arrive with your luggage if you hire one of the many private ones. You may or may not have the cabin of one of these sleek vessels to yourself, since the captains fill their boats with as many passengers as the law allows before taking off. Your porter's uncanny radar will guide you to one of the inconspicuous piers where a water taxi waits.

The price of transit by water taxi from Piazzale Roma (the road/rail terminus) to Piazza San Marco is 98€ ($157) for up to four passengers and 10€ ($16) more for each additional person. The captains can adroitly deliver you, with luggage, to the canal-side entrance of your hotel or to one of the smaller waterways within a short walking distance of your destination. You can also call for a water taxi; try the **Consorzio Motoscafi Venezia** at *C* **041/5222303;** www.motoscafivenezia.it.

BY CAR

Obviously you won't need a car in Venice, but you might want one when you leave, in order to head off to nearby cities like Padua. Most of the car-rental agencies lie near the rail station in the traffic-clogged Piazzale Roma (meaning also that you can return a rental car here when you arrive in Venice). You'll get the best rate if you reserve before leaving home.

Hertz is at Piazzale Roma 496 (*C* **800/654-3001** in the U.S., or 041-5284091; www.hertz.com). Monday to Friday from 8am to 6pm, Saturday and Sunday 8am to 1pm.

Europcar (associated with National in the U.S.) is at Piazzale Roma 496H (*C* **800/328-4567** in the U.S., or 041-5238616; www. europcar.com). From May to October, it's open Monday to Friday 8:30am to 1pm and 2 to 6pm, Saturday and Sunday 8:30am to 12:30pm; November to April, hours are Monday to Friday 8:30am to 12:30pm and 2:30 to 6pm, Saturday 8:30am to 12:30pm.

Avis is at Piazzale Roma 496G (© **800/331-1084** in the U.S., or 041-5237377; www.avis.com). It's open Monday to Friday 8am to 6:30pm, and Saturday and Sunday 8:30am to 1:30pm.

6 Money

The **euro,** the single European currency, became the official currency of Italy and 11 other participating countries on January 1, 1999.

However, the euro didn't go into general circulation until early in 2002. The old currency, the Italian lire, disappeared into history on March 1, 2002, replaced by the euro, whose official abbreviation is "EUR." The symbol of the euro is a stylized *E:* €. Exchange rates of participating countries are locked into a common currency fluctuating against the U.S. dollar.

For more details on the euro, check out **www.europa.eu.int/ euro**.

The relative value of the euro has fluctuated wildly recently. For this guide, we used a rate of $1 = 1.60€, just before the rate dropped down to 1.25€. A last-minute check is advised before beginning your trip.

4

Where to Stay

Venice has some of the most expensive hotels in the world, but we've also found some wonderful lesser-known, moderately priced places, often on hard-to-find narrow streets. However, Venice has never been known as an inexpensive destination.

Because of the age and lack of uniformity of Venice's hotels, they offer widely varying rooms. For example, it's entirely possible to stay in a hotel generally considered "expensive" while paying only a "moderate" rate—if you settle for a less desirable room. Many "inexpensive" hotels and boardinghouses have two or three rooms in the "expensive" category. Usually these are more spacious and open onto a view. Also, if an elevator is essential for you, always inquire in advance when booking a room, because they don't always exist in old buildings.

The cheapest way to visit Venice is to book into a *locanda* (small inn), which is rated below the *pensione* (boardinghouse) in official Italian hotel lingo. Standards are highly variable in these places, many of which are dank, dusty, and dark. The rooms even in many second- or first-class hotels are often cramped, because space has always been a problem in Venice. In this "City of Light," most of the rooms in any category are dark, so be duly warned. Those with lots of light and opening onto the Grand Canal carry a hefty price tag.

The most difficult times to find rooms are during the February Carnevale, around Easter, and from June to September. Because of the tight hotel situation, it's advisable to make reservations as far in advance as possible (months in advance for summer, and even a year in advance for Carnevale). Outside of those peak times, you can virtually have your pick of rooms. Most hotels, if you ask at the reception desk, will grant you a 10% to 15% discount in winter (Nov 1–Mar 15), though getting it may require a little negotiation. A few hotels close in January if there's no prospect of business.

Should you arrive without a reservation, go to one of the **AVA reservations booths,** run by the Venetian Hotel Association, with locations at the train station, the municipal parking garage at Piazzale Roma, the airport, and the information point on the mainland where the highway comes to an end. The main office is at Piazzale Roma (② **041-5238032**). To get a room, you'll have to pay a deposit that's then rebated on your hotel bill. Depending on the hotel classification, deposits are 15€ to 50€ ($24–$80) per person. All hotel reservations booths are open daily from 9am to 10pm.

See "Neighborhoods in Brief" (p. 24) to get an idea of where you might want to base yourself, whether it be in less touristy San Polo or Dorsoduro or in and around Piazza San Marco (where hotels tend to be expensive, but where you're in the heart of the action).

1 Near Piazza San Marco

VERY EXPENSIVE

Gritti Palace ⋆⋆⋆   The Gritti, in a stately Grand Canal setting, is the renovated *palazzo* (palace) of 15th-century doge Andrea Gritti. Even after its takeover by ITT Sheraton, it's still a bit starchy and has a museum aura (some of the furnishings are roped off), but for sheer glamour and history, only the Cipriani (p. 58) tops it. (Stay at the Cipriani for quiet, isolation, and more recreational facilities, but stay here for a completely central location and service that's just as good.) Guests here are more pampered than those at the Danieli, the Gritti's closest rival in the heart of Venice, but expect to pay a great deal more at the Gritti for that extra notch in service. This was Hemingway's "home in Venice," and it has drawn some of the world's greatest theatrical, literary, political, and royal figures. The variety of guest rooms seems almost limitless, from elaborate suites to small singles. But throughout, the elegance is evident. The most spacious rooms face the *campo* (square), but we prefer the big corner doubles (second and third floors) with balconies overlooking the canal.

Campo Santa Maria del Giglio, San Marco 2467, 30124 Venezia. ② **800/325-3535** in the U.S., 416/947-4864 in Canada, or 041-794611. Fax 041-5200942. www.luxury collection.com/grittipalace. 93 units. 750€–1,060€ ($1,200–$1,696) double; from 1,250€ ($2,000) suite. Rates include breakfast. AE, DC, MC, V. Vaporetto: Santa Maria del Giglio. **Amenities:** Restaurant; bar; private boat launches and sightseeing tours; salon; room service; butler service; babysitting; laundry service; dry cleaning; nonsmoking rooms. *In room:* A/C, TV, Wi-Fi, minibar, hair dryer, safe.

EXPENSIVE

Hotel Concordia ⋆   The Concordia, in a russet-colored building with stone-trimmed windows, is the only hotel with rooms overlooking St. Mark's Square (only a few do, and they command a high price). A series of gold-plated marble steps takes you to the lobby, where you'll find a comfortable bar area, good service, and elevators to whisk you to the labyrinthine halls. The (quite small) guest rooms

Where to Stay in Venice

Near the Railway Station

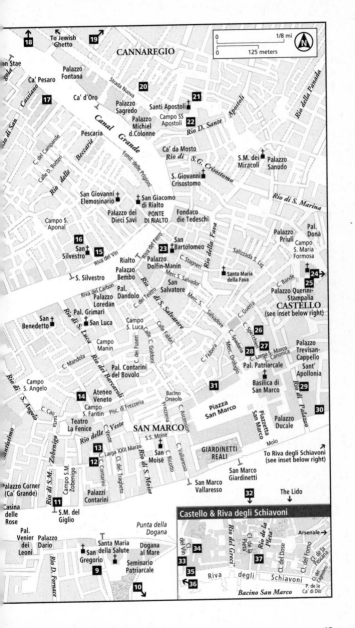

CANNAREGIO

0 — 1/8 mi
0 — 125 meters

To Jewish Ghetto

18
19

Palazzo Fontana
Ca' Pesaro
17
Ca' d'Oro
20
Palazzo Sagredo
Santi Apostoli
21
Palazzo Michiel d.Colonne
Campo SS Apostoli
22
Pescaria
Rio D. Sante Apostoli
Ca' da Mosto
Rio di S.G. Crisostomo
S.M. dei Miracoli
Palazzo Sanudo
S. Giovanni Crisostomo
San Giovanni Elemosinario
S. Giacomo di Rialto
Rio di S. Marina
Palazzo dei Dieci Savi
PONTE DI RIALTO
Fondaco die Tedeschi
Campo S. Aponal
San Bartolomeo
23
Palazzo Priuli
Pal. Donà
Campo S. Maria Formosa
16
15
San Silvestro
Rialto
Palazzo Bembo
Palazzo Dolfin-Manin
San Salvador
Santa Maria della Fava
24
25
Palazzo Querini-Stampalia
(see inset below right)
S. Silvestro
Riva del Vin
Pal. Dandolo
San Salvatore
Riva del Carbon
Palazzo Loredan
CASTELLO
San Benedetto
Pal. Grimari
San Luca
Campo S. Luca
26
27
Palazzo Trevisan-Cappello
Campo Manin
28
Pal. Patriarcale
Sant' Apollonia
Pal. Contarini del Bovolo
31
Basilica di San Marco
29
14
Ateneo Veneto
Campo S. Fantin
Bacino Orseolo
Piazza San Marco
Campo S. Angelo
Teatro La Fenice
SAN MARCO
Piazzetta San Marco
30
Palazzo Ducale
Palazzo Corner (Ca' Grande)
13
12
S.S. Moisè
San Moisè
GIARDINETTI REALI
Molo
To Riva degli Schiavoni (see inset below right)
Campo S.M. Zobenigo
Palazzi Contarini
San Marco Vallaresso
San Marco Giardinetti
32
The Lido
11
S.M. del Giglio
Casina delle Rose
Pal. Venier dei Leoni
Palazzo Dario
Santa Maria della Salute
Punta della Dogana
San Gregorio
Dogana al Mare
Seminario Patriarcale
9
10

Castello & Riva degli Schiavoni

Arsenale →
34
37
33
35
36
Riva degli Schiavoni
Bacino San Marco
P. de la Ca' di Dio

43

are decorated in a Venetian antique style, with small Murano chandeliers, coordinated fabrics, hand-painted furnishings, and marble bathrooms.

Calle Larga, San Marco 367, 30124 Venezia. © **041-5206866**. Fax 041-5206775. www.hotelconcordia.com. 57 units, some with shower only. 220€–413€ ($352–$661) double; 239€–450€ ($382–$720) suite. Rates include buffet breakfast. AE, DC, MC, V. Vaporetto: San Marco. **Amenities:** Restaurant; bar; room service; babysitting; laundry service; dry cleaning; nonsmoking rooms. *In room:* A/C, TV, Wi-Fi, minibar, hair dryer, safe.

Hotel Saturnia International ☆☆

Far superior to the Scandinavia (see below), this is one of Venice's most successful adaptations of a 14th-century *palazzo*. You're surrounded by richly embellished beauty: a grand hall with a wooden staircase, iron chandeliers, fine paintings, and beamed ceilings. The individually styled guest rooms are generally spacious and furnished with chandeliers, Venetian antiques, tapestry rugs, gilt mirrors, and carved ceilings. A few on the top floor have small balconies; others overlook the garden in back.

Calle Larga XXII Marzo, San Marco 2398, 30124 Venezia. © **041-5208377**. Fax 041-5207131. www.hotelsaturnia.it. 95 units, a few with tub or shower only. 198€–465€ ($317–$744) double; 279€–525€ ($446–$840) triple. Rates include buffet breakfast. AE, DC, MC, V. Vaporetto: San Marco. **Amenities:** Restaurant; lounge; room service; babysitting; laundry service; dry cleaning; nonsmoking rooms; 1 room for those w/limited mobility. *In room:* A/C, TV, Wi-Fi, minibar, hair dryer, safe.

Hotel Scandinavia ☆

This hotel isn't actually in San Marco (it's in neighboring Castello, just off a colorful square), but it has a convenient location not far from Piazza San Marco. The public rooms are rococo, filled with copies of 18th-century Italian chairs and Venetian-glass chandeliers. The guest rooms are of a decent size and are decorated in the Venetian style, but modern comforts have been added. The lobby lounge overlooks the *campo*. Breakfast is the only meal served, but the hotel staff will direct you to several good dining spots within a short walk of the hotel.

Campo Santa Maria Formosa, Castello 5240, 30122 Venezia. © **041-5223507**. Fax 041-5235232. www.scandinaviahotel.com. 34 units, some with shower only. 120€–240€ ($192–$384) double; 150€–300€ ($240–$480) triple. Rates include buffet breakfast. AE, DC, MC, V. Vaporetto: San Zaccaria or Rialto. **Amenities:** Bar; room service; babysitting. *In room:* A/C, TV, Wi-Fi, minibar, hair dryer, safe.

Hotel Violino d'Oro ☆

The 18th-century Palazzo Barozzi is now a restored three-story hotel. Its midsize guest rooms are handsomely furnished, with well-kept bathrooms. Two rooms and the junior suite open onto private terraces. Ms. Cristina and her family run the hotel with both style and grace.

Campiello Barozzi, San Marco 2091, 30124 Venezia. ② **041-2770841**: Fax 041-2771001. www.violinodoro.com. 26 units. 215€–315€ ($344–$504) double. Rates include breakfast. AE, MC, V. Vaporetto: San Marco. **Amenities:** Breakfast room; bar; babysitting; all nonsmoking rooms. *In room:* A/C, TV, minibar, hair dryer.

MODERATE

Ca' Dei Dogi 🏆🏆 *Finds*   This small *albergo* is reached down a maze of narrow alleyways. Set in a tranquil pocket of Venice, it lies just a short walk from the Bridge of Sighs and the Doge's Palace. This is a remarkable find in that it combines luxury and value, two elements that rarely, if ever, come together in Venice. Each of the midsize bedrooms is individually decorated, the details of decor carefully chosen for both taste and comfort. The most idyllic of the accommodations includes a small alcove and opens onto the ducal palace. Much altered over the years, the palace itself dates from the 15th century.

Corte Santa Scolastica, Castello 4242, 30122 Venezia. ② **041-2413759**. Fax 041-5285403. www.cadeidogi.it. 6 units. 130€–250€ ($208–$400) double. MC, V. Vaporetto: San Zaccaria. **Amenities:** Restaurant; bar; room service; babysitting; laundry service; dry cleaning. *In room:* A/C, TV, minibar, hair dryer, safe.

Hotel do Pozzi 🏆   A short stroll from Piazza San Marco, this small place feels more like a country tavern than a hotel. Its original structure is 200 years old and opens onto a paved courtyard with potted greenery. The sitting and dining rooms are furnished with antiques (and near-antiques) intermixed with utilitarian modern decor. Half the guest rooms open onto the street and half onto a view of an inner garden where breakfast is served in summer. Some have Venetian styling with antique reproductions; others are in a more contemporary, more sterile vein.

Corte do Pozzi, San Marco 2373, 30124 Venezia. ② **041-5207855**. Fax 041-5229413. www.hoteldopozzi.it. 35 units, some with shower only. 130€–280€ ($208–$448) double. Rates include buffet breakfast. AE, DC, MC, V. Vaporetto: Santa Maria del Giglio. **Amenities:** Dining room; bar; babysitting; laundry service/dry cleaning; nonsmoking rooms. *In room:* A/C, TV, minibar, hair dryer.

Hotel La Fenice et des Artistes *Overrated*   For decades one of the most famous hotels of Venice, this landmark is now in sad decline, although it still has its fans and one of the most desirable of all Venetian locations. Maintenance could be better, and the staff has grown complacent. This hotel offers widely varying accommodations in two connected buildings, each at least 100 years old. One is rather romantic, though timeworn, with an impressive staircase leading to the ornate rooms (one building even has its own small garden and terraces). Your satin-lined room might have an inlaid desk and a wardrobe painted in the Venetian manner to match a baroque bed frame. The main building, site of the reception desk, is the more desirable, furnished in a more typically Venetian style.

Campiello de la Fenice, San Marco 1936, 30124 Venezia. ✆ **041-5232333.** Fax 041-5203721. www.fenicehotels.it. 69 units. 135€–270€ ($216–$432) double; 200€–295€ ($320–$472) suite. Rates include buffet breakfast. AE, DC, MC, V. Vaporetto: San Marco. **Amenities:** Restaurant; bar; room service; babysitting; laundry service; dry cleaning. *In room:* A/C, TV, hair dryer, safe.

Hotel Montecarlo   This hotel, which hides behind a 17th-century facade just 2 minutes from Piazza San Marco, was significantly renovated and vastly improved in 2001. Upper halls are lined with paintings by Venetian artists, while guest rooms feature Venetian-style furniture and Venetian-glass chandeliers. Some are quite dark, the curse of many city hotels.

Calle dei Specchieri, San Marco 463, 30124 Venezia. ✆ **041-5207144.** Fax 041-5207789. www.venicehotelmontecarlo.com. 48 units. 125€–290€ ($200–$464) double. Rates include buffet breakfast. AE, DC, MC, V. Vaporetto: San Marco. **Amenities:** Restaurant; bar; room service; babysitting; laundry service; nonsmoking rooms. *In room:* A/C, TV, hair dryer, safe.

INEXPENSIVE

Hotel ai do Mori ⭐ *Value*   This 1450s town house lies about 10 paces from the heart of Venice. You'll have to balance your need for space with your desire for a view (and your willingness to climb stairs, because there's no elevator): The lower-level rooms are larger but don't have views; the third- and fourth-floor rooms are cramped but have sweeping views over the basilica's domes. Owner Antonella Bernardi frequently upgrades the building. The furniture in the guest rooms is simple and modern, and most of the street noise is muffled by double-paned windows. Try for the painters' room (if you don't mind climbing 77 steps)—you'll be rewarded with a rooftop balcony. No meals are served, but there are dozens of cafes in the neighborhood.

Calle Larga San Marco, San Marco 658, 30124 Venezia. ✆ **041-5204817.** Fax 041-5205328. www.hotelaidomori.com. 11 units, 9 with private bathroom (showers only). 60€–95€ ($96–$152) double without bathroom; 80€–150€ ($128–$240) double with bathroom. MC, V. Vaporetto: San Marco. **Amenities:** Lounge; all nonsmoking rooms. *In room:* A/C, TV, hair dryer, safe.

Locanda Armizo ⭐ *Finds*   This is a glorified B&B and a real discovery with one of the most gracious hosts in Venice, Massimiliano. He has taken an antique home of a former Venetian merchant and converted it into this little inn decorated in a typically Venetian style. The word *armizo* means "mooring" in old Venetian. The location is only a 2-minute walk from the Rialto Bridge and close to the Grand Canal where ancient ships indeed used to moor. Bedrooms have reproductions of Venetian antiques and are immaculately kept and midsize, each with a small private bathroom with shower.

Campo San Silvestro–San Polo 1104, 30100 Venezia. ⓒ **041-5206473**. Fax 041-2960384. www.locandaarmizo.com. 6 units. 69€–189€ ($110–$302) double; 90€–280€ ($144–$448) junior suite. Rates include breakfast. AE, MC, V. Vaporetto: San Silvestro. **Amenities:** Breakfast lounge; babysitting; laundry service; dry cleaning; all nonsmoking rooms. *In room:* A/C, TV, minibar, hair dryer, safe.

Locanda Fiorita 𝕽 *(Value)*   In a red-painted *palazzo*, parts of which date from the 1700s, this is a little charmer and both a winning and affordable place to stay. At the close of the century, new management took over and massively renovated the place. Everything was given a kind of faux Venetian style of the 1700s. The location is on a postage-stamp square off Campo Santo Stefano. If available, ask for room no. 1 or 10, which offers a little patio beneath a glorious wisteria vine best enjoyed in the spring. Bedrooms have style and a certain Venetian flair, giving you much comfort either in the main building or in an annex. Six other equally good bedrooms lie in a nearby annex.

San Marco 3457 (on Campiello Novo), 30124 Venezia. ⓒ **041-5234754**. Fax 041-5228043. www.locandafiorita.com. 16 units. 110€–155€ ($176–$248) double. Rates include buffet breakfast. AE, MC, V. Vaporetto: Sant'Angelo. **Amenities:** Breakfast-only room service; tour desk; babysitting; all nonsmoking rooms. *In room:* A/C, TV, Wi-Fi, hair dryer.

2 In Castello/On Riva degli Schiavoni

Several of the hotels in this section are also very close to Piazza San Marco.

VERY EXPENSIVE

Hotel Danieli 𝕽𝕽𝕽   The Cipriani is more exclusive and isolated, almost like a spa, and the Gritti coddles its guests a bit more, but the Danieli is clearly number three among the fabulous *palazzi* hotels of Venice. Comparisons between the Danieli and the Gritti are inevitable. The Danieli broods, as the Gritti sparkles. The Danieli is more baronial, and the Gritti is more like home (that is, if your home is a *palazzo*). The Danieli sprawls, whereas the Gritti is intimate.

The Danieli was built as a grand showcase by Doge Dandolo in the 14th century and in 1822 was transformed into a "hotel for kings." The atmosphere is luxurious; even the balconies opening off the main lounge are illuminated by stained-glass skylights. The guest rooms range widely in price, dimension, decor, and vistas (those opening onto the lagoon cost a lot more, but are also susceptible to the noise of Riva degli Schiavoni). You're housed in one of three buildings: a modern structure (least desirable), a 19th-century building, or the 14th-century Venetian-Gothic Palazzo Dandolo (most desirable). On the downside, although the *palazzo* rooms are the most romantic, they also are the smallest.

Riva degli Schiavoni, Castello 4196, 30122 Venezia. ✆ **800/325-3535** in the U.S. and Canada, or 041-5226480. Fax 041-5200208. www.starwoodhotels.com. 233 units. 475€–925€ ($760–$1,480) double; from 2,470€ ($3,952) suite. AE, DC, MC, V. Vaporetto: San Zaccaria. **Amenities:** Restaurant; bar; 24-hr. concierge; room service; babysitting; laundry service; dry cleaning; nonsmoking rooms. *In room:* A/C, TV, minibar, hair dryer, safe.

EXPENSIVE

Hotel Bisanzio ⟨⋆⟩   A few steps from Piazza San Marco, this hotel in the former home of sculptor Alessandro Vittoria offers good service. It has an elevator and terraces, plus a little bar and a mooring for gondolas and motorboats. The lounge opens onto a traditional courtyard. The guest rooms are generally quiet, each done up in a Venetian antique style. The most requested rooms are the eight opening onto private balconies.

Calle della Pietà, Riva degli Schiavoni 3651, 30122 Venezia. ✆ **041-5203100.** Fax 041-5204114. www.bisanzio.com. 50 units, half with shower only. 210€–330€ ($336–$528) double. Rates include buffet breakfast. AE, DC, MC, V. Vaporetto: San Zaccaria. **Amenities:** Breakfast room; bar; room service; babysitting; laundry service; dry cleaning; nonsmoking rooms. *In room:* A/C, TV, minibar, hair dryer, safe.

Locanda Vivaldi ⟨⋆⟩ ⟨*Finds*⟩   Here is a rare chance to immerse yourself in a cliché of Venetian charm: The house of the composer Antonio Vivaldi (1678–1741) has been converted into a hotel. The most original and influential Italian composer of his day, Vivaldi was *maestro de' concerti* in Venice from 1716 to 1738, during which time he lived at this house. In keeping with the spirit of the maestro, the Locanda has been decorated with baroque ornamentation. Bedrooms are comfortably lush, evoking a time gone by—but with modern conveniences such as tiled bathrooms, each with a shower/box sauna and Jacuzzi. Standard doubles have a view of the Grand Canal, while superior double units offer a lagoon view and also contain a hydromassage tub.

Riva degli Schiavoni 4152, 30122 Venezia. ✆ **041-2770477.** Fax 041-2770489. www.locandavivaldi.it. 22 units, some with shower only. 160€–525€ ($256–$840) double; 300€–770€ ($480–$1,232) suite. Rates include buffet breakfast. AE, DC, MC, V. Vaporetto: San Zaccaria. **Amenities:** Bar; room service; laundry service; dry cleaning. *In room:* A/C, TV, minibar, safe.

MODERATE

Hotel Campiello   This pink-fronted Venetian town house dates from the 1400s, but today you'll find cost-conscious Venetian-style accommodations here. This government-rated two-star hotel is better than its rating implies thanks to a spectacular location and Renaissance touches such as marble mosaic floors and carefully polished hardwoods. The guest rooms are cozy, with tidy bathrooms. The only room with a separate entrance is a ground-floor hideaway that, fortunately, has been flooded by high tides only once in the past century.

Campiello del Vin, Castello 4647, 30122 Venezia. *C* 041-5205764. Fax 041-5205798. www.hcampiello.it. 17 units (showers only). 100€–250€ ($160–$400) double; 170€–350€ ($272–$560) suite. Rates include buffet breakfast. AE, DC, MC, V. Closed 3 weeks in Jan. Vaporetto: San Zaccaria. **Amenities:** Bar; babysitting; all nonsmoking rooms. *In room:* A/C, TV, hair dryer, safe.

Hotel Savoia & Jolanda *R*   The Savoia & Jolanda occupies a prize position on Venice's premier boulevard, with a lagoon as its front yard. Although its exterior reflects old Venice, the interior is somewhat spiritless; the staff, however, makes life comfortable. Most of the modern guest rooms have a view of the boats and the Lido; they contain desks and armchairs. Some units are large enough to contain three or four beds.

Riva degli Schiavoni, Castello 4187, 30122 Venezia. *C* **041-5206644.** Fax 041-5207494. www.hotelsavoiajolanda.it. 75 units, some with shower only. 208€–425€ ($333–$680) double; 408€–620€ ($653–$992) suite. Rates include buffet breakfast. AE, DC, MC, V. Vaporetto: San Zaccaria. **Amenities:** Restaurant; bar; room service; babysitting; laundry service; dry cleaning; nonsmoking rooms. *In room:* A/C, TV, Wi-Fi, minibar, hair dryer, safe.

La Residenza *RR*   In a 14th-century building that looks a lot like a miniature Doge's Palace, this little hotel is on a residential square where children play soccer and older people feed the pigeons. You'll pass through a stone vestibule lined with ancient Roman columns before ringing another doorbell at the bottom of a flight of stairs. First an iron gate and then a door will open into an enormous salon filled with antiques, 300-year-old paintings, and some of the most marvelously preserved walls in Venice. The guest rooms are far less opulent, with contemporary pieces and small bathrooms, but beds are comfortable.

Campo Bandiera e Moro, Castello 3608, 30122 Venezia. *C* **041-5285315.** Fax 041-5238859. www.venicelaresidenza.com. 15 units (showers only). 105€–180€ ($168–$288) double. Rates include continental breakfast. MC, V. Vaporetto: Arsenale. **Amenities:** Lounge. *In room:* A/C, TV, minibar, hair dryer, safe.

INEXPENSIVE

Albergo Doni   The Doni sits about a 3-minute walk from St. Mark's. Most of its very basic guest rooms overlook either a garden with a tall fig tree or a little canal where four or five gondolas are usually tied up. Simplicity and cleanliness prevail, especially in the down-to-earth rooms. The beds, often brass, are a little worn but still comfortable, and the plumbing is antiquated but still working fine.

Calle de Vin, Castello 4656, 30122 Venezia. ℰ/fax 041-5224267. www.albergo doni.it. 13 units, 3 with private bathroom. 95€ ($152) double without bathroom; 120€ ($192) double with bathroom. Rates include continental breakfast. No credit cards. Vaporetto: San Zaccaria. **Amenities:** Breakfast room; lounge. *In room:* No phone.

Hotel Al Piave *(Value)*   For Venice, this centrally located hotel is a real bargain, and the Puppin family welcomes you with style. Although the hotel is rated only one star by the government, its level of comfort is excellent, and its decor and ambience are inviting. Even some guests who could afford to pay more select the Piave for its cozy warmth. The small but comfortable guest rooms come with well-maintained bathrooms.

Ruga Giuffa, Castello 4838–4840, 30122 Venezia. ℰ 041-5285174. Fax 041-5238512. www.hotelalpiave.com. 15 units (showers only). 120€–220€ ($192–$352) double; 180€–270€ ($288–$432) suite for 3. Rates include continental breakfast. AE, DC, MC, V. Vaporetto: San Zaccaria. **Amenities:** Lounge; all non-smoking rooms. *In room:* A/C, TV, minibar, hair dryer, safe.

3 Near the Ponte di Rialto

At the epicenter of this neighborhood is the bustling activity of the Rialto Market itself. This area is a mixed bag, with plenty of decaying apartment houses alongside tourist sights. There are some fine shops and restaurants, but also some of the worst tourist traps in Venice. Our recommendations will steer you clear of these.

MODERATE

Hotel Rialto   The Rialto opens right onto the San Marco side of the Grand Canal at the foot of the Ponte di Rialto, the famous bridge flanked with shops. Its guest rooms combine modern or Venetian furniture with ornate Venetian ceilings and wall decorations. The hotel has been considerably improved in recent years, with its furnishings upgraded and made more inviting. The most desirable and expensive doubles overlook the canal.

Riva del Ferro, San Marco 5149, 30124 Venezia. ℰ 041-5209166. Fax 041-5238958. www.rialtohotel.com. 79 units, half with showers only. 240€–340€ ($384–$544) double; 270€–600€ ($432–$960) junior suite. Rates include buffet breakfast. AE,

DC, MC, V. Vaporetto: Rialto. **Amenities:** Dining room; bar; room service; babysitting; laundry service; dry cleaning. *In room:* A/C, TV, minibar, hair dryer, safe.

Locanda Sturion ✦   You may recognize the facade of this building from a painting by Carpaccio hanging in the Gallerie dell'Accademia. In the early 1200s, the Venetian doges commissioned this site as a place where foreign merchants could stay for the night. After long stints as a private residence, the Sturion caters to visitors once again. A private entrance leads up four steep flights of marble steps, past apartments, to a labyrinth of cozy, clean, but not overly large guest rooms. Most have views over the terra-cotta rooftops of this congested neighborhood; two open onto Grand Canal views.

Calle del Sturion, San Polo 679, 30125 Venezia. ✆ **041-5236243.** Fax 041-5228378. www.locandasturion.com. 11 units. 80€–310€ ($128–$496) double; 120€–360€ ($192–$576) triple. Rates include buffet breakfast. MC, V. Vaporetto: Rialto. **Amenities:** Lounge; all nonsmoking rooms. *In room:* A/C, TV, minibar, beverage maker, hair dryer, safe.

INEXPENSIVE

Locanda Ca' le Vele ✦ *(Finds)*   One of the many—and also one of the best—little inns to open in Venice post-millennium lies within easy walking distance of the Rialto Bridge and St. Mark's Square. It opens onto the Santa Sofia Canal. Its charm is of another day, although it has been completely modernized. The elegant bedrooms are both tastefully and comfortably furnished in the classic Venetian style of exposed beams, damasks, marbles, and Murano glass chandeliers. The inn is suitable for families, as many rooms are triples and quads.

Ca le Vele, 30131 Venezia. ✆ **041-2413960.** Fax 041-2414280. www.locanda levele.com. 6 units. 70€–180€ ($112–$288) double; 110€–190€ ($176–$304) triple; 120€–220€ ($192–$352) quad; 160€–260€ ($256–$416) suite. AE, DC, MC, V. Vaporetto: Ca d'Oro. **Amenities:** Room service. *In room:* A/C, TV, minibar, hair dryer, safe.

4 In Cannaregio

This is one of our favorite sections of Venice because it affords visitors a chance to see some of the local life. Otherwise, you'd think that nobody lived here except tourists. Nearly a third of the shrinking population of Venice calls Cannaregio home.

EXPENSIVE

Boscolo Grand Hotel dei Dogi ✦✦ *(Finds)*   Once an embassy and later a convent, this is one of the hotel secrets of Venice, definitely a hidden gem. On the northern tier of Venice, dei Dogi looks across the lagoon to the mainland. As you sit in the beautiful little garden of rosebushes, you will think that you've arrived at a Venetian Shangri-La. Acquired by the Boscolo chain in 1998, the hotel lies just a short stroll down the canal from the Church of Madonna dell'Orto, where Tintoretto lies buried. Bedrooms are elegantly decorated in a palatial Venetian style, with gilt and polish. Some 18th-century frescoes decorate the walls of the bedrooms, as do antique mirrors, swag draperies, and doors intricately inlaid with veneer.

Fondamenta Madonna dell'Orto 3500, 30121 Venezia. ℂ **041-2208111.** Fax 041-722278. www.boscolohotels.com. 76 units. 179€–589€ ($286–$942) double; from 539€ ($862) junior suite; from 1,200€ ($1,920) suite. AE, DC, MC, V. Vaporetto: Madonna dell'Orto. **Amenities:** Restaurant; bar; spa; room service; babysitting; laundry service; dry cleaning; nonsmoking rooms. *In room:* A/C, TV, Wi-Fi, minibar, hair dryer, safe.

Locanda ai Santi Apostoli ⍟ *(Kids)*   If you can't afford the Gritti but you still fantasize about living in a *palazzo* overlooking the Grand Canal, near the Rialto, here's your chance. This inn isn't cheap, but it's a lot less expensive than the palaces nearby. The hotel is on the top floor of a 15th-century building, and the guest rooms, though simple, are roomy and decorated in pastels, and they often contain antiques. Naturally, the two rooms opening onto the canal are the most requested. Extra beds can often be set up in the rooms to accommodate children. This is one of three 14th- or 15th-century Venetian palaces still owned by the family that built it.

Strada Nuova, Cannaregio 4391, 30131 Venezia. ℂ **041-5212612.** Fax 041-5212611. www.locandasantiapostoli.com. 11 units (showers only). 100€–220€ ($160–$352) double; 200€–320€ ($320–$512) double with Grand Canal view; 200€–400€ ($320–$640) suite. Rates include continental breakfast. AE, DC, MC, V. Vaporetto: Ca d'Oro. **Amenities:** Breakfast room; babysitting; laundry service; dry cleaning. *In room:* A/C, TV, minibar, hair dryer.

Residenza Cannaregio ⍟ *(Finds)*   Lying in a charming, tranquil corner of Venice, this little stunner has a dramatically modern interior in spite of its ancient origins as a monastery from the 17th century. By the 19th century it had become a *squero,* a place where gondolas are built. All its former roles have been wiped away in a complete renovation of this *residenza,* with its several lounge rooms, a popular American bar (Il Grappolo), and a first-class restaurant, along with a magnificent Venetian garden. Resting under beamed ceilings, the guest rooms are like garrets with style, comfort, and drama. The use of wood, wrought iron, Venetian tiles, and ancient stones creates a certain architectural distinctiveness.

Cannaregio 3210A, 30121 Venezia. © **041-5244332.** Fax 041-2757952. www. residenzacannaregio.it. 66 units. 90€–300€ ($144–$480) double; 120€–400€ ($192–$640) suite. Rates include American-style buffet breakfast. AE, DC, MC, V. Vaporetto: San Alvise. **Amenities:** Restaurant; bar; business center; room service; babysitting; laundry service; dry cleaning; nonsmoking rooms. *In room:* A/C, TV, Wi-Fi, minibar, safe.

MODERATE

Hotel Giorgione ⓕ   Here's a modern hotel with traditional Venetian decor. The lounges and public rooms boast fine furnishings and decorative accessories, while the comfortable and stylish guest rooms are designed to coddle guests. Each unit comes with an excellent bed and a tiled bathroom. The hotel also has a typical Venetian garden. It's rated second class by the government, but the Giorgione maintains higher standards than many first-class places.

Campo SS. Apostoli, Cannaregio 4587, 30131 Venezia. © **041-5225810.** Fax 041-5239092. www.hotelgiorgione.it. 76 units, some with shower only. 150€–310€ ($240–$496) double; 250€–400€ ($400–$640) suite. Rates include buffet breakfast. AE, DC, MC, V. Vaporetto: Ca' d'Oro. **Amenities:** Bar; room service; babysitting; laundry service; dry cleaning; nonsmoking rooms; 1 room for those w/limited mobility. *In room:* A/C, TV, minibar, hair dryer, safe.

Hotel San Geremia *(Value)*   For years the small Geremia was a government-rated one-star hotel that many guests considered worthy of two-star status. In 1997, the government raised it to two stars, justifying an increase in rates. Neither grand nor well located, the Geremia still fills up every night because it offers good value for the money. Located in a modernized early-1900s setting, this hotel is a 5-minute walk from the train station. Inside, you'll find well-maintained pale-green guest rooms. They're often small, but each comes with a good bed. No elevator, but the price is appealing—and a little climb up the stairs might help you work off the pasta and gelato you polished off at lunch, right?

Campo San Geremia, Cannaregio 290A, 30121 Venezia. © **041-716245.** Fax 041-5242342. www.sangeremiahotel.com. 20 units, 14 with private bathroom (showers only). 50€–75€ ($80–$120) double without bathroom; 75€–115€ ($120–$184) double with bathroom. Rates include continental breakfast. AE, DC, MC, V. Vaporetto: Ferrovia. **Amenities:** Breakfast room; nonsmoking rooms. *In room:* TV, minibar, hair dryer, safe.

INEXPENSIVE

Hotel Abbazia   The benefit of staying here is that there's no need to transfer onto any *vaporetto*—you can walk from the rail station, about 10 minutes away. This hotel was built in 1889 as a monastery for barefooted Carmelite monks, who established a verdant garden in what's now the courtyard; it's planted with subtropical plants that thrive, sheltered as they are from the cold Adriatic winds. You'll find a highly accommodating staff and comfortable but very plain guest rooms with well-kept bathrooms. Twenty-five units overlook the courtyard, ensuring quiet in an otherwise noisy neighborhood.

Calle Priuli ai Cavaletti, Cannaregio 68, 30121 Venezia. ⓒ 041-717333. Fax 041-717949. www.abbaziahotel.com. 49 units, some with shower only. 95€–270€ ($152–$432) double; 200€–300€ ($320–$480) suite. Rates include buffet breakfast. AE, DC, MC, V. Vaporetto: Ferrovia. **Amenities:** Breakfast room; bar; room service; non-smoking rooms. *In room:* A/C, TV, minibar, hair dryer, safe.

5 In Santa Croce

The eastern part of Santa Croce is rarely visited by most tourists, but it represents a slice of authentic Venetian life. Although Santa Croce sprawls all the way to Piazzale Roma, its heart is the Campo San Giacomo dell'Orio.

MODERATE

Hotel San Cassiano Ca' Favretto ✷ The hotel's gondola pier affords views of the lacy Ca' d'Oro, perhaps Venice's most beautiful building. The hotel is a 14th-century palace (it contained the studio of 19th-c. painter Giacomo Favretto), and the owner has carefully worked to preserve the original details, such as a 6m (20-ft.) beamed ceiling in the entrance. Fifteen of the conservatively decorated guest rooms overlook one of two canals, and many are filled with antiques or high-quality reproductions. Generally the housekeeping is excellent.

Calle della Rosa, Santa Croce 2232, 30135 Venezia. ⓒ 041-5241768. Fax 041-721033. www.sancassiano.it. 35 units. 120€–439€ ($192–$702) double. Rates include buffet breakfast. AE, DC, MC, V. Vaporetto: San Stae. **Amenities:** Dining room; bar; babysitting; nonsmoking rooms. *In room:* A/C, TV, minibar, hair dryer, safe.

6 In Dorsoduro

On the opposite side of the Accademia Bridge from San Marco, Dorsoduro is one of our favorite neighborhoods of Venice, with a real flavor of the city and a dash of funky chic. Accommodations are limited, but rather special and full of character.

EXPENSIVE

Ca Maria Adele ✷ *(Finds* This whimsically decorated inn lies at the tip of the Dorsoduro district, only a short walk from St. Mark's Square. An *Il Settecentro* Venice style meets Zen minimalism here, with geometric wood furnishings resting beneath flamboyant Murano chandeliers and wood-beam rafters. The hotel sits behind the facade of a 16th-century *palazzo* facing a canal, with views looking out at the church of Santa Maria della Salute. The bedrooms are spread across four floors of the old *palazzo*. Each of the themed accommodations—the Doge's Room, the Red Room, the Oriental Room, the Black Room—has been painstakingly restored. Damask fabrics with African wood pieces create a tasteful, harmonious atmosphere.

Dorsoduro 111, 30123 Venezia. © **041-5203078.** Fax 041-5289013. www.camaria adele.it. 14 units. 310€–500€ ($496–$800) double; 410€–700€ ($656–$1,120) themed room or suite. AE, DC, MC, V. Vaporetto: Salute. **Amenities:** Lounge; room service; massage; babysitting; laundry service; dry cleaning; nonsmoking rooms. *In room:* A/C, TV, Wi-Fi, minibar, hair dryer, safe.

Ca' Pisani *⚘⚘ (Finds* The style of this boutique hotel, located near the Gallerie dell'Accademia, evokes the 1930s and 1940s, but the setting is a former Venetian nobleman's residence from the end of the 16th century. Accommodations come in a wide variety of sizes, ranging from standard doubles to spacious suites. The design is unusual for Venice in that it concentrates on the avant-garde trends that blossomed "between the wars." The lobby, for example, recalls the forms of futurism, with a wealth of marble and walnut wood. The walls in the bedrooms evoke the graphics of Mondrian. Our favorites are the two studios with loft sleeping areas. The rooms are equipped with modern technology such as electric curtains and remote-control door openings. The bathrooms are under "starlight," creating the effect of small shining stars. A roof-terrace solarium opens onto the rooftops of Venice.

Dorsoduro 979A, 30123 Venezia. © **041-2401411.** Fax 041-2771061. www. capisanihotel.it. 29 units. 213€–415€ ($341–$664) double; 294€–495€ ($470–$792) suite. Rates include buffet breakfast. AE, DC, MC, V. Vaporetto: Accademia. **Amenities:** Restaurant; bar; access to next-door gym; sauna; room service; babysitting; laundry service; dry cleaning; nonsmoking rooms; rooms for those w/limited mobility. *In room:* A/C, TV, Wi-Fi, minibar, hair dryer, safe.

DD724 *⚘⚘ (Finds* Just steps from the Peggy Guggenheim museum and the Gallerie dell'Accademia, this one-of-a-kind lodging is the brainchild of hotelier Chiara Bocchini, who wanted to create something new and different for Venice. It became a hit from the day it first opened in 2003. The odd name comes from the hotel's location in the Dorsoduro area. A house of charm and grace, it's a luxurious choice and ideal for a romantic getaway. Abstract paintings by contemporary artists hang in the tiny lobby, and the intimate breakfast area is lined with travel and art books for guests to use. (Incidentally, breakfast is cooked individually for each guest.) The bedrooms are one-of-a-kind, with beamed ceilings, velvet armchairs, Signoria di Firenze linens, and luxurious bathrooms—cozy havens rarely found in Venice.

Dorsoduro 724, 30123 Venezia. ⒸⓉ **041-2770262**. Fax 041-2960633. www.dd724.it. 7 units. 230€–410€ ($368–$656) double; 280€–520€ ($448–$832) suite. Rates include breakfast. AE, DC, MC, V. Vaporetto: Accademia. **Amenities:** Bar; room service; massage; babysitting; laundry service; dry cleaning; all nonsmoking rooms. *In room:* A/C, TV, Wi-Fi, minibar, beverage maker, hair dryer, safe.

Hotel American 𝕮 *Value*   There's nothing American about this ocher building across the Grand Canal from the most heavily touristed areas of Venice. The modest lobby is filled with murals, warm colors, and antiques. The guest rooms are comfortably furnished in a Venetian style, but they vary in size; some of the smaller ones are a bit cramped. Many rooms with their own private terraces face the canal. On the second floor is a beautiful terrace where guests can relax over drinks.

Campo San Vio, Accademia 628, 30123 Venezia. ⒸⓉ **041-5204733**. Fax 041-5204048. www.hotelamerican.com. 29 units. 80€–370€ ($128–$592) double; 130€–460€ ($208–$736) triple. Rates include buffet breakfast. AE, MC, V. Vaporetto: Accademia. **Amenities:** Breakfast room; bar; room service; babysitting; laundry service; dry cleaning; nonsmoking rooms. *In room:* A/C, TV, Wi-Fi, minibar, hair dryer, safe.

MODERATE

Hotel La Calcina   La Calcina lies in a secluded and less-trampled district that used to be the English enclave before the area developed a broader base of tourism. John Ruskin, who wrote *The Stones of Venice,* stayed here in 1877, and he charted the ground for his latter-day compatriots. This *pensione* is absolutely spotless, and the furnishings are well chosen but hardly elaborate. The guest rooms are cozy and comfortable.

Zattere al Gesuati, Dorsoduro 780, 30123 Venezia. ⒸⓉ **041-5206466**. Fax 041-5227045. www.lacalcina.com. 29 units (showers only). 110€–250€ ($176–$400) double; 140€–240€ ($224–$384) suite. Rates include buffet breakfast. AE, DC, MC, V. Vaporetto: Zattere. **Amenities:** Restaurant; bar; room service; babysitting; laundry service; dry cleaning; all nonsmoking rooms. *In room:* A/C, TV, Wi-Fi, minibar, hair dryer, safe.

Pensione Accademia 𝕮𝕮 *Value*   The Accademia is the most patrician of the *pensioni,* in a villa whose garden is bounded by the junction of two canals. The interior features Gothic-style paneling, Venetian chandeliers, and Victorian-era furniture, and the upstairs sitting room is flanked by two large windows. This place has long been a favorite of the *Room with a View* crowd of Brits and scholars; it's often booked months in advance. The guest rooms are airy and bright, decorated in part with 19th-century furniture.

Fondamenta Bollani, Dorsoduro 1058, 30123 Venezia. © **041-5210188.** Fax 041-5239152. www.pensioneaccademia.it. 27 units (showers only). 140€–300€ ($224–$480) double; 200€–330€ ($320–$528) suite. Rates include buffet breakfast. AE, DC, MC, V. Closed Jan 9–20. Vaporetto: Accademia. **Amenities:** Bar; room service; babysitting; laundry service; dry cleaning. *In room:* A/C, TV, Wi-Fi, minibar, hair dryer, safe.

INEXPENSIVE

Hotel Galleria   If you've dreamed of opening your windows to find the Grand Canal before you, step through this 17th-century *palazzo's* leaded-glass doors. But reserve way in advance—these are the cheapest rooms on the canal and possibly the most charming. Six guest rooms varying in size overlook the canal, and the others have partial views that include the Accademia Bridge.

Dorsoduro 878A (at the foot of the Accademia Bridge), 30123 Venezia. © **041-5232489.** Fax 041-5204172. www.hotelgalleria.it. 10 units, 6 with private bathroom (showers only). 115€–130€ ($184–$208) double without bathroom; 140€–185€ ($224–$296) double with bathroom. Rates include continental breakfast. No credit cards. Vaporetto: Accademia. **Amenities:** Breakfast room; babysitting; all nonsmoking rooms. *In room:* Hair dryer.

Locanda Montin ✦ *(Finds*   The Montin is an old-fashioned Venetian inn whose adjoining restaurant is one of the area's most loved. The guest rooms are cozy and quaint. Only a few units have private bathrooms, and in-room extras are scarce aside from a phone. Most guests have to share the small corridor bathrooms, which are barely adequate in number, especially if the house is full. The inn is a bit difficult to locate (it's marked by only a small carriage lamp etched with the name), but is worth the search.

Fondamenta di Borgo, Dorsoduro 1147, 31000 Venezia. © **041-5227151.** Fax 041-5200255. www.locandamontin.com. 11 units, 5 with bathroom. 85€–110€ ($136–$176) double without bathroom; 110€–150€ ($176–$240) double with bathroom. Rates include buffet breakfast. AE, DC, MC, V. Vaporetto: Accademia. **Amenities:** Restaurant; bar; laundry service; dry cleaning.

7 On Isola della Giudecca

Even though this is traditionally a blue-collar neighborhood, it contains one of the grandest pockets of posh in northeast Italy, the Cipriani. If you can afford to stay here, you'll be isolated, but just across the water from St. Mark's.

VERY EXPENSIVE

Cipriani ✦✦✦   For old-world Venetian splendor, check in to the Gritti or Danieli. But for chic, contemporary surroundings, flawless service, and refinement at every turn, the Cipriani is in a class by itself—as long as you can swing its jaw-dropping prices, some of the highest hotel rates in Europe.

Set in a 16th-century cloister on the isolated island of Giudecca (reached by private hotel launch from Piazza San Marco), this pleasure palace was opened in 1958 by Giuseppe Cipriani, the founder of Harry's Bar. The guest rooms range in design from tasteful contemporary to grand antique, but all are sumptuous and have splendid views. We prefer the corner rooms, the most spacious and most elaborately decorated. The Cipriani is the only hotel on Giudecca.

Isola della Giudecca 10, 30133 Venezia. ✆ **800/992-5055** in the U.S., or 041-5207744. Fax 041-5207745. www.hotelcipriani.com. 110 units. 870€–1,320€ ($1,392–$2,112) double; from 1,680€ ($2,688) suite. Rates include buffet breakfast. AE, DC, MC, V. Closed Oct 30–Mar 19. Vaporetto: Zitele. **Amenities:** 2 restaurants; 3 bars (including a piano bar); Olympic-size outdoor swimming pool; Venice's only tennis court; fitness center; Turkish bath and sauna; private boat shuttle; room service; massage; babysitting; laundry service; dry cleaning; nonsmoking rooms; rooms for those w/limited mobility. *In room:* A/C, TV, Wi-Fi, minibar, hair dryer, safe.

8 Near Piazzale Roma

Palazzo Odoni ✦ *Finds*   This restored Gothic palace from the 15th century lies a few steps from Piazzale Roma and the Santa Lucia railway station. It is family-run by the descendants of owners who took it over five generations ago. Modern comforts have been added without ruining the Gothic architectural features of this place, which is decorated with antiques, tapestries, and Murano glass. All the bedrooms are spacious and romantically decorated, and all the private bathrooms have been completely redone. There are almost no common areas, however.

Santa Croce 151, Fondamenta Minotto, 30135 Venezia. ✆ **041-2759454.** Fax 041-2759454. www.palazzoodoni.com. 10 units. 80€–230€ ($128–$368) double; 140€–290€ ($224–$464) junior suite. Rates include buffet breakfast. MC, V. Vaporetto: Piazzale Roma. **Amenities:** Bar; room service; all nonsmoking rooms. *In room:* A/C, TV, minibar, hair dryer, safe.

9 On the Lido

If you visit when the weather is nice, you can have a beach holiday on the Lido with time out for sightseeing in the heart of Venice.

VERY EXPENSIVE

Hotel des Bains 🟆🟆   This is the best old-world spa hotel along this fabled strip of Adriatic sand. The property was built in the grand era of European resort hotels, but long ago lost its supremacy on the Lido to the Westin Excelsior (see below). It has its own wooded park and beach with individual cabanas. Thomas Mann stayed here several times before making it the setting for *Death in Venice,* and later it was used as a set for the film. The renovated interior exudes the flavor of the leisurely life of the Belle Epoque. Guest rooms are large, each elegantly furnished with rich fabrics, Oriental rugs, antiques, and paneled walls.

Lungomare Marconi 17, 30126 Lido di Venezia. ✆ **800/228-3000** in the U.S. and Canada, or 041-5265921. Fax 041-5260113. www.sheraton.com or www.sheraton. com/desbains. 191 units. 305€–836€ ($488–$1,338) double; from 385€ ($616) junior suite; from 1,401€ ($2,242) suite. Rates include buffet breakfast. AE, DC, MC, V. Closed Nov–Mar. Vaporetto: Lido, then bus A, B, or C. **Amenities:** Restaurant; bar; outdoor pool; 2 tennis courts; fitness center; sauna; 24-hr. concierge; private boat shuttle; room service; babysitting; laundry service; dry cleaning; nonsmoking rooms. *In room:* A/C, TV, minibar, hair dryer, safe.

Westin Excelsior 🟆🟆🟆   This luxurious palace caters to the most pampered beach crowd in Europe. When the Excelsior was built, it was the world's biggest resort hotel, and its presence helped make the Lido fashionable. Today, it offers the most luxury on the Lido, although it doesn't have the antique character of the Hotel des Bains (see above). Guest rooms vary in style and amenities, but all have walk-in closets. Most of the social life takes place around the angular pool or on the flowered terraces leading up to the cabanas on the sandy beach.

Lungomare Marconi 41, 30126 Venezia Lido. ✆ **800/228-3000** in the U.S. and Canada, or 041-5260201. Fax 041-5267276. www.westin.com. 196 units. 405€– 750€ ($648–$1,200) double; from 1,326€ ($2,122) suite. Rates include breakfast. AE, DC, MC, V. Parking 35€ ($56). Closed Nov–Mar 15. Vaporetto: Lido, then bus A, B, or C. **Amenities:** 2 restaurants; 3 bars; outdoor pool; 6 tennis courts; fitness center; sauna; boat rentals; private boat shuttle; business center; room service; babysitting; laundry service; dry cleaning; nonsmoking rooms; rooms for those w/limited mobility. *In room:* A/C, TV, minibar, hair dryer, safe.

EXPENSIVE

Albergo Quattro Fontane 🟆   The Quattro Fontane is one of the most charming hotels on the Lido. The trouble is, a lot of people know that, so it's likely to be booked. This former summer home of a 19th-century Venetian family is most popular with the British, who seem to appreciate its homey atmosphere, garden, helpful staff, and bedrooms with superior luxuries, not to mention the good food served at tables set under shady trees. Many of the guest rooms are furnished with antiques; all have tile or terrazzo floors and excellent beds.

Via Quattro Fontane 16, 30126 Lido di Venezia. ℂ **041-5260227.** Fax 041-5260726. www.quattrofontane.com. 60 units. 240€–500€ ($384–$800) double. Rates include buffet breakfast. AE, DC, MC, V. Closed Nov 1–Apr 20. Vaporetto: Lido, then bus A, B, or C. **Amenities:** Restaurant; bar; tennis court; room service; babysitting; laundry service; dry cleaning; nonsmoking rooms. *In room:* A/C, TV, Wi-Fi, minibar, hair dryer, safe.

MODERATE

Hotel Belvedere *(Kids)*   The modernized Belvedere has been a family favorite since 1857. Right across from the *vaporetto* stop, the hotel is open year-round, which is unusual for the Lido, and offers simply furnished guest rooms, each with a good bed and tiled bathroom. As an added courtesy, the Belvedere offers guests free entrance to the Casino Municipale; in summer, guests can use the hotel's cabanas on the Lido.

Piazzale Santa Maria Elisabetta 4, 30126 Lido di Venezia. ℂ **041-5260115.** Fax 041-5261486. www.belvedere-venezia.com. 30 units (showers only). 80€–286€ ($128–$458) double; 100€–344€ ($160–$550) triple. Rates include buffet breakfast. AE, DC, MC, V. Vaporetto: Lido. **Amenities:** Restaurant; bar; room service; babysitting; laundry service; dry cleaning; nonsmoking rooms. *In room:* A/C, TV, hair dryer, safe.

Hotel Helvetia   This 19th-century building, on a side street near the lagoon side of the island, is an easy walk from the *vaporetto* stop. The quieter guest rooms face away from the street, and those in the older wing have Belle Epoque high ceilings and attractively comfortable furniture. The newer wing has a more conservative style. Breakfast is served, weather permitting, in a flagstone-covered walled garden behind the hotel.

Gran Viale 4, 30126 Lido di Venezia. ℂ **041-5260105.** Fax 041-5268903. www.hotelhelvetia.com. 60 units. 130€–250€ ($208–$400) double; 160€–310€ ($256–$496) triple. Rates include continental breakfast. AE, DC, MC, V. Closed Jan to mid-Apr. Vaporetto: Lido. **Amenities:** Breakfast room; bar; room service; babysitting; laundry service. *In room:* TV, hair dryer.

5

Where to Dine

Even though Venice doesn't grow much of its own produce, it's surrounded by a rich agricultural district and plentiful vineyards, and it naturally specializes in fresh seafood. Venice's restaurants are among the most expensive in Italy, but we've found some wonderful, moderately priced *trattorie* (less formal dining establishments, sometimes without printed menus).

Some restaurants still offer a *menu turistico* (tourist menu) at a set price. It includes soup (nearly always minestrone) or pasta, followed by a meat dish with vegetables, topped off by dessert (fresh fruit or cheese), plus a quarter-liter of wine or mineral water, bread, cover charge, and service (you'll still be expected to tip). Some restaurants serve a fixed-price meal called a *menu a prezzo fisso,* which rarely includes the cost of your wine but does include taxes and service.

If you want only a plate of spaghetti or something light, you can patronize any number of fast-food cafeterias (also look for a *rosticce-ria* or *tavola calda,* literally "hot table"). You don't pay a cover charge and can order as much or as little as you wish. Pizzerias are another good option for light meals or snacks. Many bars or cafe-bars also offer both hot and cold food throughout the day. If you're lunching light in the heat, ask for *panini,* rolls stuffed with meat. *Tramezzini* are white-bread sandwiches with the crust trimmed.

1 Near Piazza San Marco

VERY EXPENSIVE

Harry's Bar *(Overrated* VENETIAN   Harry's Bar no longer serves some of the best food in Venice. But because of its fab name, visitors flock here anyway, despite the painful prices. Harry, by the way, is an Italian named Arrigo, son of the late Commendatore Cipriani. Like his father, Arrigo is an entrepreneur extraordinaire. His bar is a big draw for martini-thirsty Americans, but Hemingway and Hotchner always ordered bloody marys in their day. The most famous drink, which was originally concocted here, is the Bellini (*prosecco*—a type of sparkling wine—and white-peach juice), wonderful when created

Where to Dine in Venice

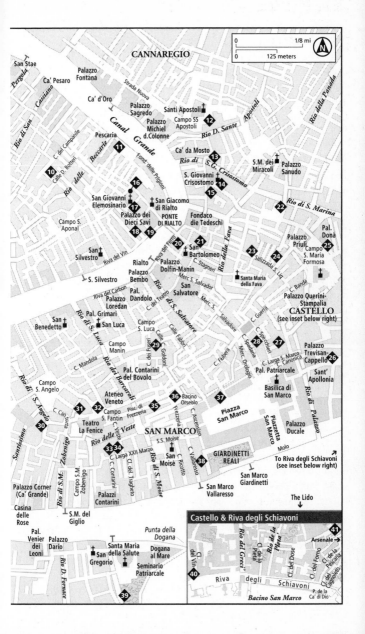

properly, though we've had a watered-down horror here in the off season (a real disappointment). You can have your choice of dining in the bar downstairs or the room with a view upstairs. Popular dishes include the Venetian fish soup, followed by the scampi Thermidor with rice pilaf or the seafood ravioli. The food is relatively simple and fresh, but often lacking flavor.

Calle Vallaresso, San Marco 1323. © 041-5285777. www.cipriani.com. Reservations required. Main courses 50€–100€ ($80–$160). AE, DC, MC, V. Apr–Oct daily 10:30am–1am; Nov–Mar daily 10:30am–11pm. Vaporetto: San Marco.

EXPENSIVE

Antico Martini ✮✮✮ VENETIAN/INTERNATIONAL Antico Martini elevates Venetian cuisine to its highest level. Elaborate chandeliers glitter and gilt-framed oil paintings adorn the paneled walls. The courtyard is splendid in summer. An excellent beginning is the *risotto di frutti di mare* ("fruits of the sea") in a creamy Venetian style with plenty of fresh seafood. For a main dish, try the *fegato alla veneziana*, tender liver fried with onions and served with polenta, a yellow cornmeal mush. The chefs are better at regional dishes than at international ones. The restaurant has one of the city's best wine lists, featuring more than 350 choices. The yellow Tocai is an interesting local wine and especially good with fish dishes.

Campo San Fantin, San Marco 1983. © 041-5224121. Reservations required. Main courses 25€–65€ ($40–$104); fixed-price 6-course menu 106€ ($170). AE, DC, MC, V. Thurs–Mon noon–2:30pm and 7–11:30pm. Vaporetto: San Marco or Santa Maria del Giglio.

La Caravella ✮✮ VENETIAN/INTERNATIONAL La Caravella has an overblown nautical atmosphere and a leather-bound menu that may make you think you're in a tourist trap—but you're not. The restaurant contains four dining rooms and a courtyard that's open in summer. The decor is rustically elegant, with frescoed ceilings, flowers, and wrought-iron lighting fixtures. You might begin with an antipasti *misto de pesce* (assortment of fish) with olive oil and lemon juice, or perhaps the prawns with avocado. Star specialties are *granceola* (Adriatic sea crab on carpaccio) and chateaubriand for two. The best item to order, however, is one of the poached-fish options, such as bass, priced according to weight and served with a tempting sauce. The ice cream in champagne is a soothing finish.

In the Hotel Saturnia International, Calle Larga XXII Marzo, San Marco 2397. © 041-5208901. Reservations required. Main courses 30€–35€ ($48–$56). AE, DC, MC, V. Daily noon–3pm and 7–11pm. Vaporetto: San Marco.

Quadri *@@@* INTERNATIONAL   One of Europe's most famous restaurants, the Quadri is even better known as a cafe (p. 162); its elegant premises open onto Piazza San Marco, where a full orchestra often adds to the magic. Many diners come just for the view and are surprised by the high-quality cuisine and impeccable service (and the whopping tab). The Antico Martini serves better food, though the skills of Quadri's chef are considerable. He's likely to tempt you with such dishes as tagliolini with lobster sauce or grilled sea bass and anglerfish with grilled vegetables. Filet of hake emerges under an aromatic herb crust, or you can also enjoy veal medallions with chanterelles, potato pie, and chopped black olives. Dessert specialties are "baked" ice cream and lemon mousse with fresh strawberry sauce.

Piazza San Marco, San Marco 120–124. ⓒ **041-5289299.** Reservations required. Main courses 36€–53€ ($58–$85). AE, DC, MC, V. Nov–Mar Tues–Sun noon–2:30pm and 7–10:30pm; Apr–Oct daily noon–2:30pm and 7–10:30pm. Vaporetto: San Marco.

MODERATE

Centrale Restaurant & Lounge VENETIAN/MEDITER-RANEAN   Only a 1-minute walk from Piazza San Marco in the center of Venice, this restaurant lies in a historical *palazzo* dating from 1659. The facade has three showcase windows on Piscina Frezzeria, plus an antique door opening directly onto the water canal, Rio dei Barcaroli, should you arrive by gondola. Its location is divine—just 30m (98 ft.) from La Fenice opera house. Spike Lee and other celebrities visiting Venice might be seen lingering for hours (at least until the un-Venetian hour of 2am), enjoying after-theater cocktails in the lounge, with a backlit crystal bar and busy fabrics. The intelligent, flavorful cuisine features such delights as risotto with scampi and champagne; black tagliolini flavored with squid ink served with raw scampi; or lobster ravioli. Chefs make a delightful beef carpaccio and also satisfy the palate with a beef filet with a green or pink peppercorn sauce served with steamed fresh vegetables.

Piscina Frezzeria, San Marco 1659B. ⓒ **041-2960664.** Reservations required. Main courses 22€–35€ ($35–$56). AE, DC, MC, V. Daily 7pm–2am. Vaporetto: San Marco.

Da Ivo *@* TUSCAN/VENETIAN   Da Ivo draws a faithful crowd. The rustic atmosphere is cozy and relaxing, the well-set tables bathed in candlelight. Florentines head here for fine Tuscan cookery, but regional Venetian dishes are also served. In season, game, prepared according to ancient traditions, is cooked over an open charcoal grill. Try homemade *tagliatelle* (flat noodles) topped with slivers of *tartufi bianchi,* the unforgettable pungent white truffle from Piedmont.

Dishes change according to the season and the availability of ingredients, but are likely to include swordfish, anglerfish, or cuttlefish in its own ink.

Calle dei Fuseri, San Marco 1809. ✆ **041-5285004.** Reservations required. Main courses 30€–43€ ($48–$69). AE, DC, MC, V. Mon–Sat noon–2:30pm and 7–10:30pm. Closed Jan 6–Feb 10. Vaporetto: San Marco.

Do Forni ✿ VENETIAN   Centuries ago, this was where bread was baked for monasteries, but today it's the busiest restaurant in Venice, even when the rest of the city slumbers under a wintertime Adriatic fog. It's divided into two sections, separated by a narrow alley. The locals prefer the front part, which is decorated in *Orient Express* style. The larger section in back is like a country tavern, with ceiling beams and original paintings. The English menu (with at least 80 dishes, prepared by 14 cooks) is entitled "Food for the Gods" and lists specialties such as tagliolini pasta with fresh scampi and asparagus or Venetian-style cuttlefish stewed in its own ink.

Calle dei Specchieri, San Marco 457. ✆ **041-5232148.** Reservations recommended. Main courses 22€–33€ ($35–$53). AE, DC, MC, V. Daily noon–4pm and 7pm–midnight. Vaporetto: San Marco.

Ristorante da Raffaele ✿ ITALIAN/VENETIAN   The Raffaele has long been a favorite canal-side spot. It's often overrun with tourists, but the veteran kitchen staff handles the onslaught well. The restaurant offers the kind of charm and atmosphere unique to Venice, with its huge inner sanctum and high-beamed ceiling, 17th- to 19th-century pistols and sabers, wrought-iron chandeliers, a massive fireplace, and hundreds of copper pots. The food is excellent, beginning with a choice of tasty antipasti or well-prepared pastas. Specialties include risotto with scampi and radicchio; octopus with potato salad; or homemade green noodles with "blue swimmer" crab. The grilled meats are wonderful. Finish with a tempting dessert.

Calle Larga XXII Marzo (Fondamenta delle Ostreghe), San Marco 2347. ✆ **041-5232317.** Reservations recommended Sat–Sun. Main courses 15€–30€ ($24–$48). AE, DC, MC, V. Fri–Wed 11:30am–2:30pm and 6:30–10pm. Closed Dec 10–Jan. Vaporetto: San Marco or Santa Maria del Giglio.

Taverna la Fenice ✿✿ ITALIAN/VENETIAN   Opened in 1907, when Venetians were flocking in record numbers to hear the *bel canto* performances in nearby La Fenice opera house (which burned down a few years ago), this taverna is one of Venice's most romantic restaurants. The interior is suitably elegant, but the preferred spot in fine weather is outdoors beneath a canopy. The service is both smooth and efficient. The most appetizing beginning is the

selection of seafood antipasti—the fish is fresh from the Mediterranean. You might enjoy the *risotto con scampi e arugula, tagliatelle*
with cream sauce and exotic mushrooms, or sea bass baked under a
potato crust.

Campiello de la Fenice, San Marco 1939. ℃ **041-5223856**. Reservations required.
Main courses 24€–35€ ($38–$56). AE, DC, MC, V. Tues–Sun 7–11pm. Vaporetto:
San Marco.

Trattoria La Colomba ✵ VENETIAN/INTERNATIONAL
This is one of Venice's most distinctive *trattorie*, its history going
back at least a century. Modern paintings adorn the walls; they
change periodically and are usually for sale. Menu items are likely to
include at least five daily specials based on Venice's time-honored
cuisine, as well as *risotto di funghi del Montello* (risotto with mushrooms from the local hills of Montello) and *baccalà mantecato* (milk-
simmered dry cod seasoned with onions, anchovies, and cinnamon
and served with polenta). The fruits and vegetables served are, for
the most part, grown on the lagoon islands.

Piscina Frezzeria, San Marco 1665. ℃ **041-5221175**. Reservations recommended.
Main courses 35€–50€ ($56–$80). AE, DC, MC, V. Fri–Wed noon–3pm; daily
7–11pm. Closed Wed Nov–Apr. Vaporetto: San Marco or Rialto.

INEXPENSIVE
Le Chat Qui Rit *(Value)* VENETIAN/PIZZA   This self-service cafe-
teria/pizzeria offers food prepared "just like mama made." It's very
popular because of its low prices. Dishes might include various fried
fish or perhaps cuttlefish simmered in stock and served on a bed of
yellow polenta. You can also order a steak grilled very simply, flavored with oil, salt, and pepper or a little garlic and herbs. Main-dish
platters are served rather quickly after you order them.

Calle Frezzeria, San Marco 1131. ℃ **041-5229086**. Main courses 6€–20€ ($9.60–
$32); pizzas 8€–11€ ($13–$18). AE, DC, MC, V. Nov–Mar Sun–Fri 11am–9:30pm;
Apr–Oct daily 11am–9:30pm. Vaporetto: San Marco.

Osteria alle Botteghe VENETIAN/ITALIAN   Once you've
located the bigger-than-life Campo Santo Stefano, you'll find this
osteria a great choice for a light snack or an elaborate meal. Stand-up
hors d'oeuvres *(cicchetti)* and fresh sandwiches can be enjoyed at the
bar or the window-side counter; more serious diners can choose
from pasta dishes or *tavola calda* (a buffet of prepared dishes like eggplant parmigiana, lasagna, and fresh cooked vegetables in season,
reheated when you order) and repair to tables in the back. Classic
dishes include cuttlefish with polenta or a platter of fried squid. Vege-
tarians will be happy with the vegetable lasagna.

Something Sweet

If you're in the mood for some tasty gelato, head to the **Gelateria Paolin,** Campo Stefano Morosini (℃ 041-5225576), which offers 20 flavors. It has stood on the corner of this busy square since the 1930s, making it Venice's oldest ice-cream parlor. You can order your gelato to go or eat it at one of the sidewalk tables (it costs more if you sit at a table). April to October, it's open daily 10am to midnight; November to March, hours are daily 10am to 8:30pm.

One of the city's finest pastry shops is the **Pasticceria Marchini,** Ponte San Maurizio, San Marco 676 (℃ 041-5229109), whose cakes, muffins, and pastries are the stuff of childhood memories for many locals. The high-calorie output of the busy kitchens is displayed behind glass cases and sold by the piece for eating at the bar (there are few tables) or by the kilogram for takeout. The pastries include traditional versions of *torte del Doge,* made from almonds and pine nuts; *zaleti,* made from a mix of cornmeal and eggs; and *bigna,* akin to zabaglione, concocted from chocolate and cream. It's open daily 8:30am to 8:30pm.

Calle delle Botteghe, San Marco 3454. ℃ **041-5228181.** Reservations recommended. Main courses 10€–20€ ($16–$32); fixed 2-course menu 18€ ($29). AE, DC, MC, V. Daily 11am–4pm; Tues–Sun 7–11pm. Vaporetto: Accademia or Sant'Angelo.

Trattoria da Fiore *(Value* VENETIAN/ITALIAN Don't confuse this *trattoria* with the well-known and very expensive Osteria da Fiore. You might not eat better here, but you'll be a lot happier when your bill arrives. Start with the house specialty, *penne alla Fiore* (prepared with olive oil, garlic, and seven in-season vegetables), and you might be content to call it a night. Or skip right to another popular specialty, *fritto misto,* comprising more than a dozen varieties of fresh fish and seafood. The *zuppa di pesce,* a delicious bouillabaisse-like soup, is stocked with mussels, crab, clams, shrimp, and chunks of fresh tuna. The Bar Fiore next door is a great place for an afternoon snack or light lunch (open 10:30am–10:30pm).

Calle delle Botteghe, San Marco 3461. ℃ **041-5235310.** Reservations suggested. Pasta dishes 10€–15€ ($16–$24); main courses 18€–30€ ($29–$48). MC, V. Wed–Mon noon–3pm and 7–10pm. Vaporetto: Accademia.

2 In Castello

EXPENSIVE

Do Leoni 🐾🐾 VENETIAN/INTERNATIONAL   For years, this restaurant was known by the French version of its name, Les Deux Lions. Set in the elegant Londra Palace, it offers a panoramic view of a 19th-century equestrian statue ringed with heroic women taming (you guessed it) lions. The restaurant is filled with scarlet and gold, a motif of lions patterned into the carpeting, and reproductions of English furniture. Lunches are brief buffet-style affairs, in which diners serve themselves from a large choice of hot and cold Italian and international food. The appealing candlelit dinners are more formal, emphasizing Venetian cuisine. The chef's undeniable skill is reflected in such dishes as fried shrimp on polenta perfumed with garlic for an appetizer, followed by such main courses as Irish sirloin steak with braised artichoke bottoms or mixed fish grilled with boiled vegetables. If the weather permits, you can dine out on the *piazza* overlooking the lions and their masters.

In the Londra Palace, Riva degli Schiavoni, Castello 4171. © 041-5200533. Reservations required. Main courses 24€–36€ ($38–$58). Guests of the Londra Palace receive 10%–30% discount. AE, DC, MC, V. Restaurant daily noon–3pm and 7:30–11pm. Bar daily 10am–12:30am. Vaporetto: San Zaccaria.

MODERATE

Al Mascaron VENETIAN   Crowd into one of the three loud, boisterous dining rooms here, where you'll probably be directed to sit next to a stranger at a long trestle table. The waiters will come by and slam down copious portions of fresh-cooked local specialties: deep-fried calamari, spaghetti with lobster, monkfish in a salt crust, pastas, savory risottos, and Venetian-style calves' liver (which locals prefer rather pink), plus the best seafood of the day made into salads. There's also a convivial bar, where locals drop in to spread the gossip of the day, play cards, and order *vino* and snacks.

Calle Lunga Santa Maria Formosa, Castello 5225. © 041-5225995. Reservations recommended. Main courses 15€–28€ ($24–$45). No credit cards. Mon–Sat noon–3pm and 7:30–11pm. Closed Jan. Vaporetto: Rialto or San Marco.

Al Nuovo Galeon *Value* VENETIAN   Sometimes it's a good idea to go where your waiter takes his family to eat on his day off. Such a choice might be this restaurant in the Castello neighborhood with a typical Venetian square outside. With its two dining rooms, it's decorated just like the interior of a 16th-century ship. The location is a 15-minute walk east of Piazza San Marco. The chef prepares good-value, wholesome food made with market-fresh ingredients. Specialties include scampi in *saorone* (fried scampi marinated in a sweet-and-sour sauce with lightly sautéed onions) or else a filet of turbot with curried vegetables. Our favorite is a large platter of seafood with such delights as spider crab, octopus, squid, sea bass, shrimp, and a couple of fish we don't recognize.

Via Garibaldi 1308, Castello. © **041-5204656.** Reservations recommended. Main courses 15€–22€ ($24–$35). AE, MC, V. Wed–Sun 12:30–2:30pm and 7:30–9:30pm. Closed Dec 9–Jan 22. Vaporetto: Ciardini.

Nuova Rivetta *Value* SEAFOOD   Nuova Rivetta is an old-fashioned *trattoria* where you get good food at a good price. The most popular dish is *frittura di pesce,* a mixed-fish fry that includes squid or various other "sea creatures" from the day's market. Other specialties are gnocchi stuffed with spider crab, pasticcio of fish (a main course), and spaghetti flavored with squid ink. The most typical wine is sparkling *prosecco,* whose bouquet is refreshing and fruity with a slightly sharp flavor; for centuries, it has been one of the most celebrated wines of the Veneto.

Campo San Filippo, Castello 4625. © **041-5287302.** Reservations required. Main courses 10€–18€ ($16–$29). AE, MC, V. Tues–Sun 10am–10pm. Closed July 23–Aug 20. Vaporetto: San Zaccaria.

Restaurant da Bruno VENETIAN   On a narrow street about halfway between the Rialto Bridge and Piazza San Marco, this "country taverna" grills its meats on an open-hearth fire. You get your antipasti at the counter and watch your prosciutto being prepared—paper-thin slices of spicy ham wrapped around breadsticks *(grissini).* In season, Bruno does some of Venice's finest game dishes. A typical Venetian dish prepared well here is *zuppa di pesce* (fish soup). Other specialties are beef filet with pepper sauce, scampi and calamari, veal scaloppine with wild mushrooms, and mixed grilled fish with lobster.

Calle del Paradiso, Castello 5731. © **041-5221480.** Main courses 13€–33€ ($21–$53); fixed-price menu 15€–30€ ($24–$48). AE, DC, MC, V. Daily noon–3pm and 6:30–11pm. Vaporetto: San Marco or Rialto.

Ristorante Corte Sconta SEAFOOD   The Corte Sconta is behind a narrow storefront you'd otherwise ignore if you didn't know about this place. This modest restaurant boasts a multicolored marble floor, plain wooden tables, and not much of an attempt at decoration. It has become well known, however, as a gathering place for artists, writers, and filmmakers. As the depiction of the satyr chasing the mermaid above the entrance implies, it's a fish restaurant, serving a variety of grilled creatures (much of the "catch" is largely unknown in North America). The fresh fish is flawlessly fresh; the gamberi, for example, is placed live on the grill. A great start is marinated salmon with arugula and pomegranate seeds in olive oil.

Calle del Pestrin, Castello 3886. (C) 041-5227024. Reservations required. Main courses 15€–25€ ($24–$40). MC, V. Tues–Sat 12:30–2:30pm and 7:30–9:30pm. Closed Jan 7–Feb 7 and July 15–Aug 15. Vaporetto: Arsenale.

Ristorante Masaniello VENETIAN/NEAPOLITAN   Set adjacent to a charming square, immediately behind the much more expensive dining facilities of the also-recommended Danieli Hotel, this is an immaculate, charming, and well-managed restaurant with relatively affordable prices (for hyperexpensive Venice). It was named after Masaniello, leader of the Neapolitan fishermen who led a "peoples' revolt" against the city's oppressive political regime in the 17th century, and who is remembered throughout Italy today as a folk hero. Its menu items, many inspired by the cuisine of the Amalfi coast, in southern Italy, remind residents of foggy and rain-soaked Venice throughout the year that, indeed, sunnier climes lie nearby. The best examples include *gatto di patate* (cakes made from mashed potatoes, layered with ham and cheese), grilled octopus with a savory tomato sauce, pasta with squid or with fried eggplant, many different preparations of fresh fish and grilled meats, and homemade desserts *(dolci della casa)*.

San Marco, Campo San Stefano 2801. (C) 041-5209003. Reservations not necessary. Main courses 23€–25€ ($37–$40). AE, DC, MC, V. Wed–Mon noon–3pm and 7–11pm. Vaporetto: San Zaccaria.

3 Near the Ponte di Rialto
EXPENSIVE
Al Graspo de Ua (R) SEAFOOD/VENETIAN   "The Bunch of Grapes" is a great place for a special meal. Decorated in old taverna style, it offers several air-conditioned dining rooms. One has a beamed ceiling, hung with garlic and copper bric-a-brac. Among Venice's best fish restaurants, it's hosted biggies like Liz Taylor, Jeanne Moreau, and Giorgio de Chirico. You can help yourself to all the hors d'oeuvres you want (the menu tells you it's "self-service mammoth"). Next try the *gran fritto dell'Adriatico,* a mixed treat of deep-fried fish, the grilled tuna, or the tagliolini with lobster. The desserts are also good, especially the peach Melba.

Calle Bombaseri, San Marco 5094. (C) 041-5200150. Reservations required. Main courses 28€–38€ ($45–$61). AE, DC, MC, V. Tues–Sun noon–3pm and 7–11pm. Closed Aug 5–20. Vaporetto: Rialto.

MODERATE

Fiaschetteria Toscana *(★ Value* VENETIAN   There may be some rough points in the service at this hip restaurant (the staff is frantic), but lots of local foodies come here to celebrate special occasions or to soak in the see-and-be-seen atmosphere. The dining rooms are on two levels; the upstairs is somewhat more claustrophobic. In the evening, the downstairs is especially appealing, with its romantic candlelit ambience. Menu items include *frittura della Serenissima* (mixed platter of fried seafood with vegetables), veal scallops with lemon Marsala sauce and mushrooms, ravioli stuffed with whitefish and herbs, and several kinds of Tuscan-style beefsteak.

Campo San Giovanni Crisostomo, Cannaregio 5719. ℂ 041-5285281. Reservations required. Main courses 15€–30€ ($24–$48). AE, DC, MC, V. Wed 7:30–10:30pm; Thurs–Mon 12:30–2:30pm and 7:30–10:30pm. Closed last week in July and 1st 3 weeks of Aug. Vaporetto: Rialto.

Il Milion VENETIAN   With a tradition extending back more than 300 years and a location near the rear of San Giovanni Crisostomo, this restaurant is named after the book written by Marco Polo, *Il Milion,* describing his travels. In fact, it occupies a town house once owned by members of the explorer's family. The bar, incidentally, is a favorite with some of the gondoliers. The menu items read like a who's who of well-recognized Venetian platters, each fresh and well prepared. Some of the best examples include small lamb kidneys sautéed with garlic and gin or slices of veal sautéed in a white-wine sauce. One of the best pasta dishes is taglioni with spider crab, or you might order broiled scampi served on an arugula salad.

Corte Prima al Milion, Cannaregio 5841. ℂ 041-5229302. Reservations recommended. Main courses 10€–22€ ($16–$35). AE, MC, V. Fri–Tues noon–3pm and 6:30–11pm; Thurs 6:30–11pm. Closed 3 weeks in Aug. Vaporetto: Rialto.

Il Sole Sulla Vecia Cavana *(★ Finds* SEAFOOD   This restaurant is off the tourist circuit and well worth the trek through the winding streets. A *cavana* is a place where gondolas are parked, a sort of liquid garage, and the site of this restaurant was such a place in the Middle Ages. When you enter, you'll be greeted by brick arches, stone columns, terra-cotta floors, framed modern paintings, and a photo of 19th-century fishermen relaxing after a day's work. The menu specializes in seafood, such as a mixed grill from the Adriatic, fried scampi, fresh sole, three types of risotto (each with seafood), and a spicy *zuppa di pesce. Antipasti di pesce Cavana* is an assortment of just about every sea creature. The food is authentic and seems prepared for the Venetian palate—not necessarily for the visitor's.

Rio Terrà SS. Apostoli, Cannaregio 4624. ☎ **041-5287106**. Main courses 10€–23€ ($16–$37). AE, DC, MC, V. Tues–Sun noon–3pm and 6:30–10:30pm. Vaporetto: Ca' d'Oro.

L'Osteria di Santa Marina ☀ *Finds* VENETIAN/ITALIAN

Near Ponte di Rialto, this discovery is the domain of Agostino Doria and Danilo Baldan, the latter a Cipriani (of New York) alum. Together, they've forged their own place, combining a rustic yet classic decor. You'll feel right at home in the warm and cozy setting, partaking of their savory cuisine. The cuisine is light, full-flavored, and impertinently inventive as evidenced by the lasagna, served crepe-style with fresh shrimp and purple radicchio. The ravioli with turbot and mussels in a crayfish sauce has subtly intermingled flavors. Incidentally, all the pasta is homemade. Other standout dishes include veal cheeks braised with potatoes, fried soft-shell crabs and artichokes, grilled fish, and shellfish skewers with smoked bacon.

Campo Santa Marina 5911. ☎ **041-5285239**. Reservations recommended. Main courses 18€–25€ ($29–$40). AE, DC, MC, V. Tues–Sat 12:30–2:30pm; Mon–Sat 7:30–9:30pm. Closed Jan 10–25 and 2 weeks in Aug (dates vary). Vaporetto: Rialto.

Poste Vecie ☀ SEAFOOD

This charming restaurant is near the Rialto open-air market and connected to the rest of the city by a small, privately owned bridge. It opened in the early 1500s as a post office, and the kitchen used to serve food to fortify the mail carriers. Today, it's the oldest restaurant in Venice, with a pair of intimate rooms (both graced with paneling, murals, and 16th-c. mantelpieces) and a courtyard. Menu items include fresh fish from the nearby markets; a salad of shellfish and exotic mushrooms; tagliolini flavored with squid ink, crabmeat, and fish sauce; and the *pièce de résistance, seppie* (cuttlefish) *à la veneziana* with polenta. If you don't like fish, calves' liver or veal shank with ham and cheese are also well prepared.

Pescheria Rialto, San Polo 1608. ☎ **041-721822**. Reservations recommended. Main courses 15€–30€ ($24–$48). AE, DC, MC, V. Wed–Mon noon–3pm and 7–10:30pm. Vaporetto: Rialto.

Ristorante Al Mondo Novo VENETIAN/SEAFOOD

In a Renaissance building, with a dining room outfitted in a regional style, this restaurant offers professional service and a kindly staff. Plus, it stays open later than many of its nearby competitors. Locals who frequent the place always order the fresh fish because the owner is a wholesaler in the Rialto fish market. Menu items include a selection of seafood, prepared fried or charcoal-grilled. Other options include risotto with shrimp and arugula or spaghetti with shellfish.

Salizzada di San Lio, Castello 5409. ✆ **041-5200698**. Reservations recommended. Main courses 18€–31€ ($29–$50). AE, DC, MC, V. Daily 11:30am–11pm. Vaporetto: Rialto or San Marco.

Trattoria alla Madonna VENETIAN   No, this place has nothing to do with *that* Madonna. It opened in 1954 in a 300-year-old building and is one of Venice's most characteristic *trattorie*, specializing in traditional Venetian recipes and grilled fresh fish. A good beginning might be the *antipasto frutti di mare*. Pasta, polenta, risotto, meats (including *fegato alla veneziana*, liver with onions), and many kinds of irreproachably fresh fish are widely available. Many creatures of the sea are displayed in a refrigerated case near the entrance.

Calle della Madonna, San Polo 594. ✆ **041-5223824**. Reservations recommended but not always accepted. Main courses 15€–23€ ($24–$37). AE, MC, V. Thurs–Tues noon–3pm and 7:15–10pm. Closed Dec 24–Jan 2 and Aug 4–17. Vaporetto: Rialto.

INEXPENSIVE

Ai Tre Spiedi *(Value)* VENETIAN   Venetians bring their visiting friends here to make a good impression without breaking the bank, and then swear them to secrecy. Rarely will you find as pleasant a setting and as appetizing a meal as in this casually elegant *trattoria* with exposed-beam ceilings and some of the most reasonably priced fresh-fish dining that will keep meat-eaters happy as well. If you order a la carte, ask the English-speaking waiters to estimate the cost of your fish entree, since it'll typically appear priced by the *etto* (100g).

Salizzada San Cazian, Cannaregio 5906. ✆ **041-5208035**. Main courses 14€–18€ ($22–$29). AE, MC, V. Tues–Sat noon–2:30pm and 7–9:30pm; Sun 12:30–3:30pm. Vaporetto: Rialto.

Rosticceria San Bartolomeo *(Value)* VENETIAN/ITALIAN   This *rosticceria* (rotisserie delicatessen) is Venice's most popular fast-food place and has long been a blessing for cost-conscious travelers. Downstairs is a *tavola calda* where you can eat standing up, but upstairs is a restaurant with waiter service. Typical dishes are *baccalà alla vicentina* (codfish simmered in herbs and milk), deep-fried mozzarella (which the Italians call *in carrozza*), and *seppie con polenta* (squid in its own ink sauce, served with polenta). Everything is accompanied by typical Veneto wine.

Calle della Bissa, San Marco 5424. ✆ **041-5223569**. Main courses 8€–17€ ($13–$27). AE, DC, MC, V. Tues–Sun 9am–9pm (daily Easter–Nov 14 and for Carnevale). Vaporetto: Rialto.

Tiziano Bar SANDWICHES/PASTA/PIZZA   The Tiziano Bar is a *tavola calda:* There's no waiter service, and you eat standing at a counter or sitting on one of the high stools. The place is known in

Venice for selling pizza by the yard. From noon to 3pm, it serves hot pastas such as rigatoni and cannelloni. Throughout the day, you can order sandwiches or perhaps a plate of mozzarella.

Salizzada San Crisostomo, Cannaregio 5747, in front of the Sanctuary. ✆ 041-5235544. Main courses 8€–12€ ($13–$19). No credit cards. Daily 8am–10:30pm. Vaporetto: Rialto.

4 In Santa Croce

MODERATE

Trattoria Antica Besseta ✸ *Finds* VENETIAN   If you manage to find this place (go with a good map), you'll be rewarded with true Venetian cuisine at its most unpretentious. Head for Campo San Giacomo dell'Orio; then negotiate your way across infrequently visited squares and winding alleys. Push through saloon doors into a bar area filled with modern art. The dining room is hung with paintings and illuminated with wagon-wheel chandeliers. Nereo Volpe, his wife, Mariuccia, and one of their sons are the guiding force, the chefs, the buyers, and even the "talking menus." The food depends on what looked good in the market that morning, so the menu could include roast chicken, fried scampi, *fritto misto,* spaghetti in sardine sauce, various roasts, and a selection from the day's catch. You might start your meal with the fish soup flavored with curry. The Volpe family produces two kinds of their own wine, a pinot blanc and a cabernet.

Campo SS. de Ca' Zusto, Santa Croce 1395. ✆ 041-721687. Reservations required. Main courses 13€–25€ ($21–$40). AE, MC, V. Thurs–Mon noon–2:30pm; Wed–Mon 7–10:30pm. Vaporetto: Riva di Biasio.

5 In San Polo

EXPENSIVE

Osteria da Fiore ✸✸✸ *Finds* SEAFOOD   The breath of the Adriatic seems to blow through this place, though how the wind finds this little restaurant tucked away in a labyrinth is a mystery. Imaginative cuisine is served, depending on the availability of fresh fish and produce. If you have a love of maritime foods, you'll find everything from scampi (a sweet Adriatic prawn, cooked in as many ways as there are chefs) to *granzeola,* a type of spider crab. You might also sample fried calamari, risotto with scampi, *tagliata* (sliced beef) with rosemary, *masenette* (tiny green crabs you eat shell and all), and *canoce* (mantis shrimp). For wine, we suggest *prosecco,* with a distinctive golden-yellow color and a bouquet that's refreshing and fruity.

Calle del Scaleter, San Polo 2202. ✆ **041-721308**. Reservations required. Main courses 35€–45€ ($56–$72). AE, DC, MC, V. Tues–Sat 12:30–2:30pm and 7:30–10:30pm. Closed 3 weeks in Aug and Dec 25–Jan 14. Vaporetto: San Tomà.

INEXPENSIVE

Al Pesador VENETIAN   If you want to blend in with the locals head just 100m (328 ft.) from the Rialto Bridge to this little *trattoria* in San Polo. The location is right off Campo San Giacometo, a charming square where many young people and young-at-heart Venetians hang out devouring bottles of wine from the Beneto. Around the corner from the square stands Al Pesador where in-the-know diners go for food and drink. This is a trendy spot for well-prepared but non-fussy food such as lasagna with leeks or turbot in a fish sauce. Turbot also appears imaginatively with chestnuts and grapefruit. You can also order various versions of carpaccio—tuna, scorpion fish, or wild sea bass.

San Polo 125. ✆ **041-5239492**. Reservations required. Main courses 12€–20€ ($19–$32). MC, V. Apr–Oct Tues–Sun 10am–2pm; off season Tues–Sun 11am–3:30pm and 6pm–2am. Vaporetto: Rialto.

Antiche Carampane VENETIAN/SEAFOOD   Venetians might call this little *trattoria "molto romantic."* In a tranquil little corner just past Campo San Polo, it takes its name from the slang word for the prostitutes who worked their trade around here back in medieval times. Today it attracts politicians and show-business personalities who are attracted to its intimate atmosphere and a menu based on classic Venetian dishes, most often freshly caught seafood. Start with the antipasti of the house, a large platter of fresh seafood to be consumed raw like sushi or cooked. In fair weather, dine on the terrace enjoying such dishes as spaghetti in a lightly spiced seafood sauce or baked filet of turbot in a citrus sauce, even fried soft-shell crabs.

San Polo 1911. ✆ **041-5240165**. Reservations recommended. Main courses 15€–21€ ($24–$34). AE, DC, MC, V. Tues–Sat 12:30–2:30pm and 7:30–10:30pm. Closed Jan 7–18 and 2 weeks in Aug. Vaporetto: San Silvestro.

6 In Dorsoduro

EXPENSIVE

Lineadombra 🎭🎭 *Finds*   Venice doesn't look entirely as it did at the time of the doges. There is such a thing as Nouveau Venice, as exemplified by this modern restaurant with sleek contemporary lines. In Dorsoduro, it faces the Canale della Giudecca. In fair weather, you can sit out on the deck on cushy chairs. Here you will enjoy one of the most scenic spots in Venice behind the Church of the Salute. The chefs blend their creativity and imagination, turning out a mouthwatering range of freshly made dishes. The best of these include grilled scallops with a zucchini, yogurt, and a saffron sauce or else tortelloni filled with spinach and ricotta. Baked turbot comes with a velvety sauce made with fresh asparagus. Every dish is a feast for the eye and palate, especially a *mille-feuille* of scampi with onions and green apples.

Ponte dell'Umilta, Dorsoduro 19. ℂ 041-2411881. Reservations required. Main courses 19€–34€ ($30–$54). AE, DC, MC, V. Thurs–Tues 12:30–3pm and 7:30–10pm. Closed Jan 15–Feb 15. Vaporetto: Salute.

MODERATE

La Furatola SEAFOOD   La Furatola is very much a neighborhood hangout, but it has captured the imagination of local foodies. The simple dining room occupies a 300-year-old building, along a narrow flagstone-paved street that you'll need a good map and a lot of patience to find. Perhaps you'll have lunch here after a visit to San Rocco, a short distance away. The specialty is fish brought to your table in a wicker basket so you can judge its size and freshness by its bright eyes and red gills. A display of seafood antipasti is set out near the entrance. A standout is the baby octopus boiled and eaten with a drop of red-wine vinegar. Eel comes with a medley of mixed fried fish, including baby cuttlefish, prawns, and squid rings.

Calle Lunga San Barnaba, Dorsoduro 2870A. ℂ 041-5208594. Reservations required. Main courses 20€–30€ ($32–$48). AE, DC, MC, V. Fri–Sun 12:30–2:30pm; Fri–Mon 7:30–10:30pm. Closed Jan and Aug. Vaporetto: Ca' Rezzonico.

Locanda Montin ✦ INTERNATIONAL/ITALIAN   The Montin opened after World War II and has hosted Ezra Pound, Jackson Pollock, Mark Rothko, and the artist friends of the late Peggy Guggenheim. More recent visitors have included everybody from Brad Pitt to Mick Jagger. It's owned and run by the Carretins, who have covered the walls with paintings donated by or bought from their many friends and guests. The arbor-covered garden courtyard is filled with regulars, many of whom allow their favorite waiter to select most of the items for their meal. The frequently changing menu includes a variety of salads, grilled meats, and fish caught in the Adriatic.

Fondamenta di Borgo, Dorsoduro 1147. ℂ 041-5227151. Reservations recommended. Main courses 10€–25€ ($16–$40). AE, DC, MC, V. Thurs–Tues 12:30–2:30pm; Thurs–Mon 7:30–10pm. Closed 10 days in mid-Aug and Tues in July–Aug and Nov–Mar. Vaporetto: Accademia.

INEXPENSIVE

La Bitta ⚑ ITALIAN   Close to the Accademia, this is a mom-and-pop operation in a small storefront off Campo San Barnaba. The decor is rustic, the furniture wooden, and the menu propped on a table easel. Market-fresh specialties are based on the shopping that morning. The menu changes daily, and might include carpaccio of smoked beef or gnocchi with Gorgonzola and speck (a type of Italian raw ham). In summer the menu might tempt you with chicken salad with vegetables of the season; or in autumn you might gravitate to the roast partridge with a *peverada* sauce (made with stock, spices, bread crumbs, and ox marrow). A hazelnut chocolate mousse will finish off a meal nicely. La Bitta is also a wine bar, with some 70 offerings, all bottles from northeast Italy.

Calle Lunga San Barnaba, Dorsoduro 2753A. ℂ 041-5230531. Reservations recommended. Main courses 10€–20€ ($16–$32). No credit cards. Mon–Sat 6:30–11pm. Closed mid-July to mid-Aug. Vaporetto: Cà Rezzonico.

Muro Vino e Cucina INTERNATIONAL   In the heart of the Rialto open-air market, close to the Rialto Bridge, this restaurant is one of the few in Venice that aims for high modernism—all polished steel and sharp angles. Josef Klostermaier, a former professional ice hockey player, is already one of the rising chefs of Venice. He mostly specializes in whatever was fresh at the market that day. The bar is downstairs, with the restaurant on the second floor, opening onto a view. You might begin with a soup of cabbage, turnip, fresh tomato, and fresh tuna. There is a certain creativity to his cookery, as evoked by the tuna tartare with a mango carpaccio. Justifiably favorite main dishes include filet of beef with a mushroom carpaccio and giant shrimp flavored with ham and served with polenta.

San Polo 222. ℂ 041-5237495. Reservations recommended. Main courses 14€–25€ ($22–$40). AE, DC, MC, V. Mon–Sat 9am–3pm and 5pm–2am. Vaporetto: Rialto.

7 On Isola della Giudecca

VERY EXPENSIVE

Fortuny ⚑⚑⚑ ITALIAN   The grandest of the hotel restaurants, Fortuny offers a sublime but relatively simple cuisine, with the freshest of ingredients used by one of the best-trained staffs along the Adriatic. This isn't the place to bring the kids—in fact, children 7 and under aren't allowed (a babysitter can be arranged). You can dine on the extensive terrace overlooking the lagoon, or in the formal room with Murano chandeliers and Fortuny curtains when the weather is nippy. Freshly made pasta is a specialty, and it's among the finest we've ever sampled. Chef's specialties include gooseliver terrine with dried fruits as an appetizer or sautéed king prawns coated with sesame. Highlights of the main courses include roast turbot with a lemon-and-caper sauce or sea bass baked in a salt crust. Meat eaters might go for the rack of lamb flavored with tarragon or the classic sliced calves' liver sautéed with onions in the Venetian way.

In the Hotel Cipriani, Isola della Giudecca 10. ℂ 041-5207744. www.hotel cipriani.com. Reservations required. Main courses 24€–46€ ($38–$74). AE, DC, MC, V. Daily 12:30–3pm and 8–10:30pm. Closed Nov–Mar. Vaporetto: Zitelle.

EXPENSIVE

Harry's Dolci ✦ INTERNATIONAL/ITALIAN   The people at the famed Harry's Bar (p. 61) have established their latest enclave far from the maddening crowds of Piazza San Marco on this little-visited island. From the quay-side windows of this chic place, you can watch seagoing vessels, from yachts to lagoon barges. White linens and uniformed waiters grace a modern room, where no one minds if you order only coffee and ice cream or perhaps a selection from the large pastry menu (the zabaglione cake is divine). Popular items are carpaccio Cipriani, chicken salad, club sandwiches, gnocchi, and house-style cannelloni. The dishes are deliberately kept simple, but each is well prepared.

Fondamenta San Biago 773, Isola della Giudecca. ℂ 041-5224844. Reservations recommended, especially Sat–Sun. Main courses 28€–34€ ($45–$54); fixed-price menu 56€–69€ ($90–$110). AE, MC, V. Wed–Mon noon–3pm; Wed–Sun 7–10:30pm. Closed Nov 1–Mar 30. Vaporetto: Santa Eufemia.

8 On the Lido

MODERATE

Favorita SEAFOOD   Occupying two rustic dining rooms and a garden, Favorita has thrived here since the 1920s, operated by the Pradel family, now in their third generation of ownership. Their years of experience contribute to flavorful, impeccably prepared seafood and shellfish dishes, many of them grilled. Try the *bavette* (spaghetti-like pasta) with baby squid and eggplant, potato-based gnocchi with crabs from the Venetian lagoon, or grilled versions of virtually every fish in the Adriatic, including eel, sea bass, turbot, and sole.

Via Francesco Duodo 33, Lido di Venezia. ℂ 041-5261626. Main courses 14€–23€ ($22–$37). AE, DC, MC, V. Wed–Sun noon–2:30pm; Tues–Sun 7:30–10:30pm. Vaporetto: Lido di Venezia.

Ristorante Belvedere VENETIAN   Outside the big hotels, the best food on the Lido is served at the Belvedere, across from the *vaporetto* stop. It attracts a lot of locals, who come here knowing they can get some of the best fish along the Adriatic. Tables are placed outside, and there's a glass-enclosed portion for windy days. The main dining room is attractive, with cane-backed bentwood chairs and big windows. In back, reached through a separate entrance, is a busy cafe. Main dishes include the chef's special sea bass, grilled dorade (or sole), and fried scampi. You might begin with the special fish antipasti or spaghetti with fish ragout.

Piazzale Santa Maria Elisabetta 4, Lido di Venezia. (*C*) **041-5260115**. Reservations recommended. Main courses 11€–18€ ($18–$29). AE, DC, MC, V. Tues–Sun noon–2:30pm and 7–9:30pm. Closed Nov 4–Easter. Vaporetto: Lido.

9 The Lagoon Islands of Murano, Burano & Torcello

ON MURANO

Ai Vetrai VENETIAN   Ai Vetrai entertains and nourishes its guests in a large room not far from the Canale dei Vetrai. If you're looking for fish prepared in the local style, with arguably the widest selection on Murano, this is it. Most varieties of crustaceans and gilled creatures are available on the spot. However, if you phone ahead and order food for a large party, as the Venetians sometimes do, the owners will prepare what they call "a noble fish." You might begin with spaghetti in green clam sauce and follow with *grigliata mista di pesce,* a dish that combines all the seafood of the Adriatic or other types of grilled or baked fish accented with vegetables.

Fondamenta Manin 29. (*C*) **041-739293**. Reservations recommended. Main courses 12€–20€ ($19–$32). DC, MC, V. Daily 9am–4pm; Oct–May Sat–Sun 6:30–10pm; June–Sept Fri–Tues 6:30–10pm. Closed Jan. Vaporetto: Line 41.

ON BURANO

Trattoria Da Romano VENETIAN   If you're on the island at mealtime, you may want to join a long line of people who enjoy this rather simple-looking spot around the corner from the lace school. It was founded in 1920. You can enjoy a superb dinner here, perhaps *fritto misto di pesce,* a mixed-fish fry from the Adriatic with savory bits of mullet, squid, and shrimp, or risotto *nero de seppia* (flavored with squid ink).

Via Baldassare Galuppi 221, Burano. (*C*) **041-730030**. Reservations recommended. Main courses 15€–20€ ($24–$32). AE, MC, V. Wed–Mon noon–3pm and 6:30–9pm. Closed Dec 15–Jan 31. Vaporetto: Line 12 or 52.

ON TORCELLO

Locanda Cipriani 𝔊𝔊 VENETIAN   This place is operated by the same folks behind the Hotel Cipriani and Harry's Bar (actually by the very cosmopolitan Bonifacio Brass, nephew of Harry Cipriani). This artfully simple *locanda* (small inn) is deliberately rustic, light-years removed from the family's grander venues. Menu items are uncompromisingly classic, with deep roots in family tradition. A good example is *filleto di San Pietro alla Carlina* (filet of John Dory in the style of Carla, a late and much-revered matriarch, who made the dish for decades using tomatoes and capers). Also look for carpaccio Cipriani, risotto *alla Torcellano* (with fresh vegetables and herbs from the family's garden), fish soup, *tagliolini verdi gratinati* (pasta with ham and a creamy cheese sauce), and a traditional roster of veal, liver, fish, and beef dishes. Diners can sit on the outdoor terrace in summer.

Piazza San Fosca 29, Torcello. *C* **041-730150.** Reservations required. Main courses 22€–33€ ($35–$53). AE, DC, MC, V. Wed–Mon noon–3pm; Fri–Sat 7–10pm. Closed Jan. Vaporetto: Line 12 or 14.

6

Exploring Venice

Centuries ago, in an effort to flee barbarians, Venetians left dry dock and drifted out to a flotilla of "uninhabitable" islands in the lagoon. Survival was difficult enough, but no Venetian has ever settled for mere survival. The remote ancestors of the present inhabitants ended up creating the world's most beautiful city. To your children's children, however, Venice may be nothing more than a legend: It's sinking at a rate of about 6.3 centimeters (2½ in.) per decade. Experts estimate that if no action is taken soon, one-third of the city's art will deteriorate hopelessly within the next decade or so. Clearly, Venice is in peril. One recent headline proclaimed, "The Enemy's at the Gates."

But for however long Venice lasts, decaying or not, it will be one of the highlights of your trip through Italy. It lacks the speeding cars and roaring Vespas of Rome; instead, you make your way through the city either by boat or on foot. The situation would be ideal if it weren't for the hordes of tourists that descend every year, overwhelming the squares and making the streets almost impossible to navigate. In the sultry summer heat of the Adriatic, the canals become a smelly stew. Steamy and overcrowded July and August are the worst times to visit; May, June, September, and October are much better.

Although Venice is one of the world's most enchanting cities, you do pay a price, literally and figuratively, for all this beauty. Venice is virtually selling its past to the world, even more so than Florence, and anybody who has been here leaves complaining about the outrageous prices, which can be double what they are elsewhere in the country. Since the 19th century, Venice has thrived on its visitors, but these high prices have forced out many locals. They've fled across the lagoon to dreary Mestre, an industrial complex launched to help boost the regional economy.

Today, the city is trying belatedly to undo the damage its watery environs and tourist-based economy have wrought. In 1993, after a 30-year hiatus, the canals were again dredged in an attempt to reduce water loss and reduce the stench brought in with the low tides. In an effort to curb residential migration to Mestre, state subsidies are now being offered to the citizens of Venice as an incentive not only to stay, but also to renovate their crumbling properties.

Despite all its problems and relatively modest plans (so far) for saving itself, Venice still endures. But for how long? That is the question.

In the pages ahead, we'll explore the city's great art and architecture. But, unlike Florence, Venice rewards its guests with treasures even if they never duck inside a museum or church. Take some time just to stroll and let yourself get lost in this gorgeous city.

1 St. Mark's Square (Piazza San Marco)

Piazza San Marco ⋒⋒⋒ was the heart of Venice in the heyday of its glory as a seafaring republic. If you have only a single day in Venice, you need not leave the square, as some of the city's major attractions, like St. Mark's Basilica and the Doge's Palace, are centered here or nearby.

The traffic-free square, frequented by visitors and pigeons and sometimes even by Venetians, is a source of both bewilderment and interest. If you rise at dawn, you can almost have the *piazza* to yourself, and as you watch the sun come up, the sheen of gold mosaics glistens with a mystical beauty. At around 9am, the overstuffed pigeons are fed by the city (if you're caught under the whir, you'll think you're witnessing a remake of Hitchcock's *The Birds*). At midafternoon, the tourists reign supreme, and it's not surprising in July to witness a scuffle over a camera angle. At sunset, when the two Moors in the clock tower strike the end of another day, lonely sailors begin a usually frustrated search for those hot spots that characterized the Venice of yore. Later in the evening, you should stop for an espresso at the Caffè Florian and sip while listening to the orchestra play.

Thanks to Napoleon, the square was unified architecturally. The emperor added the Fabbrica Nuova facing the basilica, thus bridging the Old and New Procuratie on either side. Flanked with medieval-looking palaces, the Sansovino Library, elegant shops, and colonnades, the square is now finished—unlike Piazza della Signoria in Florence.

If Piazza San Marco is Europe's drawing room, then the *piazza's* satellite, **Piazzetta San Marco** ⋒, is Europe's antechamber. Hedged in by the Doge's Palace, Sansovino Library, and a side of St. Mark's, the tiny square faces the Grand Canal and is graced by two tall granite columns. One is surmounted by a winged lion, representing St. Mark; the other is topped by a statue of a man taming a dragon, supposedly the dethroned patron saint Theodore. Both columns came from the East in the 12th century.

During Venice's heyday, dozens of victims either lost their heads or were strung up here, many of them first being subjected to torture that would've made the Marquis de Sade flinch. One, for example, had his teeth hammered in, his eyes gouged out, and his hands cut off before being strung up. Venetian justice became notorious throughout Europe. If you stand with your back to the canal, looking toward the south facade of St. Mark's, you'll see the so-called *Virgin and Child of the Poor Baker,* a mosaic honoring Pietro Fasiol (also Faziol), a young man unjustly sentenced to death on a charge of murder.

To the left of the entrance to the Doge's Palace are four porphyry figures, whom, for want of a better description, the Venetians called "Moors." These puce-colored fellows are huddled close together, as if afraid. Considering the decapitations and tortures that have occurred on the *piazzetta,* it's no wonder.

St. Mark's Basilica (Basilica di San Marco) ★★★ Dominating Piazza San Marco is the Church of Gold (Chiesa d'Oro), one of the world's greatest and most richly embellished churches, its cavernous candlelit interior gilded with mosaics added over some 7 centuries. The basilica is a conglomeration of styles, though it's particularly indebted to Byzantium. In fact, it looks as if it were moved intact from Istanbul. Like Venice, St. Mark's is adorned with booty from every corner of the city's once far-flung mercantile empire: capitals from Sicily, columns from Alexandria, porphyry from Syria, and sculpture from old Constantinople.

The basilica is capped by a dome that, like a spider plant, sends off shoots, in this case a quartet of smaller-scale bulbed cupolas. Spanning the facade is a loggia, surmounted by replicas of the four famous St. Mark's horses, the *Triumphal Quadriga.* The facade's rich marble slabs and mosaics depict scenes from the lives of Christ and St. Mark. One of the mosaics re-creates the entry of the evangelist's body into Venice—according to legend, St. Mark's body, hidden in a pork barrel, was smuggled out of Alexandria in A.D. 828 and

---

Tips **A St. Mark's Warning**

A dress code for men and women prohibiting shorts, bare arms and shoulders, and skirts above the knee is strictly enforced at all times in the basilica. You *will* be turned away. In addition, you must remain silent and cannot take photographs.

shipped to Venice. The evangelist dethroned Theodore, the Greek saint who up until then had been the patron of the city that had outgrown him.

In the **atrium** are six cupolas with mosaics illustrating scenes from the Old Testament, including the story of the Tower of Babel. The interior of the basilica, once the private chapel and pantheon of the doges, is a stunning wonderland of marble, alabaster, porphyry, and pillars. You'll walk in awe across the undulating multicolored ocean floor, patterned with mosaics.

To the right is the **baptistery,** dominated by the Sansovino-inspired baptismal font, upon which John the Baptist is ready to pour water. If you look back at the aperture over the entry, you can see a mosaic of the dance of Salome in front of Herod and his court. Salome, wearing a star-studded russet-red dress and three white fox tails, is dancing under a platter holding John the Baptist's head. Her glassy face is that of a Madonna, not an enchantress.

After touring the baptistery, proceed up the right nave to the doorway to the oft-looted **treasury** *(tesoro)* ✖. Here you'll find the inevitable skulls and bones of some ecclesiastical authorities under glass, plus goblets, chalices, and Gothic candelabra. The entrance to

What to See & Do in Venice

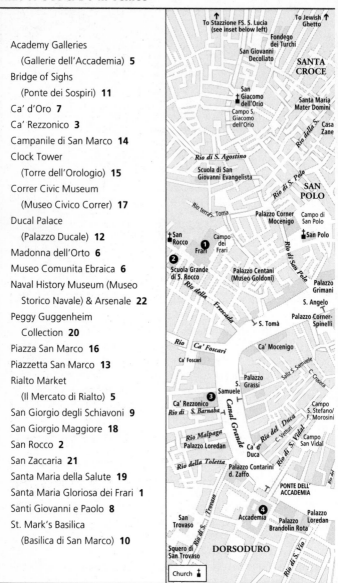

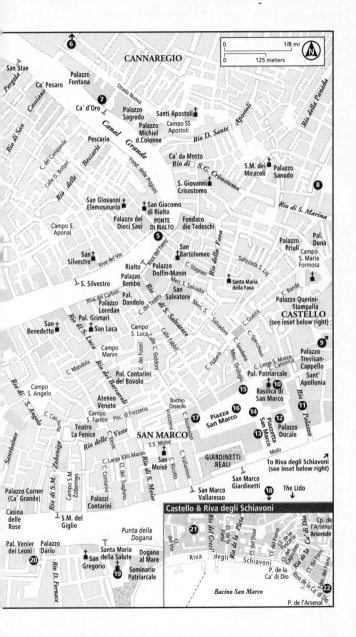

the **presbytery** is nearby. In it, on the high altar, the alleged sarcophagus of St. Mark rests under a green marble blanket and is held by four Corinthian alabaster columns. Behind the altar is the rarest treasure at St. Mark's: the **Pala d'Oro** ⟨⟨⟨, a Byzantine-style golden altar screen measuring 3×1.2m (10×4 ft.). It's set with 300 emeralds, 300 sapphires, 400 garnets, 90 amethysts, and 1,300 pearls, plus rubies and topazes accompanying 157 enameled rondels and panels. Second in importance is the 10th-century *Madonna di Nicopeia,* a bejeweled icon taken from Constantinople and exhibited in its own chapel to the left of the high altar.

On leaving the basilica, head up the stairs in the atrium to the **Marciano Museum** and the **Loggia dei Cavalli.** The star of the museum is the world-famous *Triumphal Quadriga* ⟨⟨⟨, four horses looted from Constantinople by Venetian crusaders during the sack of that city in 1204. These horses once surmounted the basilica, but were removed because of pollution damage and subsequently restored. This is the only *quadriga* (a quartet of horses yoked together) to have survived from the classical era. It's believed to have been cast in the 4th century. Napoleon once carted these much-traveled horses off to Paris for the Arc de Triomphe du Carrousel, but they were returned to Venice in 1815. The museum, with its mosaics and tapestries, is especially interesting, but also be sure to walk out onto the loggia for a view of Piazza San Marco.

Piazza San Marco. ⟨⟩ 041-5225205. www.basilicasanmarco.it. Basilica free; treasury 3€ ($4.80); presbytery 2.50€ ($4); Marciano Museum 3€ ($4.80). Basilica and presbytery Apr–Sept Mon–Sat 9:30am–5pm, Sun 2–5pm; Oct–Mar Mon–Sat 10am–4:45pm, Sun 1–4:45pm. Treasury Mon–Sat 9:30am–4:45pm; Sun 2–5pm. Marciano Museum Apr–Sept Mon–Sat 10am–5pm, Sun 2–4:30pm; Oct–Mar Mon–Sat 10am–4:45pm, Sun 2–4:30pm. Vaporetto: San Marco.

Campanile di San Marco ⟨⟨   One summer night in 1902, the bell tower of St. Mark's, suffering from years of rheumatism in the damp Venetian climate, gave out a warning sound that sent the fashionable coffee drinkers in the *piazza* below scurrying for their lives. But the campanile gracefully waited until the next morning, July 14, before tumbling into the *piazza.* The Venetians rebuilt their belfry, and it's now safe to climb to the top. Unlike Italy's other bell towers, where you have to brave narrow, steep spiral staircases to reach the top, this one has an elevator so that you can get a pigeon's-eye view. It's a particularly good vantage point for viewing the cupolas of the basilica.

Piazza San Marco. ⟨⟩ 041-5224064. www.basilicasanmarco.it. Admission 8€ ($13). July–Sept daily 9am–9pm; Oct and Apr–June daily 9am–7pm; Nov–Mar daily 9:30am–3:30pm. Closed Jan 7–31. Vaporetto: San Marco.

Clock Tower (Torre dell'Orologio)   The two Moors striking the bell atop this Renaissance clock tower, soaring over the Old Procuratie, are one of the most characteristic Venetian scenes. The clock under the winged lion not only tells the time, but also is a boon to the astrologer: It matches the signs of the zodiac with the position of the sun. If the movement of the Moors striking the hour seems slow in today's fast-paced world, remember how many centuries the poor wretches have been at their task without time off. The Moors originally represented two European shepherds, but after having been reproduced in bronze, they've grown darker with the passing of time. As a consequence, they came to be called "Moors" by the Venetians.

The base of the tower has always been a favorite meeting point for Venetians and is the entrance to the ancient **Mercerie** (from the word for merchandise), the principal souklike retail street of both high-end boutiques and trinket shops that zigzags its way to the Rialto Bridge.

Piazza San Marco. ✆ **041-5209070.** www.museicivicveneziani.it. Admission 12€ ($19). Visits in English Mon–Wed 10am, 11am, and 1pm; Thurs–Sun 2pm, 3pm, and 5pm. Vaporetto: San Marco.

Ducal Palace & Bridge of Sighs (Palazzo Ducale & Ponte dei Sospiri) ✶✶✶   You enter the Palace of the Doges through the magnificent 15th-century **Porta della Carta** ✶✶ at the *piazzetta*. This Venetian Gothic *palazzo* gleams in the tremulous light somewhat like a frosty birthday cake in pinkish-red marble and white Istrian stone. Italy's grandest civic structure, it dates to 1309, though a 1577 fire destroyed much of the original building. That fire made ashes of many of the palace's masterpieces and almost spelled doom for the building itself, because the new architectural fervor of the post-Renaissance was in the air. However, sanity prevailed. Many of the greatest Venetian painters of the 16th century contributed to the restored palace, replacing the canvases or frescoes of the old masters.

If you enter from the *piazzetta*, past the four porphyry Moors, you'll be in the splendid Renaissance courtyard, one of the most recent additions to a palace that has benefited from the work of many architects with widely varying tastes. To get to the upper loggia, you can take the **Giants' Stairway (Scala dei Giganti),** so called because of the two Sansovino statues of mythological figures.

If you want to understand something of this magnificent palace, the fascinating history of the 1,000-year-old maritime republic, and the intrigue of the government that ruled it, search out the infrared **audio guide** at the entrance, costing 5€ ($8). Unless you can tag along with an English-language tour group, you may otherwise miss out on the importance of much of what you're seeing.

After climbing the Sansovino stairway, you'll enter some get-acquainted rooms. Proceed to the **Sala di Antecollegio,** housing the palace's greatest works, notably Veronese's *Rape of Europa,* to the far left on the right wall. Tintoretto is well represented, with his *Three Graces* and *Bacchus and Ariadne.* Some critics consider the latter his supreme achievement. The ceiling in the adjoining **Sala del Collegio** bears allegorical paintings by Veronese. As you proceed to the right, you'll enter the **Sala del Senato o Pregadi,** with its allegorical painting by Tintoretto in the ceiling's center.

It was in the **Sala del Consiglio dei Dieci,** with its gloomy paintings, that the dreaded Council of Ten (often called the Terrible Ten, for good reason) used to assemble to decide who was in need of decapitation. In the antechamber, bills of accusation were dropped in the lion's mouth.

The excitement continues downstairs. You can wander through the once-private apartments of the doges to the grand **Maggior Consiglio,** with Veronese's allegorical *Triumph of Venice* on the ceiling. The most outstanding feature, however, is over the Grand Council chamber: Tintoretto's *Paradise,* said to be the world's largest oil painting. *Paradise* seems to have an overpopulation problem, perhaps reflecting Tintoretto's too-optimistic point of view (he was in his seventies when he began this monumental work and died 6 years later). The second grandiose hall, which you enter from the grand chamber, is the **Sala dello Scrutinio,** with paintings telling of Venice's past glories.

Reentering the Maggior Consiglio, follow the arrows on their trail across the **Bridge of Sighs (Ponte dei Sospiri)** ⟨⟨, linking the Doge's Palace with the Palazzo delle Prigioni. Here you'll see the cellblocks that once lodged the prisoners who felt the quick justice of the Terrible Ten. The changing roster of the Terrible Ten comprised a series of state inquisitors appointed by the city of Venice to dispense justice to the citizens. This often meant torture on the rack, even for what could be viewed as minor infractions. The reputation of the Terrible Ten for the ferocity of their sentences became infamous in Europe. The "sighs" in the bridge's name stem from the sad laments of the numerous victims forced across it to face certain torture and possible death. The cells are somber remnants of the horror of medieval justice.

If you're really intrigued by the palace, you may want to check out the **Secret Trails of the Palazzo Ducale (Itinerari Segreti del Palazzo**

Ducale). These 16€ ($26) guided tours, given by appointment only, are so popular they've been introduced in English; tours start daily at 9:55am, 10:45am, and 11:35am (you must reserve in advance at the ticket-buyers' entrance or by calling ℭ **041-5209070**). You'll peek into otherwise restricted quarters and hidden passageways of this enormous palace, such as the doge's private chambers and the torture chambers where prisoners were interrogated. The tour is offered in Italian daily at 10am and noon.

Piazzetta San Marco. ℭ **041-2715911**. www.museiciviciveneziani.it. Admission 12€ ($19); includes admission to Civic Museum, reviewed below. Apr–Oct daily 9am–7pm; Nov–Mar daily 9am–5pm. Closed Jan 1 and Dec 25. Vaporetto: San Marco.

2 The Grand Canal (Canal Grande) ★★★

Peoria may have its Main Street, Paris its Champs-Elysées, New York City its Fifth Avenue—but Venice, for uniqueness, tops them all with its **Canal Grande.** Lined with *palazzi* (many in the Venetian Gothic style), this great road of water is filled with *vaporetti* (public motorboats), motorboats, and gondolas. The boat moorings are like peppermint sticks. The canal begins at Piazzetta San Marco on one side and Longhena's La Salute church opposite. At midpoint, it's spanned by the **Ponte di Rialto (Rialto Bridge),** site of **Il Mercato di Rialto (Rialto Market;** see below). Eventually, the canal winds its serpentine course to the rail station.

Some of the most impressive buildings along the Grand Canal have been converted into galleries and museums. Others have been turned into cooperative apartments, but often the lower floors are now deserted. (Venetian housewives aren't as incurably romantic as foreign visitors. A practical lot, these women can be seen stringing up their laundry to dry in front of thousands of tourists.)

The best way to see the Grand Canal is to board *vaporetto* **no. 1** (push and shove until you secure a seat at the front of the vessel). Settle yourself in and prepare for a view that can thrill even the most experienced world traveler.

Il Mercato di Rialto ★★   The most famous bridge of Venice, Ponte di Rialto, is home to its most famous market, sprawling across the bridge and into the outlying streets. The bridge itself dates from 1588 and was designed by Antonio da Ponte. The market is the major showcase for the produce grown on the islands of the lagoon and for the fresh fish from the bordering Adriatic. You can see boats from such islands as Burano and Pellestrina, arriving at the Rialto to

---

Tips **Venice by Gondola**

You and your gondolier have two major agreements to reach: the price and the length of the ride. If you aren't careful, you're likely to be taken on both counts. It's a common sight to see a gondolier huffing and puffing to take his passengers on a "quickie," often reducing an hour to 15 minutes.

The "official" rate is 110€ ($176) per hour, but we've never known anyone to honor it. The actual fare depends on how well you stand up to the gondolier, *beginning* at 73€ ($117) for up to 50 minutes. Most gondoliers will ask at least double the "official" rate and reduce your trip to 30 to 40 minutes or even less. Prices go up after 8pm. In fairness to them, we must say their job is hard and has been overly romanticized: They row boatloads of tourists across hot, smelly canals with such endearments screamed at them as, "No sing! No pay!" And these fellows have to make plenty of cash while the sun shines, because their work ends when the first cold winds blow in from the Adriatic.

A word to the wise: Try to schedule your gondola ride at high tide. Otherwise, you'll have an eye-level view of scum and gunk on the sides of the canals, exposed at low tide.

Two major stations where you can hire gondolas are **Piazza San Marco** (© 041-5200685) and **Ponte di Rialto** (© 041-5224904).

---

unload their catch of the day. Sea bass, sardines, clams, and sturgeon form just some of the catch.

At the Ponte di Rialto (Rialto Bridge). Market Mon–Sat 7am–2pm. Vaporetto: Rialto.

3 Museums & Galleries

Academy Galleries (Gallerie dell'Accademia) ⚹⚹⚹ The glory that was Venice lives on in this remarkable collection of paintings spanning the 13th to 18th centuries. The hallmark of the Venetian school is color and more color. From Giorgione to Veronese, from Titian to Tintoretto, with a Carpaccio cycle thrown in, the Accademia has samples of its most famous sons—often their best

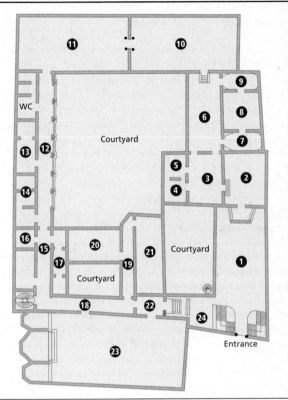

Venetian painters: 14th century **1**

Giovanni Bellini and
   Cima da Conegliano **2**

Late 15th century to
   early 16th century **3**

Italian painters: 15th century **4**

Giovanni Bellini and Giorgione **5**

16th century **6**

Lorenzo Lotto and Salvodo **7**

Palma the Elder **8**

16th-century schools of painting **9**

Titian, Veronese, and Tintoretto **10**

Veronese, Tintoretto, and Tiepolo **11**

18th-century landscape painters **12**

Tintoretto and Bassano **13**

Renovators of the 17th century **14**

Minor painters of the
   18th century **15**

Giambattista Piazzetta **16**

Longhi, Canaletto, Carriera,
   and Guardi **17**

18th-century painters and
   engravers **18**

15th-century painters **19**

Gentile Bellini and Vittorio
   Carpaccio **20**

Vittorio Carpaccio **21**

Bookshop **22**

Venetian painters: 15th century **23**

Albergo Room and Titian **24**

work. Here we've highlighted only some of the most-renowned masterpieces for the first-timer in a rush.

You'll first see works by such 14th-century artists as Paolo and Lorenzo Veneziano, who bridged the gap from Byzantine art to Gothic (see the latter's *Annunciation*). Next, you'll view Giovanni Bellini's *Madonna and Saint* (poor Sebastian, not another arrow) and Carpaccio's fascinating yet gruesome work of mass crucifixion. As you move on, head for the painting on the easel by the window, attributed to the great Venetian artist Giorgione. On this canvas, he depicted the Madonna and Child, along with the mystic St. Catherine of Siena and John the Baptist (a neat trick for Catherine, who seems to have perfected transmigration to join the cast of characters).

Two of the most important works with secular themes are Andrea Mantegna's armored *St. George,* with the slain dragon at his feet, and Hans Memling's 15th-century portrait of a young man. A most unusual *Madonna and Child* is by Cosmé Tura, the master of Ferrara, who could always be counted on to give a new twist to an old subject.

The Madonnas and bambini of **Giovanni Bellini** 🎨🎨, an expert in harmonious color blending, are the focus of another room. None but the major artists could stand the test of a salon filled with the same subject, but under Bellini's brush, each Virgin achieves her individual spirituality. **Giorgione's *Tempest* 🎨🎨🎨**, displayed here, is the single most famous painting at the Accademia. It depicts a baby suckling at the breast of its mother, while a man with a staff looks on. What might have emerged as a simple pastoral scene by a lesser artist comes forth as rare and exceptional beauty. Summer lightning pierces the sky, but the tempest seems to be in the background, far away from the foreground figures, who are unaware of the approaching danger.

You can see the masterpiece of Lorenzo Lotto, a melancholy portrait of a young man, before coming to a room dominated by **Paolo Veronese's *The Banquet in the House of Levi* 🎨🎨**. This is really a "Last Supper," but was considered a sacrilege in its day, so Veronese was forced to change its name and pretend it was a secular work. (Impish Veronese caught the hot fire of the Inquisition by including dogs, a cat, midgets, Huns, and drunken revelers in the mammoth canvas.) Four large paintings by Tintoretto, noted for their swirling action and powerful drama, depict scenes from the life of St. Mark. Finally, painted in his declining years (some have suggested in his 99th year, before he died from the plague) is **Titian's majestic *Pietà.***

After an unimpressive long walk, search out **Canaletto's *Porticato.*** Yet another room is heightened by **Gentile Bellini's stunning**

portrait of St. Mark's Square ⊀, back in the days (1496) when the houses glistened with gold. All the works in this salon are intriguing, especially the re-creation of the Ponte de Rialto and a covered wood bridge by Carpaccio.

On your way out, look for Titian's ***Presentation of the Virgin,*** a fitting farewell to this galaxy of great Venetian art.

Campo della Carità, Dorsoduro. ⓒ 041-5222247. www.gallerieaccademia.org. Admission 6.50€ ($10) adults, free for children 11 and under. Mon 8:15am–2pm; Tues–Sun 8:15am–7:15pm. Closed Jan 1 and Dec 25. Vaporetto: Accademia.

Ca' d'Oro ⊀⊀⊀ The only problem with the use of this building as an art museum is the fact that the Ca' d'Oro is so opulent, its architecture and decor compete with the works contained within. It was built in the early 1400s, and its name translates as "House of Gold," though the gilding that once covered its facade eroded away long ago, leaving softly textured pink-and-white stone carved into lacy Gothic patterns. The building was restored in the early 20th century by philanthropist Baron Franchetti, who attached it to a smaller nearby *palazzo* (Ca' Duodo), today part of the Ca' d'Oro complex. The interconnected buildings contain the baron's valuable private collection of paintings, sculpture, and furniture.

Enter into the stunning courtyard with a multicolored patterned marble floor. Proceed upstairs to the lavishly appointed *palazzo.* One of the gallery's major paintings is Titian's voluptuous **Venus.** She coyly covers one breast, but what about the other?

The masterpiece of the collection is Andrea Mantegna's icy-cold **St. Sebastian** ⊀, the central figure of which is riddled with what must be a record number of arrows. You'll also find works by Carpaccio here. If you walk onto the loggia, you'll have one of the grandest views of the Grand Canal, a panorama that inspired even Lord Byron—when he could take his eyes off the ladies.

For a delightful break, step out onto the loggia, overlooking the Grand Canal, for a view of the aquatic waterway and the *pescheria* (fish market), a timeless vignette of an unchanged city.

Cannaregio 3931–3932. ⓒ 041-5238790. www.cadoro.org. Admission 5€ ($8). Mon 8:15am–1:30pm; Tues–Sun 8:15am–7:15pm. Closed Jan 1, May 1, and Dec 25. Vaporetto: Ca' d'Oro.

Ca' Rezzonico ⊀⊀ This 17th- and 18th-century palace along the Grand Canal is where Robert Browning set up his bachelor headquarters and eventually died in 1889. Pope Clement XIII also stayed here. It's a virtual treasure house, known for its baroque paintings and furniture. First you enter the **Grand Ballroom,** with its allegorical ceiling, and then you proceed through lavishly embellished rooms with Venetian chandeliers, brocaded walls, portraits of patricians, tapestries, gilded furnishings, and touches of chinoiserie. Eventually you come to the **Throne Room,** with its allegorical ceilings by Giovanni Battista Tiepolo.

On the first floor, you can walk out onto a **balcony** for a view of the Grand Canal as the aristocratic tenants of the 18th century saw it. Another group of rooms follows, including the library. In these salons, look for a bizarre collection of paintings: One, for example, depicts half-clothed women beating up a defenseless naked man (one Amazon is about to stick a pitchfork into his neck, another to crown him with a violin). In the adjoining room, another woman is hammering a spike through a man's skull.

Upstairs is a survey of 18th-century Venetian art. As you enter the main room from downstairs, head for the **first salon** on your right (facing the canal), which contains the best works, paintings from the brush of Pietro Longhi. His most famous work, *The Lady and the Hairdresser* ☆☆, is here. Others depict the life of the idle Venetian rich. On the rest of the floor are bedchambers, a chapel, and salons, some with badly damaged frescoes.

Fondamenta Rezzonico, Dorsoduro 3136. © 041-2410100. www.museicivici veneziani.it. Admission 6.50€ ($10). Nov–Mar Wed–Mon 10am–5pm; Apr–Oct Wed–Mon 10am–6pm. Closed Jan 1, May 1, and Dec 25. Vaporetto: Ca' Rezzonico.

Correr Civic Museum (Museo Civico Correr) ☆☆ This museum traces the development of Venetian painting from the 14th to 16th centuries. On the second floor are the robes once worn by the doges, plus some fabulous street lanterns and an illustrated copy of *Marco Polo in Tartaria.* You can see Cosmè Tura's *Pietà* ☆☆, a miniature of renown from the genius in the Ferrara school. This is one of his more gruesome works, depicting a bony, gnarled Christ sprawled on the lap of the Madonna. Farther on, search out Schiavone's *Madonna and Child* (no. 545), our candidate for ugliest bambino ever depicted on canvas (no wonder his mother looks askance).

One of the most important rooms boasts three masterpieces: a *Pietà* by **Antonello da Messina,** a *Crucifixion* by **Flemish Hugo van der Goes,** and a *Madonna and Child* by **Dieric Bouts,** who depicted the baby suckling at his mother's breast in a sensual manner. The star attraction of the Correr is the **Bellini salon,** which includes works by founding padre Jacopo and his son, Gentile. But the real master of the household was the other son, Giovanni, the major painter of the 15th-century Venetian school (look for his *Cru-cifixion* and compare it with his father's treatment of the same subject). A small but celebrated portrait of St. Anthony of Padua by Alvise Vivarini is here, plus works by Bartolomeo Montagna. The most important work is **Vittore Carpaccio's *Two Venetian Ladies*** 𝒦𝒦, though their true gender is a subject of much debate. In Venice they're popularly known as "The Courtesans." A lesser work, *St. Peter,* depicting the saint with the daggers piercing him, hangs in the same room.

The entrance is under the arcades of Ala Napoleonica at the western end of the square.

In the Procuratie Nuove, Piazza San Marco. ℂ 041-2405211. www.museicivici veneziani.it. Admission (including admission to Ducal Palace, reviewed above) 12€ ($19). Apr–Oct daily 9am–7pm; Nov–Mar daily 9am–5pm. Closed Jan 1 and Dec 25. Vaporetto: San Marco.

Naval History Museum (Museo Storico Navale) & Arsenale 𝒦

The Naval History Museum is filled with cannons, ships' models, and fragments of old vessels dating to the days when Venice was supreme in the Adriatic. The prize exhibit is a gilded model of the *Bucintoro,* the great ship of the doge that surely would have made Cleopatra's barge look like an oil tanker. In addition, you'll find models of historic and modern fighting ships, local fishing and rowing craft, and a collection of 24 Chinese junks, as well as a number of maritime *ex voto* (offerings left at shrines) from churches of Naples.

If you walk along the canal as it branches off from the museum, you'll arrive at the Ships' Pavilion, where historic vessels are displayed. Proceeding along the canal, you'll soon reach the Arsenale, guarded by stone lions, Neptune with a trident, and other assorted ferocities. You'll spot it readily enough because of its two towers flanking the canal. In its day, the Arsenale turned out galley after galley at speeds usually associated with wartime production.

Campo San Biasio, Castello 2148. ℂ 041-5200276. Admission 1.55€ ($2.50). Mon–Fri 8:45am–1:30pm; Sat 8:45am–1pm. Closed holidays. Vaporetto: Arsenale.

Peggy Guggenheim Collection (Collezione Peggy Guggen-heim) 𝒦𝒦𝒦 This brilliant modern-art collection reveals both the foresight and the critical judgment of its founder. It's housed in an unfinished *palazzo,* the former Venetian home of Peggy Guggenheim, who died in 1979. In the tradition of her family, Peggy Guggenheim was a lifelong patron of contemporary painters and sculptors. In the 1940s, she founded the avant-garde Art of This Century Gallery in New York, impressing critics not only with the

Moments   Carnevale

Venetians take to the *piazzas* and streets for the pre-Lenten holiday of **Carnevale**. The festival traditionally marked the unbridled celebration that preceded Lent, the period of penitence and abstinence prior to Easter. It lasts about 5 to 10 days today, and culminates in the Friday through Tuesday before Ash Wednesday.

In the 18th-century heyday of Carnevale, well-heeled revelers came from all over Europe to take part in the festivities. Masks became ubiquitous, affording anonymity and pardoning a thousand sins: They permitted the fishmonger to attend the ball and dance with the baroness. The doges condemned the festival and the popes denounced it, but nothing could dampen the Venetian Carnevale spirit until Napoleon arrived in 1797 and put an end to the fun.

Resuscitated in 1980 by local tourism powers to fill the empty winter months, Carnevale is calmer now, though just barely. In the 1980s, it attracted an onslaught of what seemed to be the entire student population of Europe, backpackers who slept in the squares and the train station. Politicians and city officials adopted a middle-of-the-road policy that helped establish Carnevale's image as neither a backpackers' free-for-all outdoor party nor a continuation of the exclusive private balls in the Grand Canal *palazzi* available only to a very few.

Each year, the festival opens with a series of lavish balls and private parties, most of which aren't open to the public. But the candlelit **Doge's Ball (Ballo del Doge)** is a dazzling exception, traditionally held the Saturday before Shrove Tuesday in the 15th-century Palazzo Pisani Moretta on the Grand Canal. Historic costumes are a must (you can rent them). Of course, this ball isn't exactly cheap—it costs 550€ ($880) per person—but it's the extravagant experience of a lifetime. If you're interested in finding out more

high quality of the artists she sponsored, but also with her methods of displaying them.

As her private collection increased, she decided to find a larger showcase and selected Venice. While the Solomon R. Guggenheim and arranging for a costume rental, contact Antonia Saut-ter at the Ballo del Doge (© **041-5233851** or 041-5224426; fax 041-5287543; www.ballodeldoge.com).

Even if you don't attend a ball, there's still plenty of fun to be had in the streets. Musical and cultural events, many of them free of charge, appeal to all tastes, nationalities, ages, and budgets. The city's dozens of squares host every-thing from reggae to jazz to chamber music; special art exhibits are mounted at numerous museums and galleries. The recent involvement of international corporate spon-sors has met with a mixed reception, but it seems to be the wave of the future.

Carnevale is not for those who dislike crowds. The crowds, in fact, are what it's all about. All of life becomes a stage, and everyone is on it. It's a chance to relive the glory days of the 1700s, when Venetian life was at its most extravagant, which is why masks and costumes place an emphasis on the historical. Groups travel in coordinated get-ups that range from a contemporary passel of Felliniesque clowns to the court of the Sun King in all its wigged-out glory. You might see the Three Musketeers rid-ing the *vaporetto,* or your waiter may be dressed as a nun. The places to be seen in costume are the cafes lining Piazza San Marco. Don't expect to be seated at a full-view win-dow seat unless your costume is straight off the stage of the local opera house.

The merrymakers carry on until Shrove Tuesday, when the bells of San Francesco della Vigna toll at midnight. But before they do, the grand finale features fireworks over the lagoon. The city is the quintessential set, the perfect venue; Hollywood could not create a more evocative loca-tion. This is a celebration of history, art, theater, and drama. Venice and Carnevale were made for each other.

Museum was going up in New York City according to Frank Lloyd Wright's specifications, she was creating her own gallery here. You can wander through and enjoy art in an informal and relaxed way.

Max Ernst was one of Peggy Guggenheim's early favorites (she even married him), as was Jackson Pollock (she provided a farmhouse where he could develop his technique). Displayed here are works by Pollock and Ernst, as well as Picasso (see his 1911 cubist *The Poet*), Duchamp, Chagall, Mondrian, Brancusi, and Dalí, plus a garden of modern sculpture with Giacometti works (some of which he struggled to complete while resisting the amorous intentions of Marlene Dietrich).

Temporary modern-art shows may be presented during winter. In the new wing are a museum shop and a cafe, overlooking the sculpture garden.

In the Palazzo Venier dei Leoni, Calle Venier dei Leoni, Dorsoduro 701. ⓒ 041-2405411. www.guggenheim-venice.com. Admission 10€ ($16) adults, 5€ ($8) students, free for children 11 and under. Wed–Mon 10am–6pm. Vaporetto: Accademia.

4 Churches & Guild Houses

Much of the great art of Venice lies in its churches and *scuole* (guild houses or fraternities). Most of the guild members were drawn from the rising bourgeoisie. The guilds were said to fulfill both the material and the spiritual needs of their (male) members, who often engaged in charitable works in honor of the saint for whom their *scuole* were named. Many of Venice's greatest artists, including Tintoretto, were commissioned to decorate these guild houses. Some created masterpieces you can still see today. Narrative canvases that depicted the lives of the saints were called *teleri*.

Madonna dell'Orto ⓐ At this church, a good reason to walk to this remote northern district, you can pay your final respects to **Tintoretto.** The brick structure with a Gothic front is famed not only because of its paintings by that artist but also because the great master is buried in the chapel to the right of the main altar. At the high altar are his *Last Judgment* (on the right) and *Sacrifice of the Golden Calf* (on the left). Over the doorway to the right of the altar is Tintoretto's superb portrayal of the presentation of Mary as a little girl at the temple. The composition is unusual in that Mary isn't the focal point; rather, a pointing woman bystander dominates the scene.

The first chapel to the right of the main altar contains a masterly work by Cima de Conegliano, showing the presentation of a sacrificial lamb to the saints (the plasticity of St. John's body evokes Michelangelo). In the first chapel on the left, as you enter, notice the large photo of Giovanni Bellini's *Madonna and Child*. The original, which was noteworthy for its depiction of the eyes and mouths of the mother and child, was stolen in 1994; the photograph was installed in its place. In the apse, flanking an *Annunciation,* the work of Palma Giovane, is the *Vision of the Cross to St. Peter,* by Tintoretto, and the *Beheading of St. Paul,* also by Tintoretto.

Campo dell'Orto, Cannaregio 3512. © 041-2750462. Admission 3€ ($4.80). Mon–Sat 10am–5pm. Vaporetto: Madonna dell'Orto.

San Giorgio degli Schiavoni 🦋🦋 At the St. Antonino Bridge (Fondamenta dei Furlani) is the second important guild house to visit. Between 1502 and 1509, Vittore Carpaccio painted a pictorial cycle here of exceptional merit. His works of **St. George and the Dragon** are our favorite art in all Venice and certainly the most delightful. For example, in one frame St. George charges the dragon on a field littered with half-eaten bodies and skulls. Gruesome? Not at all. Any moment you expect the director to call "Cut!"

Calle dei Furlani, Castello. © 041-5228828. Admission 4€ ($6.40). Nov–Mar Tues–Sun 10am–12:30pm, Tues–Sat 3–6pm; Apr–Oct Tues–Sun 9:30am–12:30pm, Tues–Sat 3:30–6:30pm. Last entrance 20 min. before closing. Vaporetto: San Zaccaria.

San Giorgio Maggiore 🦋 This church, on the little island of San Giorgio Maggiore, was designed by the great Renaissance architect **Palladio**—perhaps as a consolation prize, since he wasn't chosen to rebuild the burned-out Doge's Palace. The logical rhythm of the Vicenza architect plays out here on a grand scale. But inside, it's almost too stark; Palladio wasn't much on gilded adornment. The chief art hangs on the main altar: two epic paintings by **Tintoretto,** the *Fall of Manna* to the left and the far more successful *Last Supper* to the right. It's interesting to compare Tintoretto's *Cena* with that of Veronese at the Accademia. Afterward, you may want to take the elevator (for 3€/$4.80) to the top of the belfry for a view of the greenery of the island itself, the lagoon, and the Doge's Palace across the way. It's unforgettable.

Isola San Giorgio Maggiore, across from Piazzetta San Marco. © 041-5227827. Free admission. Apr–Oct daily 9:30am–12:30pm and 2:30–6pm; Nov–Mar daily 10am–12:30pm and 2:30–4:30pm. Closed for Mass on Sun and feast days 10:45am–noon. Vaporetto: Take the Giudecca-bound vaporetto on Riva degli Schiavoni and get off at the 1st stop, right in the courtyard of the church.

San Rocco 🦋🦋🦋 Of all Venice's *scuole,* none is as richly embellished as this one, filled with epic canvases by **Tintoretto.** Known for paintings of mystical spirituality and phantasmagoric light effects, he won a competition to decorate this darkly illuminated early-16th-century building and began painting in 1564. The work stretched on until his powers as an artist waned; he died in 1594. The paintings sweep across the upper and lower halls, mesmerizing you with a kind of passion play. In the grand hallway, they depict New Testament scenes, devoted largely to episodes in the life of Mary (the *Flight into Egypt* is among the best). In the top gallery are works illustrating scenes from the Old and New Testaments, the most renowned being those devoted to the life of Christ. In a separate room is Tintoretto's masterpiece: his mammoth *Crucifixion.* In it he showed his dramatic scope and sense of grandeur as an artist, creating a deeply felt scene that fills you with the horror of systematic execution, thus transcending its original subject matter.

Campo San Rocco, San Polo. ✆ 041-5234864. Admission 5.50€ ($8.80) adults, 1.50€ ($2.40) children. Mar 28–Nov 2 daily 9am–5:30pm; Nov 3–30 and Mar 1–27 daily 10am–4pm; Dec–Feb Mon–Fri 10am–1pm, Sat–Sun 10am–4pm. Closed Easter and Dec 25–Jan 1. Ticket office closes 30 min. before last entrance. Vaporetto: San Tomà.

Santa Maria della Salute 𝄞𝄞 Like the proud landmark it is, La Salute, the pinnacle of the baroque movement in Venice, stands at the mouth of the Grand Canal overlooking Piazzetta San Marco and opening onto Campo della Salute. One of Venice's most historic churches, it was built by Baldassare Longhena in the 17th century as an offering to the Virgin for delivering the city from the plague. Longhena, almost unknown when he got the commission, dedicated half a century to working on this church and died 5 years before the long-lasting job was completed. Surmounted by a great cupola, the octagonal basilica makes for an interesting visit: It houses a small art gallery in its sacristy (tip the custodian), which includes a marriage feast of Cana by Tintoretto, allegorical paintings on the ceiling by Titian, a mounted St. Mark, and poor St. Sebastian with his inevitable arrow.

Campo della Salute, Dorsoduro. ✆ 041-2743911. Free admission (but offering is expected); sacristy 2€ ($3.20). Mar–Nov daily 9am–noon and 3:30–5:30pm. Vaporetto: Salute.

⌒Tips A Note on Museum Hours

As throughout Italy, visiting hours in Venice's museums are often subject to major variations. Many visitors who have budgeted only 2 or 3 days for Venice express disappointment when, for some unknown reason, a major attraction closes abruptly. When you arrive in town, check with the tourist office for the latest list of hours of operation.

Santa Maria Gloriosa dei Frari ⟨⟨   Known simply as the Frari, this Venetian Gothic church is only a short walk from the San Rocco and is filled with great art. The best work is **Titian's *Assumption*** over the main altar—a masterpiece of soaring beauty depicting the ascension of the Madonna on a cloud puffed up by floating cherubs. In her robe, and especially in the robe of one of the gaping saints below, "Titian red" dazzles as never before.

On the first altar to the right as you enter is Titian's second major work here: *Madonna Enthroned,* painted for the Pesaro family in 1526. Although lacking the power and drama of the *Assumption,* it nevertheless is brilliant in its use of color and light effects. But Titian surely would turn redder than his Madonna's robes if he could see the latter-day neoclassical tomb built for him on the opposite wall. The kindest word for it: large.

Facing the tomb is a memorial to Canova, the Italian sculptor who led the revival of classicism. To return to more enduring art, head to the sacristy for a 1488 Giovanni Bellini triptych on wood; the Madonna is cool and serene, one of Bellini's finest portraits of the Virgin. Also see the almost primitive-looking woodcarving by Donatello of St. John the Baptist.

Campo dei Frari, San Polo. ℭ 041-2750462. Admission 3€ ($4.80). Mon–Sat 9am–6pm; Sun 1–6pm. Vaporetto: San Tomà.

Santi Giovanni e Paolo ⟨⟨   This great Gothic church (also called Zanipolo) houses the **tombs** of many doges. It was built during the 13th and 14th centuries and contains works by many of the most noted Venetian painters. As you enter (right aisle), you'll find a retable by Giovanni Bellini (which includes a St. Sebastian filled with arrows). In the Rosary Chapel are Veronese ceilings depicting New Testament scenes, including *The Assumption of the Madonna.* To the right of the church is one of the world's best-known **equestrian statues,** that of Bartolomeo Colleoni, sculpted in the 15th century by Andrea del Verrocchio. The bronze has long been acclaimed as his masterpiece, though it was completed by another artist. The horse is far more beautiful than the armored military hero, who looks as if he had just stumbled onto a three-headed crocodile.

To the left of the pantheon is the **Scuola di San Marco,** with a stunning Renaissance facade (it's now run as a civic hospital). The church requests that Sunday visits be of a religious nature rather than for sightseeing.

Campo SS. Giovanni e Paolo, Castello 6363. ℭ 041-5235913. Admission 2.50€ ($4). Daily 7:30am–6:30pm. Vaporetto: Rialto or Fondamenta Nuove.

San Zaccaria ✶✶   Behind St. Mark's is this Gothic church with a Renaissance facade, filled with works of art, notably Bellini's restored *Madonna Enthroned* (second altar to the left). Many have found this to be one of Bellini's finest Madonnas, and it does have beautifully subdued coloring, though it appears rather static. Many worthwhile works lie in the main body of the church, but for a view of even more of them, apply to the sacristan for entrance to the church's museum, housed in an area once reserved exclusively for nuns. Here you'll find artwork by Tintoretto, Titian, Il Vecchio, and Anthony Van Dyck. The paintings aren't labeled, but the sacristan will point out the names of the artists. If you save the best for last, you can see the faded **frescoes of Andrea del Castagno** in the shrine honoring San Tarasio.

Campo San Zaccaria, Castello. ℂ **041-5221257.** Admission 2€ ($3.20) to crypt and treasury. Mon–Sat 10am–noon; daily 4–6pm. Vaporetto: San Zaccaria.

5 The Lido ✶✶

The white sands of the Lido have drawn artists and literary types for centuries, and today they still attract a bikini-clad crowd that includes the occasional celeb. The Lido is a resort area complete with deluxe hotels, a casino, and stratospheric prices.

The Lido is past its heyday, however. A chic crowd still checks in to the Excelsior Palace and the Hotel des Bains, but the beach strip is overrun with tourists and opens onto polluted waters. (For swimming, guests use their hotel pools, though they still stroll along the Lido sands and enjoy the views.)

Even if you aren't planning to stay in this area, you should still come over and explore for an afternoon. There's no denying the appeal of a beach so close to one of the world's most romantic cities. The strips of beachfront in front of the big hotels on the Lido are technically considered private, and the public is discouraged from using the facilities. But because you can use the beachfront on either side of their property, no one seems to really care about shooing nonguests away.

If you don't want to tread on the beachfront property of the rarefied hotels (which have huts lining the beach like those of some tropical paradise), you can try the **Lungomare G. d'Annunzio (Public Bathing Beach)** at the end of the Gran Viale (Piazzale Ettore Sorger), a long stroll from the *vaporetto* stop. You can book cabins *(camerini)* and enjoy the sand here. Rates change seasonally.

To reach the Lido, take *vaporetto* no. 1, 52, or 82 (the ride takes about 15 min.). The boat departs from a landing stage near the Doge's Palace.

6 The Ghetto ★★

The Ghetto of Venice, called the **Ghetto Nuovo** ★, was instituted in 1516 by the Venetian Republic in the Cannaregio district. It's considered to be the first ghetto in the world and also the best kept. The word *geto* comes from the Venetian dialect and means "foundry" (originally there were two iron foundries here where metals were fused). At one time, Venetian Jews were confined to a walled area and obliged to wear red or yellow marks sewn onto their clothing and distinctive-looking hats. The walls that once enclosed and confined the ghetto were torn down long ago, but much remains of the past.

There are five synagogues in Venice, each built during the 16th century and each representing a radically different aesthetic and cultural difference among the groups of Jews who built them. The oldest is the **German Synagogue** (Sinagoghe Grande Tedesca), restored after the end of World War II with funds from Germany. Others are the **Spanish Synagogue** (Sinagoghe Spagnola, the oldest continuously functioning synagogue in Europe), the **Italian Synagogue** (Sinagoghe Italiana), the **Levantine-Oriental Synagogue** (Sinagoghe Levantina, aka the Turkish Synagogue), and the **Canton Synagogue** (Sinagoghe del Canton).

The best way to visit the synagogues is to take one of the guided tours departing from the **Museo Comunità Ebraica,** Campo di Ghetto Nuovo 2902B (✆ **041-715359**). It contains a small but worthy collection of artifacts pertaining to the Jewish community of Venice and costs 8.50€ ($14). From June to September, the museum is open Sunday through Friday from 10am to 7pm (Oct–May until 6pm). However, the museum is by no means the focal point of your experience: More worthwhile are the **walking tours of the Jewish cemetery** that begin here, costing 10€ ($16), with free entrance to the museum. The 50-minute tours include visits to the interiors of three of the five synagogues (the ones you visit depend on various factors). From June to September, the tours depart hourly Sunday through Friday from 10:30am to 5:30pm (Oct–May until 3:30pm). *Note:* The Museo Comunità Ebraica is closed January 1, December 25, and during Jewish holidays.

7 Organized Tours

Tours through the streets and canals of Venice are distinctly different from tours through other cities of Italy because of the complete absence of traffic. You can always wander at will through the labyrinth of streets, but many visitors opt for a guided tour to at least familiarize themselves with the city's geography.

American Express, Calle San Moisè, San Marco 1471 (© **041-5200844**), near St. Mark's, offers an array of guided tours. It's open Monday through Friday from 9am to 5:30pm and Saturday from 9am to 12:30pm. Call ahead to make reservations. The offerings include a daily 2-hour guided tour of the city for 33€ ($53), an Evening Serenade Tour that's accompanied by musicians in gondolas for 40€ ($64), and a tour of the islands of the lagoon for 20€ ($32).

8 The Lagoon Islands of Murano, Burano & Torcello

If you're exploring these islands for the day and are looking for a good lunch spot, see p. 80 for a few suggestions.

MURANO 🏵🏵

For centuries, glass blowers on the island of Murano have turned out those fantastic chandeliers prized so highly by Victorian ladies. They also produce heavily ornamented glasses so ruby red or so indigo blue you can't tell if you're drinking blackberry juice or pure grain alcohol. Happily, the glass blowers are still plying their trade, though increasing competition (notably from Sweden) has compelled a greater degree of sophistication in design.

Murano remains the chief expedition from Venice, but it's not the most beautiful nearby island (Burano and Torcello are far more attractive).

You can combine a tour of Murano with a trip along the lagoon. To reach Murano, take *vaporetto* **no. 5 or 13** at Riva degli Schiavoni, a short walk from Piazzetta San Marco. The boat docks at the landing platform at Murano, where the first furnace awaits conveniently. It's best to go Monday through Friday between 10am and noon if you want to see some glass-blowing action.

On your way to Murano, you can hop off the *vaporetto* for a look at the cemetery island of **San Michele.** Celebrities buried here include impresario Sergei Diaghilev (1872–1929), who introduced western Europe to Russian ballet, and composer Igor Stravinsky (1882–1971). Also on the island is the 15th-century **Church of San Michele,** with its handsome white classical facade and richly decorated interior. It was the first church in Venice to be built in the Renaissance style.

THE GLASS FACTORIES & OTHER SIGHTS

As you stroll through Murano, you'll find that the factory owners are only too glad to let you come in and see their age-old craft. Bargaining

---

Moments **A Special Glass Museum**

Call for an appointment to visit the **Barovier & Toso Museum,** Palazzo Contarini, Fondamenta Vetrai 28, Murano (*©* **041-739049**), where Angelo Barovier displays rare glass from his private collection, acquired over half a century. The museum is open (providing you call in advance) during foundry hours, Monday to Friday 10am to noon and 2 to 5pm.

---

is expected. Don't—repeat, *don't*—pay the marked price on any item. That's merely the starting figure at which to begin negotiations.

However, the prices of made-on-the-spot souvenirs aren't negotiable. For example, you may want to buy a horse streaked with blue. The artisan takes a piece of incandescent glass, huffs, puffs, rolls it, shapes it, snips it, and behold—he has shaped a horse. The showrooms of Murano also contain a fine assortment of Venetian crystal beads, available in every hue. You may find some of the best work to be the experiments of apprentices.

While on the island, you can visit the Renaissance *palazzo* housing the **Museo del Vetro di Murano,** Fondamenta Giustinian 8 (*©* **041-739586;** www.museiciviciveneziani.it), which contains a spectacular collection of Venetian glass. From April through October, it's open Thursday through Tuesday from 10am to 6pm (Nov–Mar to 5pm). Admission is 5.50€ ($8.80).

If you're looking for something different, head to **San Pietro Martire,** Fondamenta Vetrai (*©* **041-739704**), which dates from the 1300s but was rebuilt in 1511 and is richly decorated with paintings by Tintoretto and Veronese. Its proud possession is a *Madonna and Child Enthroned* by Giovanni Bellini, plus two superb altarpieces by the same master. The church lies right before the junction with Murano's Grand Canal, about 228m (748 ft.) from the *vaporetto* landing stage. It's open daily from 9am to noon and 3 to 6pm; it is closed for Mass on Sunday morning.

Even more notable is **Santa Maria e Donato,** Campo San Donato (*©* **041-739056**), open Monday through Saturday from 9am to noon and 3:30 to 7pm, Sunday from 3:30 to 7pm. Dating from the 7th century but reconstructed in the 1100s, this building is a stellar example of Venetian Byzantine style, despite its 19th-century restoration. The interior is known for its mosaic floor (a parade of peacocks and eagles, as well as other creatures) and a 15th-century ship's-keel ceiling. Over the apse is an outstanding mosaic of the Virgin against a gold background from the early 1200s.

BURANO 𝕽𝕽

Burano became world-famous as a center of lace making, a craft that reached its pinnacle in the 18th century. The visitor who can spare a morning to visit this island will be rewarded with a charming fishing village far removed in spirit from the grandeur of Venice but only half an hour away by ferry.

Boats leave from Fondamenta Nuove, overlooking the Venetian graveyard (which is well worth the trip all on its own). To reach Fondamenta Nuove, take *vaporetto* **no. 52** from Riva degli Schiavoni. Once you land at Burano, you'll discover that the houses of the islanders come in varied colors: sienna, robin's-egg or cobalt blue, barn red, butterscotch, and grass green.

Check out the **Scuola di Merletti di Burano,** "Museo del Merletto," San Martino Destra 183 (℗ **041-730034;** www.museicivici veneziani.it), in the center of the village at Piazza Baldassare Galuppi. From November to March, the museum is open Wednesday to Monday from 10am to 4pm (Apr–Oct to 5pm). Admission is 4€ ($6.40). The Burano School of Lace was founded in 1872 as part of a movement aimed at restoring the age-old craft that had earlier declined, giving way to such lace-making centers as Chantilly and Bruges. On the second floor, you can see the lace makers at work. Handmade lace items are available for purchase.

After visiting the lace school, walk across the square to the **Duomo** and its leaning **campanile** (inside, look for the *Crucifixion* by Tiepolo). See it while you can, because the bell tower is leaning so precariously it looks as if it may topple at any moment.

TORCELLO 𝕽𝕽

Of all the islands of the lagoon, Torcello, the so-called "Mother of Venice," offers the most charm. If Burano is behind the times, Torcello is positively antediluvian. You can stroll across a grassy meadow, traverse an ancient stone bridge, and step back into that time when the Venetians first fled from invading barbarians to create a city of Neptune in the lagoon.

To reach Torcello, take *vaporetto* **LN** from Fondamenta Nuove on Murano. The trip takes about 45 minutes. *Warning:* If you go to Torcello on your own, don't listen to the gondoliers who hover at the ferry quay. They'll tell you that the cathedral and the *locanda* (inn) are miles away. Actually, they're both reached after a leisurely 12- to 15-minute stroll along the canal.

Torcello has two major attractions: a church with Byzantine mosaics, and a *locanda* that converts day-trippers into inebriated angels of praise. Below, the spiritual nourishment; see p. 80 for the alcoholic and culinary sustenance.

Cattedrale di Torcello, also called **Santa Maria Assunta Isola di Torcello** (© **041-730084**), was founded in A.D. 639. It stands in a lonely meadow beside an 11th-century campanile. The **Byzantine mosaics** are the stars here. Clutching her child, the weeping Madonna in the apse is a magnificent sight, and on the opposite wall is a powerful *Last Judgment.* Byzantine artisans, it seems, were at their best in portraying hell and damnation. In their *Inferno,* they've re-created a virtual human stew with the fires stirred by wicked demons. Reptiles slide in and out of the skulls of cannibalized sinners. The church is open daily March to October, from 10:30am to 5:30pm (Nov–Feb to 5pm). Admission is 6€ ($9.60).

7

Venice Strolls

Y̶ou'll spend a lot of your time in Venice walking. You'll probably even get lost once or twice, but that's part of the fun. When you want a little more guidance, though, the two walking tours outlined in this chapter will help you organize your time and link together some of the major sights, while showing you some hidden gems and secret spots along the way.

WALKING TOUR 1	PIAZZA SAN MARCO & THE DOGE'S PALACE

by Thomas Worthen

Start:	Basilica of San Marco.
Finish:	Basilica of San Marco.
Time:	About 3 hours or more.
Best Times:	Mornings (9 or 9:30am).
Worst Times:	Afternoons, when crowds gather.

This is the heart of Venice, and there's enough to keep you busy for a week. Here you'll find the Basilica of San Marco, which was the spiritual heart of Venice, and the Doge's Palace, which was its political center. These are two of the world's great cultural treasures. The other buildings that surround the *piazza* have much to offer as well.

Piazza San Marco may be the most beautiful plaza in the world. It has always been Venice's ceremonial gathering place. It's a wonderful place to stroll, to window-shop, to listen to the cafe orchestras, and to watch pigeons attack visitors. In the height of the tourist season, you may want to ignore our itinerary and just go to what's open and available, because there can be a line just to get into the:

❶ Basilica of San Marco
It was built in A.D. 832 to house the relics of St. Mark, brought here from Alexandria in Egypt by two Venetian merchants—or grave robbers, depending on your point of view. According to the legend, they took the holy man's body from its shrine in Alexandria with the help

of some local Christians to prevent the precious relic from being desecrated by the Muslim rulers of Egypt. St. Mark himself was said to have made a few timely appearances to bless and abet the enterprise. The legend inspired many works of art, but it's at least as likely that the ruling doge at the time, Giustiniano Participazio, actually commissioned the theft to enhance his own prestige and that of Venice. In any event, relics could not be owned but merely possessed, so *robbery* would certainly be too strong a word for this translocation of a spiritual treasure.

The Venetians based the design of their new church on that of the Church of the Apostles in Constantinople (then the richest city in Christendom) in order to announce architecturally that Venice was one of the great cities of the world, with one of the holiest relics. The church, built to honor St. Mark, is the most magnificent in Venice. The basic structure you see today is mainly the result of a rebuilding that took place from around 1063 to 1094. The process of clothing the basilica in marble and mosaic took more than 2 additional centuries.

Take a moment to look at:

1a The principal facade

This facade was originally plain brick. The columns, sculpture, and sheets of marble that cover it now are pure show. Since they're mainly spoils from elsewhere, they have a slightly hodgepodge quality, but because of careful attention to symmetry, the variety of colors and shapes is a delight. Venetian sculptors made free copies of some of the imported (or stolen) reliefs to maintain this symmetry. The large Byzantine relief of Hercules carrying a boar on the far left, just past the leftmost portal, is balanced by a Venetian carving of Hercules with a stag, on the far right. The Venetian imitation is less dignified and less classical, but it is also sharper, more energetic, and more decorative, like Venice itself.

Stand just in front of the central doorway, and look up at the **three stone arches,** two below and one above the large mosaic of the Last Judgment. Here the sculptors were at their most original. The inner arch was created first and has the simplest figures carved in the lowest relief. As the sculptors proceeded to the second and third arches, they became progressively more confident, and the relief of the carving becomes more pronounced, as well as more complex and naturalistic.

The outer faces of the upper two arches show such pious subjects as virtues and prophets. The insides of the arches—the parts you have to get underneath to see—are most interesting for the scenes

Walking Tour 1: Piazza San Marco & the Doge's Palace

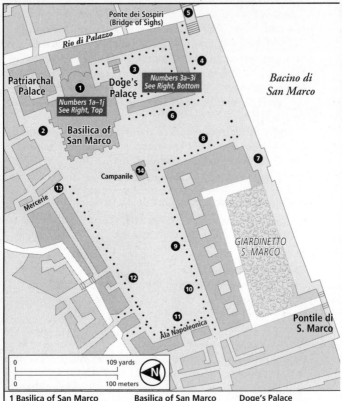

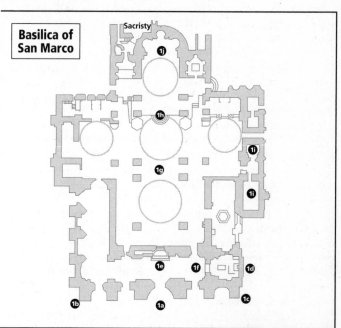

Basilica of San Marco

Sacristy

1j

1h

1j

1g

1i

1e   1f

1d

1b   1a   1c

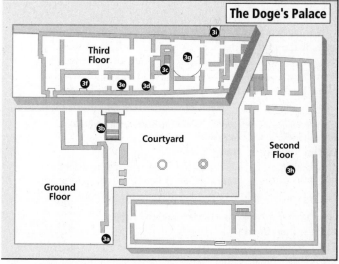

The Doge's Palace

3j

Third Floor

3g

3c

3f   3e   3d

3b

Courtyard

Second Floor

3h

Ground Floor

3a

they give us of 13th-century Venetian life. In the second arch, the inner face depicts the months, each illustrated with the appropriate zodiac sign and a typical seasonal labor. The inside of the third arch, the one surrounding the mosaic, shows a number of specifically Venetian occupations, such as fishing (in the lower right) and ship-building (in the lower left), just above the seated man with crutches. According to tradition, that seated man was the architect of San Marco; however, he probably represents old age, when men can no longer practice their occupations.

Only around the year 1400 were the standing saints added to the very top of the facade.

Above the central portal, in front of the large window, are statues of four horses, the *Triumphal Quadriga.* These were the most spec-tacular of the trophies sent from Constantinople by Doge Enrico Dandolo, and when they were installed here, they were the only free-standing works of sculpture on the facade. As one of Venice's great-est treasures, they became something of a symbol of the republic's greatness. According to legend, the Four Horses of St. Mark's once stood at the hippodrome in Constantinople, and before that they decorated Nero's arch in Rome. Napoleon had them carted off to Paris after he seized Venice in 1797. In Paris they graced the Arc de Triomphe du Carousel for 18 years, but they were returned to Venice after the Battle of Waterloo. What you see today are actually copies, made in 1982. The originals are in the church's museum.

The four semicircular mosaics above the side doors illustrate the story of the theft of the body of St. Mark, while the four large mosaics on the second story depict the death and resurrection of Jesus Christ. Most of them were made in the 17th century as replace-ments for the original Byzantine-style mosaics, which were then totally out of fashion.

One 13th-century mosaic mercifully escaped destruction, the one above the doorway on the far left, which shows:

1b The Relic of St. Mark

This lovely mosaic shows the relic of St. Mark being carried into the church. It depicts San Marco as it was around 1260 when the mosaic was laid and when the topmost part of the facade was much simpler.

Go to the other end of the main facade, where you'll find the:

1c Pietra del Banda

This is a short red column, really no more than a platform, which was probably brought from Acre late in the period of the Crusades. Officials would announce public decrees while standing upon this perch. It was severely battered in 1902 when the bell tower collapsed and a lot of the rubble slid onto it.

Now go around the corner to the side of the church facing the Doge's Palace and the lagoon to see:

1d The south facade

The south facade is a showcase for some of the finest loot. The most distinctive piece is the dark-red porphyry relief carving with four grim men, at the corner adjacent to the palace (near no. 3b, below). These four are the Tetrarchs, who ruled the Roman Empire around A.D. 300; these sculptures, too, were brought from Constantinople. A Venetian legend says that these are four Muslims who were turned to stone as they tried to carry off the treasury of San Marco, the exterior of which they adorn.

About 15 feet from the south facade are two highly decorated squared shafts. It had always been thought that they were trophies taken from the Genoese at Acre, but recently it has been proved that they came from a 6th-century church in Constantinople, destroyed by the Crusaders.

Return to the main facade and enter the church through the main door. As you do so, admire the 6th-century bronze doors with the lion's heads. (No prizes for guessing where the doors came from.) Inside the doorway is the:

1e Narthex

This is the porch of the church. It's a different world—dimmer, more delicately adorned, and with a soft, uncanny glow of golden light coming from the mosaics in the vaults overhead. The low late-afternoon sun shining into the narthex can turn this effect into a glittering blaze. On either side of the entryway into the church are miniature columns framing mosaic niches. These mosaics, from around 1100, the oldest surviving in San Marco, present us with austere but colorful Byzantine saints.

The larger mosaic in the half-dome above the door shows *St. Mark in Ecstasy* (1545). Here is a very different, boldly Renaissance conception of a saint, three-dimensional and energetic. It was designed by Titian, who wisely left the time-consuming and demanding job of inserting little cubes of stone and glass in wet mortar to a professional mosaicist.

The mosaics in the vaults that cap the narthex to the right and left depict scenes from the Old Testament.

Now go to your right (as you entered the narthex), and stand beneath the dome. When you look up into the dome, you will see the:

1f Story of Creation

Each of the 6 days of the Creation as described in the Book of Genesis is represented by the appropriate number of dainty little winged women. The reason for this odd bit of symbolism is made clear if, while standing beneath the dome, you face 45 degrees to the right of the door leading back into the *piazza* and look up at the middle row of scenes in the dome. Here you'll see the Lord blessing the Sabbath Day and making her holy.

A number of threadlike red lines runs through the mosaics (you can see them clearly in the scene closest to the door to the church). The red lines outline sections of the mosaic that, because of their ruinous condition, had to be filled in by restorers. You can see similarly outlined areas in many of the other older mosaics.

Now return to the part of the narthex just before the main entrance to the church. If you're up to climbing 44 steep steps, then, with the soft glow of the narthex mosaics fresh in your mind, enter the small door to the left of the central portal and climb up to the **museum** (there's an admission fee of 3€/$4.80), which contains ancient paintings, manuscripts, and fabrics that were used in church services. The unfinished brick vaults in the smaller rooms will help you imagine what the entire building must have looked like before it was covered with mosaics. The museum is especially worthwhile for the views you'll have of the *piazza* and the interior of the church.

In the room to the right of the top of the stairs, you can study fragments of 14th-century mosaics close up. The faces are lined with small squares of reds, greens, and blues as intense as in a painting by Matisse. When seen from across the room, the brilliant colors make the faces vivid, but blend together in such a way that they're hardly visible individually.

Continue still farther into the museum and you'll come to the originals of the *Triumphal Quadriga,* the four magnificent horses brought from Constantinople in 1204, which were once on the facade of the building. In ancient Rome they had been harnessed to a bronze chariot carrying a bronze Roman emperor holding the reins.

If the church is extremely crowded, you might begin your tour from the balcony; otherwise, descend the stairs, go through the main door, and enter the church proper. The first part of the church is the:

1g Nave

If you come in the dead of winter and are very lucky, you may have the entire place to yourself, but more likely you'll find yourself in a dense throng with too many guides. Don't abandon hope (or the building). Find a place to sit (you may have to go well into the church before you find an empty bench), and take time to gaze about.

The church is cross-shaped, covered by five domes. Three of the domes march in succession from the main door to the high altar. Another dome is above each of the arms of the cross (the transepts). The lower part of the church is covered with stone that's flatter and simpler than that in the porch. The alabaster columns are all functional. The walls are covered with sheets of marble, cut and arranged so that their veining creates symmetrical patterns.

In the nave's vaults the Venetian mosaicists created their greatest masterpieces, all surrounded by a golden aura that W. B. Yeats called "God's holy fire." Light is important mainly to illumine and reflect off the mosaics; therefore, the windows were placed at the very bottom of the domes to be as unobtrusive as possible. There's a large circular Gothic rose window in the south transept that seems very out of place in this Byzantine-style building; it was added to provide light for ducal ceremonies and for the display of relics.

The three major domes between the door and the altar depict three forms of interaction between God and humanity. In the large dome immediately above as you enter the church is the Descent of the Holy Spirit, in the form of a dove, on the disciples. The great dome in the center of the church shows the Ascension of Christ into heaven. In the dome above the sanctuary is still another image of Christ, this time with the prophets who foretold his coming.

The arches between the domes and some of the walls have scenes from the life of Christ. On the arch between the first and second domes are some of the most beautiful narrative scenes in San Marco, illustrating Christ's death and resurrection with Byzantine restraint. On the right is the Crucifixion. On the top are the holy women visiting the empty tomb on Easter morning. On the left, opposite the Crucifixion, is Christ's journey to hell to liberate the souls of the righteous of the Old Testament. This last scene was the usual way of illustrating Christ's resurrection in Byzantine art.

The lesser domes, arches, and walls depict various saints and stories connected with St. Mark.

Many of the original mosaics have been replaced in the last 500 years. Sometimes the mosaicist simply copied the composition that had been here before. The apse above the high altar is Renaissance in date (1506) but very Byzantine in style. More often an artist was commissioned to design a new composition of the same subject, and these changes were generally for the worse.

Move on now to the:

1h Sanctuary barrier and pulpits

The culmination of any church is its sanctuary, the place around the altar reserved for the priests and choir. The rest of the church, where the congregation stands, is focused on it. It's separated architecturally by being raised up and enclosed by a screen. The stone slabs that form the parapet of the screen have, however, been put on hinges so that they can be opened for services (today's congregation has a much better view of the sanctuary than did earlier congregations).

Beneath the sanctuary is a many-columned crypt designed to contain the shrine of St. Mark. It's well below water level and was generally flooded until an impressive job of sealing, completed in 1993, rendered it dry for the first time in centuries. The crypt is accessible only for prayer.

On top of the screen, in the center, is a silver crucifix flanked by statues of Mary and John the Evangelist, and flanking this group are the 12 Apostles. These handsome Gothic figures were installed in 1396.

Immediately in front of the screen on either side are pulpits. The one on the left, the green stone wedding cake topped with a bulging parapet and a canopy, was for reading the Bible. The reddish pulpit on the right was for the presentation of the doge to the people and the display of holy relics. In the 18th century, when the choir of San Marco was world-famous, musicians would crowd into it to play for services.

Walk into the transept, beneath the dome, and turn right between the columns. In front of you is the:

1i Treasury

The treasury (admission fee 2€/$3.20) has the world's best collection of Byzantine treasures, together with a number of masterpieces made in Venice itself.

The very best treasure, however, is in the sanctuary, and it requires still another admission fee (1.50€/$2.40). As you leave the treasury, move toward your right in the direction of the sanctuary, following the signs that say PALA D'ORO. The turnstile just beyond the ticket seller is more or less where the doge's throne would have been placed when the doge attended the service.

After you pay, go around to the back of the high altar to see the:

1j Pala d'Oro (Golden Altarpiece)

The altarpiece is a stunning conglomeration of Byzantine enameling, gold, and jewels. According to a 1796 inventory, its decorations include 1,300 pearls, 400 garnets, 300 sapphires, 300 emeralds, 90 amethysts, 75 balases, 15 rubies, 4 topazes, and 2 cameos. Begun around 1105, it reached its present appearance only in 1342, enlarged and enriched through several centuries. It was made to face into the nave, and still does on the major feasts. Generally, however, it's turned in the opposite direction so that you can't look for free.

While you're in the sanctuary, admire the four richly carved alabaster columns that support the stone canopy above the altar. The figures in the arches illustrate the life of Christ. Scholars have argued about whether the columns were made in Constantinople in the 6th century or Venice in the 13th. The latter date is probably correct, but it hardly matters. Like so much else in San Marco, they're unique.

You'll probably leave the church on the side opposite the Doge's Palace, which will bring you to the:

② Piazzetta dei Leoni (Small Square of the Lions)

The square is named for the two battered red Verona stone beasts (1722) that guard the well. Facing it, beneath the large arch (to your right if you left the church through the side door), is the noble tomb of Venice's 19th-century hero, Daniele Manin, who led the short-lived revival of the Venetian Republic from 1848 to 1849.

Now it's time to circle back to the other chief treasure of Venice, the:

③ Doge's Palace

The palace was begun in or shortly after A.D. 811 as a castle for the first duke, Agnolo Participazio. It has undergone several rebuildings and expansions, so no traces of the original structure are visible. The gracious Gothic structure you see today was not begun until around 1340 and was constructed in various stages over the next 100 years.

This palace remained the home of the doges (dukes) for almost a millennium, until the fall of the Venetian Republic in 1797; but the doge's actual living quarters were effectively reduced to four rooms. The purpose of the 14th-century rebuilding was to accommodate the various councils, offices, courts, prisons, and armories that were needed to make the palace not merely the town hall of the city of Venice but capital of the Venetian Empire as well. Unlike other medieval Italian governmental buildings, it's not a fortress. Its open loggias, picturesque decorations, and graceful structure bear witness to the security that the Venetian rulers felt here in the center of their stable, prosperous state.

There is sculpture at each corner of the building. On the level of the upper loggia is a protecting archangel. On the lower level are symbolic biblical scenes: *The Judgment of Solomon* is nearest the basilica, and *Adam and Eve* is at the opposite end of the facade near the *piazzetta*. There are delicate bits of symbolic sculpture on the capitals. Look for the ninth arch from the left on the upper loggia. Between these columns of red stone, death sentences were read.

The principal entrance to the palace, between the palace and the basilica, is the:
3a Porta della Carta (Paper Door)
The door may have gotten its name from the professional scribes who set up shop near here. It was built under Doge Francesco Foscari (in office 1423–57). Doge Foscari began the series of conquests of the mainland of Venice—conquests that ultimately turned Venice from an aggressive city of merchant gentlemen in the 14th century into a conservative city dominated by a landed aristocracy in the 18th. Foscari built this impressive and elaborate late-Gothic entrance to the Doge's Palace, with a statue of himself kneeling before a winged lion, the symbol of St. Mark and of Venice itself.

After Napoleon conquered Venice in 1797, the French paid the chief stonemason, one Giacomo Gallini, 982 ducats to destroy all the lions of St. Mark in Venice. Though Giacomo took the money, this was one of the few lions his masons got around to chiseling off. It seems appropriate that the effigy of the man who began Venice's mainland empire should have been effaced by order of the man who destroyed it. The lion and the statue of the doge that you see today are 19th-century replacements.

Go through the entrance to the enormous stairway you see before you, the:
3b Scala dei Giganti (Stairway of the Giants)
The stairway and the facade of the courtyard on that side were constructed after a fire gutted the east wing of the palace in 1483, to designs by Antonio Rizzo. The project was finished in 1501, but Rizzo didn't get to see it through—he had to flee Venice in 1489 when his overseers suspected that he was keeping about 15% of the construction funds for himself. The carved decoration here is derived from ancient Rome, but it's as delicate and charming—and as expensive and overdone—as the late-Gothic entryway that leads to it.

The magnificent stairway takes its name from the two oversize statues of Neptune and Mars, carved by Jacopo Sansovino in 1554, that symbolize Venice's domination of the sea and the land. The stairway was principally a stage for such ceremonies as the coronation of the doge and the reception of important foreign dignitaries. Curiously, there's a jail cell beneath the stairs.

To go any farther, you'll need to pay, but it's well worth it—the council rooms are decorated with some of the best art that Venice has produced.

Your tour through the Palazzo Ducale will have to follow the path laid out for you. The following are some of the highlights and are (probably) in the order that you'll encounter them. But be warned that the mandatory path occasionally changes.

You'll first encounter the:

3c Scala d'Oro (Golden Stairs)

This is the white-and-gold stairway that rises from the second floor. It was designed by Jacopo Sansovino and added to the palace between 1554 and 1558 to give important dignitaries a splendid access to the major reception and council rooms.

At the top of the stairs, turn right, and you'll be in the:

3d Sala dei Quattro Porti (Room of the Four Doors)

This is really a staging area for three of the most important meeting rooms. The best thing in it is the painting on the long wall immediately to your right as you enter, *Doge Antonio Grimani Kneeling before Faith,* begun by Titian around 1555.

The next room on the itinerary is the:

3e Antecollegio

This room has the loveliest collection of paintings in the palace. On the walls before you and behind you as you enter the room are four allegories (1577) by Tintoretto, filled with spiraling figures that are at once austere and sensuous. Each allegory combines pagan gods (symbolic of properties particularly propitious for Venice) with the four seasons to suggest that Venice is favored under all seasons and circumstances. If you face the door you came through, you'll see on your left, in winter, Vulcan, god of craftsmen. On your right are the three Graces in spring. Facing the opposite direction on your right is Ceres, goddess of prosperity, harvest, and summertime, separated by Wisdom (Minerva) from the harms of War (Mars). On your left, Bacchus, god of wine and of autumn, is married to Ariadne.

On the wall opposite the windows, on your right, is Jacopo Bassano's *Return of Jacob into Canaan.* To the left of it is Veronese's stunningly elegant and beautiful *Rape of Europa* (1580). We see the Phoenician princess, Europa, climbing in all innocence on the back of a white bull, who is Jupiter in disguise. Then, in several more distant scenes, we see him carrying her to the shore and across the Mediterranean, toward Crete, one of Venice's major possessions.

Next comes the:

3f Sala del Collegio

With its richly decorated ceiling and walls, this may well be the single most beautiful room in the palace. On the walls are glorifications of the virtues and piety of various 16th-century doges. Though there's a redundancy of Virgins and Christs, each work separately is quite handsome. As you enter, all the paintings to your right and behind you are by Tintoretto. The painting facing you is by Veronese, celebrating Doge Sebastian Falier and the Battle of Leponto (1581–82). Veronese also painted the allegorical scenes in the ceiling (1575–78); the large painting above the raised tribune is *Venice Enthroned, Honored by Justice and Peace.* The smaller figures in the ceiling represent the virtues of Venice. The woman knitting a spider web on your right, in the second ceiling panel from the entrance wall, for instance, is Dialectic, weaving (allegorically) a web of words.

The next room is a larger hall for the senate. The paintings (1585–95) are more extensive, if not necessarily of higher quality.

The exit returns you to the Room of the Four Doors. The painting on the easel is *Venice Honored by Neptune* (1745–50), by Tiepolo, one of the more recent paintings in the palace; the version above the windows is a copy. Next follows the:

3g Sala del Consiglio dei Dieci (Room of the Council of Ten)

The most powerful committee in Venice once met in this room. This council actually consisted of 17 people: the Council of Ten itself, the doge, and the doge's six counselors. The room's ceiling would be even more spectacular if the central painting hadn't been carted off to Paris during the Napoleonic occupation and replaced by a copy.

After this room, the tour can vary. You'll probably pass through the armory, and you may see fragments of some of the older works of art in the building, if that section is open. The two following sites are among the most memorable parts of the palace, though you may or may not see them in this order.

3h Sala del Maggior Consiglio (Room of the Great Council)

This room was originally constructed between 1340 and 1355, but after being gutted by fire in 1577, it was completely rebuilt. It needed to be big, because it had to seat every enfranchised citizen of Venice—all noblemen over the age of 25. Their average number was around 1,500, and their primary function was to elect the officials in the other councils. There were nine double rows of seats, arranged back-to-back and running lengthwise down the hall. (The specific arrangement of seats can be seen in a display at the far end of the room.)

The ensemble of the decoration may be more spectacular than its parts, but two of the paintings are wonderful: The enormous scene on the end wall is *Paradise* (1588–94), by Tintoretto, one of the largest paintings on canvas in the world. The oval painting on the ceiling above it is the *Triumph of Venice,* by Paolo Veronese, the perfect embodiment of Venice's self-conception—elegant, wealthy, aristocratic, and most serene.

On the walls immediately beneath the ceiling are portraits of the doges. The most famous is the one who isn't here. Opposite *Paradise,* on the left, one of the portraits seems to be covered with a veil, and a text reads: "Here is the place of Marin Falier, beheaded for his crimes." In 1355, after a year in office, Doge Marin Falier attempted to overthrow the republic in an effort to replace his ceremonial power with real power, but he underestimated the efficiency of the Venetian bureaucrats.

After passing through small barren corridors, you'll come to the:
3i Bridge of Sighs and the New Prisons (1566–1614)
The bridge served as the link between the court and torture rooms in the Doge's Palace and the prisons on the other side of a small canal. The name "Bridge of Sighs" was a 19th-century romantic invention, but it's certainly appropriate and evocative.

The prisons continued to be used until 1919. The most famous prisoner here was Daniele Manin, the Venetian patriot who was imprisoned here by the Austrians and later released in the 1848 rebellion. The famous and daring escape of another prisoner, Casanova, was made from an older prison, under the roof of the palace.

Much has been written about the evils of the Venetian judicial system, its use of secret denunciations and trials, political imprisonment, and torture. The *piazzetta* in front of the Doge's Palace was the traditional spot for state executions, and even in the republic's eminently civilized later centuries, these spectacles were gruesome. In 1595, Fynes Moryson, an Elizabethan traveler, witnessed the execution of two young men who were the sons of senators. Their hands were cut off and their tongues ripped from their throats before they were beheaded. Their crime had been a night of public drunkenness and wild behavior—their sentence may have had more to do with their failure to uphold standards expected of patricians than with their actual crimes. William Lithgow, a Scottish visitor to Venice in 1610, reported seeing a friar "burning quick [that is, alive] at St. Mark's pillars for begetting 15 young noble nuns with child, and all within one year."

Still, similar methods were standard for the period, and the rulers of Venice instinctively avoided fanaticism. For its time, Venice had one of the world's more equitable judicial systems. In the 18th century, the republic became the second country in the world to outlaw judicial torture.

At the end of your tour of the palace, you'll find yourself in the large courtyard. Note the two fantastically elaborate wellheads (1556 and 1559), made of expensive bronze, not cheap stone.

After you leave the palace, you'll be beside the:

❹ South facade of the palace

This was built before the facade near the basilica, and the sculptural details are even better. Each capital is elaborately carved, and each is different.

The bridge next to this corner is the:

❺ Ponte del Paglia (Bridge of Straw)

It was named not for the building material but for the cargo that was brought here. It offers a fine view of the Bridge of Sighs. Drowned bodies used to be placed nearby for relatives to claim, or, if unclaimed, to be buried by a charitable institution.

The sculpture at this corner of the Doge's Palace is the *Drunkenness of Noah,* whose three sons are just around the corner. Since those sons were supposed to have been the ancestors of all the races on the earth, this scene may suggest the breadth of Venetian trading enterprises.

Now go to the opposite end of the palace, to the two enormous columns, and you'll be in:

❻ Piazzetta San Marco

This is the sea entrance to San Marco and the palace, with the two columns forming its gateway. This was the site of a variety of ceremonies and celebrations. From here the doge entered his ceremonial boat, *Bucentoro,* for his annual Marriage with the Sea ceremony on Ascension Day. During Carnevale, acrobats used to form huge human pyramids and some daredevil would slide down a rope to the *piazzetta* from the top of the campanile.

The enormous monolithic columns were trophies brought from the eastern Mediterranean in the 12th century and dedicated to Venice's patron saints. The one with the winged lion on the top is the **Column of St. Mark.** The lion was probably made around 300 B.C. in what is today southeastern Turkey, but the wings are Venetian additions. The other column supports St. Theodore, the pre-Mark patron saint of Venice; it's a hodgepodge of antique fragments standing on a Venetian dragon. Executions took place between the two columns, and to this day, some Venetians are reluctant to walk between them.

The large building opposite the Doge's Palace is the library designed by Jacopo Sansovino, beginning in 1536, and called, appropriately, the Sansovino Library (see no. 8, below). It's a glorious building. Using nothing but white stone and shadows, Sansovino achieved an effect as rich and lush as that of its polychromatic neighbors. No surprise that it was influential—and you'll see echoes of it along the Grand Canal.

If you go around the library, along the water and away from the Doge's Palace, the next building you'll come to is the:

❼ Zecco (mint)

The shiny gold coins minted here were called *zecchini*, which gives us our word *sequin*. The facade of this knobby building is radically different from that of the library; strangely, the two were designed by the same man, Sansovino. The ponderous and rough stones suggest that the building is so strong that the gold within is safe. Originally it had only two stories, but because the furnaces made it intolerably hot, a third story was added in 1554 to help with ventilation.

The next part of the tour is a stroll alongside and through the porticoes that surround the Piazzetta and Piazza San Marco. Begin in the nearest one, the portico beneath the:

❽ Sansovino Library

At no. 7 Piazzetta San Marco is the entrance to the library itself, which is also called the Biblioteca Marciana, or Library of St. Mark. Its greatest treasure is its collection of books printed in Venice; until the end of the republic, Venice was the most important book-printing center in Italy, at one time producing more books than the rest of the world combined. Its most famous press was that of Aldus Manutius, known especially for his beautiful and scrupulously correct editions of Greek and Latin classics.

No. 13A is the entrance to the **old library,** generally opened only for special exhibits. If the door is open, by all means go up, if only to see the richly decorated rooms with paintings by Veronese, Tintoretto, and Titian, among others. With a place this beautiful for study, it's surprising that Venice didn't produce more great writers.

No. 17 is the entrance to the **Museo Archeologico,** which has an excellent collection of sculpture from ancient Greece (the Venetian Empire included many possessions in what is today Greece) and Rome.

Shortly after, the portico takes a left-hand turn, and you'll be in the:

❾ Procuratie Nuove

Built after 1586, it was conceived as a sort of extension of the Sansovino Library, with one floor too many. It served as the residence for the procurators, the most honored officials in Venice after the doge. Today it houses some of the city's more elegant shops and, on the upper floors, the Correr Museum (see below).

No. 52 leads into a courtyard with the best collection of wellheads in Venice and with an excellent explanatory text in English, just inside the door from the portico. If a doorkeeper should question your purpose, indicate that you want to see the *vere da pozzo* (wellheads).

> **TAKE A BREAK**
> A few doors down is the **Caffè Florian,** Piazza San Marco 56–59 (© 041-5205641), a coffee shop that has been here since the middle of the 18th century. Casanova claimed to have stopped here for coffee after breaking out of his cell in the Doge's Palace, before fleeing Venice. From 1815 to 1866, during the years of the Austrian occupation, the Caffè Florian was a bastion of Venetian patriots. During the rebellion against Austria from 1848 to 1849, the Florian for a time called itself the Manin, in honor of the leader of the insurrection. Later in the century, according to author John Ruskin, it was a place where "the idle Venetians of the middle classes lounge, and read empty journals." It's a real pleasure to sit at an outdoor table or in one of the hyperdecorated rooms and while away an hour, but it's a pleasure that doesn't come cheap.

Now turn into the portico that runs at a right angle to the one you've been in, the:

❿ Museo Civico Correr

This is really several connected museums. There are temporary exhibition galleries, with tickets sold at the foot of the stairs in the tourist season. This part is almost always worthwhile since the Correr hosts some of the finest temporary exhibitions in Venice. The first room of the exhibition hall is a magnificent neoclassical ballroom of 1822, designed by Lorenzo Santi, with pieces of sculpture by Venice's great neoclassical sculptor, Antonio Canova.

The main floor of the Correr Museum is dedicated to Venetian civilization, in both its more stately and its more intimate forms. Objects range from battle standards to *zoccoli,* the foot-high shoes that many upper-class women and prostitutes once tottered about in. Painted scenes range from ducal processions to battles between rival Venetian mobs.

The museum continues on the next floor with the **Picture Gallery (Quadreria),** which features an excellent collection of earlier Venetian art, including what may be the earliest surviving Venetian panel painting (on a chest from around 1250). It's especially strong in paintings of the 14th and 15th centuries, and includes not only works by such Venetian artists as the Bellinis (Jacopo, Gentile, and Giovanni) and Carpaccio, but also some small masterpieces by their northern European contemporaries.

A grand, though chilly, neoclassical stairway rises from the passageway to the second floor and the:

⓫ Ala Napoleonica (Napoleonic Wing)

This is the wing opposite the basilica. It was rebuilt (1808–14) under Napoleon to make a formal entrance and a ballroom for the royal residence that he had constructed into the Procuratie Nuove. In the middle of this wing is a large passageway named for the Church of San Gimignano, torn down in 1808 for the greater glory of the French ruler. A representation of the facade of the church is set in the pavement in the middle of the passageway.

The last wing bordering the *piazza* is the:

⓬ Procuratie Vecchie

Built between 1514 and 1526, this was the older residence of the procurators. Now there are elegant shops on the ground floor.

Shortly after you turn into this wing you'll come upon two arches on your left that open into the **Bacino Orseolo,** which has probably the largest conglomeration of gondolas in the city, so if you're interested in hiring one (and can afford it), this is a good staging point.

TAKE A BREAK
Continuing down the portico of the Procuratie Vecchie, you'll pass several cafes with orchestras, including **Quadri,** Piazza San Marco 120–124 (✆ **041-5289299**), which the occupying Austrians patronized in the first half of the 19th century, while Venetian patriots were at Florian, across the *piazza*. Now the bands occasionally seem at loggerheads, but not the clientele.

At the end of the portico is the:

⓭ Torre dell'Orologio (Clock Tower)

The tower was designed by Mauro Codussi and constructed between 1496 and 1499, with the two side wings added at a later time. It tells the time (to within 5 min.), the phases of the moon, and the place of the sun in the zodiac. The clock is the city's most wondrous and beloved timepiece. At the top of the tower is a balustraded terrace from which two mechanical bronze statues, called "Moors" because of the dark color of the bronze, faithfully strike the hour on a massive bell. Just below, against a field of golden stars, a winged lion of St. Mark looks out over the *piazza* and lagoon with his book open to the words "Peace unto you . . ." Below the lion, a niche contains a statue of the Madonna and Child. On Epiphany (Jan 6) and during the Feast of the Ascension, the clock's hourly pageant expands to include the Magi, led by an angel, who emerge from the doors on either side of the niche and bow before the figure of the Madonna. Legend has it that the eyes of the creators of the clock, Paolo and Carlo Rainieri, were put out to prevent them from ever matching this achievement for other patrons, but in actuality the two master clockmakers received only solid praise and very solid pensions.

The arch beneath the tower marks the beginning of the Mercerie, the main shopping drag that connects San Marco and the Rialto.

Now that you've seen the *piazza* from the ground, you may want to see it from above. Return to the:

⑭ Campanile (Bell Tower)

It collapsed on July 14, 1902, harming no one or nothing, apparently, but the watchman's cat. In the reconstruction, the original design (1511–14, by Bartolomeo Bon) was followed faithfully, but with a much more sophisticated understanding of building principles. It's unlikely to fall again soon.

At the base of the tower is a loggia that was begun in 1538 by Jacopo Sansovino, flattened in 1902, and carefully reconstructed by piecing together the original fragments as much as possible. It's a real jewel box and is decorated with some of Sansovino's finest statues. Originally it was a sort of clubhouse for nobles; now it's the entrance to the elevator going up the tower.

This is one of the two great tower views in Venice (the other is across the water at San Giorgio Maggiore). If the line here isn't too long, you can complete your tour of the *piazza* with a different perspective on what you've seen.

WALKING TOUR 2	THE ACCADEMIA BRIDGE TO PIAZZA SAN MARCO

by Robert Ullian

Start:	Accademia Bridge.
Finish:	Piazza San Marco.
Time:	Two or more hours, depending on time spent exploring museums or galleries.
Best Times:	Weekday mornings or late afternoons.
Worst Times:	Midday or Sunday, when most places are closed.

Much of this walk avoids the parts of San Marco that visitors generally see anyway. Instead, it leads down side streets that take you into hidden neighborhoods and enclaves of interesting shop windows and galleries. The walk includes a visit to one church with a wonderful interior and a quick look at the exterior of another, but basically this is an odyssey of twisting explorations and small, unusual discoveries.

To start this tour, take *vaporetto* (public motorboat) no. 1 to the Accademia stop and climb to the top of the:

❶ Accademia Bridge

This wooden structure was built in the 1930s (and redone in the 1980s) to replace the first Accademia Bridge, an iron span constructed by the Austrians in 1854. For both patriotic and aesthetic reasons, Venetians seem not to have fond memories of the original, which was demolished when traffic on the Grand Canal needed higher clearance. Most Venetians envision a permanent stone bridge here someday, but in recent years a proposal for a transparent plastic bridge that wouldn't obstruct the vistas has gained some attention.

Coming from the Accademia side of the bridge, the view to the right is spectacular. Looking back toward the Dorsoduro side of the Grand Canal, the vista includes the white domes and towers of Longhena's baroque masterpiece, the Church of Santa Maria della Salute (completed in 1681).

Ahead, on the invitingly gardened San Marco side of the Grand Canal, the first building to the right of the bridge is the 15th-century:

❷ Palazzo Franchetti

This *palazzo* (palace) is adorned with lavish Gothic tracery and a large, beautifully tended canal-side garden. Heavily renovated in 1896 by the same Baron Franchetti who restored the Ca' d'Oro, the Palazzo Franchetti, though sumptuous, is not admired by purists.

Walking Tour 2: The Accademia Bridge to San Marco

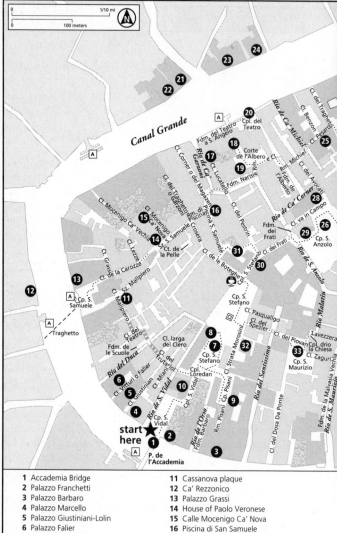

1 Accademia Bridge
2 Palazzo Franchetti
3 Palazzo Barbaro
4 Palazzo Marcello
5 Palazzo Giustiniani-Lolin
6 Palazzo Falier
7 Campo Santo Stefano
8 Palazzo Loredan
9 Palazzo Pisani
10 Church of San Vidal
11 Cassanova plaque
12 Ca' Rezzonico
13 Palazzo Grassi
14 House of Paolo Veronese
15 Calle Mocenigo Ca' Nova
16 Piscina di San Samuele
17 Grand Canal palace land entrance
18 Corte dell'Albero
19 Nardi Houses
20 Teatro Sant'Angelo

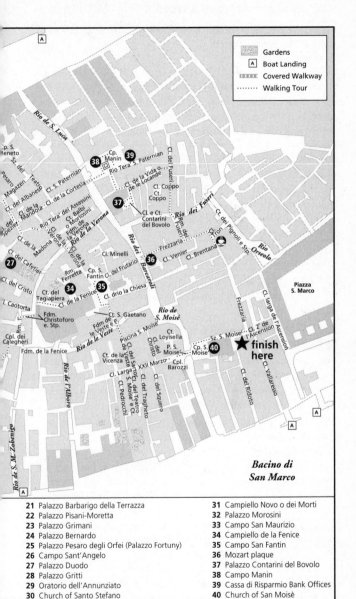

21 Palazzo Barbarigo della Terrazza
22 Palazzo Pisani-Moretta
23 Palazzo Grimani
24 Palazzo Bernardo
25 Palazzo Pesaro degli Orfei (Palazzo Fortuny)
26 Campo Sant'Angelo
27 Palazzo Duodo
28 Palazzo Gritti
29 Oratorio dell'Annunziato
30 Church of Santo Stefano

31 Campiello Novo o dei Morti
32 Palazzo Morosini
33 Campo San Maurizio
34 Campiello de la Fenice
35 Campo San Fantin
36 Mozart plaque
37 Palazzo Contarini del Bovolo
38 Campo Manin
39 Cassa di Risparmio Bank Offices
40 Church of San Moisè

The next two buildings to the right of the *palazzo,* separated from it by a narrow side canal, compose the:

❸ Palazzo Barbaro

This was once the home of the family whose portraits appear on the baroque facade of the nearby Church of Santa Maria Zobenigo. The older, closer part dates from 1425. The second part of the house, added in 1694, included a much-needed ballroom. In 1882, the upper two floors of Palazzo Barbaro were bought by Mr. and Mrs. Daniel Curtis of Boston, noted patrons of the arts. Robert Browning was invited to give recitations in the library. Henry James stayed while writing *The Aspern Papers;* he also used the *palazzo* as a setting for *The Wings of the Dove.* Claude Monet and John Singer Sargent each had a studio in the *palazzo,* and Whistler did a residence here. Cole Porter visited in 1923 before moving to a floating nightclub moored outside the Salute.

From the left side of the Accademia Bridge, the first house on the San Marco side of the Grand Canal is the:

❹ Palazzo Marcello

This is now the German Consulate, with a lush, overgrown garden to its side.

The large white *palazzo* immediately beyond is the:

❺ Palazzo Giustiniani-Lolin

The architect Longhena completed this *palazzo* in 1623, when he was in his early twenties. The sculptural baroque extravagances (like those on the Salute church) that later became Longhena's hallmark are scarcely evident in this restrained, classic facade.

The next house to the left (if you stretch your neck to look and step back a bit toward the Dorsoduro side of the bridge) is the:

❻ Palazzo Falier

Though the two roofed terrace wings might seem to be a modern addition, they're actually rare surviving examples of an old architectural form the Venetians called a *liago.* Such structures appear in Carpaccio's *Miracle of the Holy Cross* (in the Accademia), which depicts the busy area of the Rialto Bridge as it looked approximately 500 years ago. A branch of the Falier family produced Marin Falier, who, in 1355, became the only doge in the history of the republic to be executed (he plotted to overthrow the republic and seize complete power). Palazzo Falier was built in the early 15th century.

Directly ahead as you proceed across the bridge, you'll see the campanile of the Church of San Vidal, the parish church originally built in the 9th century by the Falier family, whose connection to this part of town is very ancient. Follow the way around to the right and then left, past the imposing pseudo-Palladian facade of the deconsecrated Church of San Vidal, and enter the spacious, sunny:

❼ Campo Santo Stefano

Also called Campo Francesco Morosini, this is the heart of the area this walk will explore. For now, we'll stay near the wellhead at the end of the *campo* (square) closest to the Accademia Bridge.

This fashionable *campo,* surrounded by a number of Venice's most unusual *palazzi,* was inhabited by some of the republic's noblest families. It was also the address of some notable courtesans. For centuries, Venice's vast community of prostitutes was one of its main tourist attractions. In the late 16th century, a directory for visitors was published, listing the names, addresses, and specialties of more than 11,000 such professionals (a copy can be seen at the Marciana Library). The *campo* was also the scene of bull-baiting spectacles; in 1802 the collapse of a grandstand here caused many injuries and led to the banning of this "sport" throughout Venice. A statue in the center of the *campo* commemorates Nicolo Tommaseo, who, along with Daniele Manin, led the insurrection against Austria from 1848 to 1849.

From the wellhead, you are opposite the very long, low-slung Renaissance facade of the:

❽ Palazzo Loredan

After the fall of the republic in 1797, the *palazzo* was used to house a number of public institutions. Since 1892 it has been the home of the Veneto Institute of Science, Letters, and Arts. Check out the lavish Neptune door knocker on the main entrance, just beneath the central second-story row of eight balconied windows.

In the corner of the *campo* opposite the Palazzo Loredan is the immense:

❾ Palazzo Pisani

Palazzo Pisani was begun in 1614 and continued to grow until the mid–18th century. With its formal, Romanesque-baroque style, this *palazzo* is unusual because its principal facade has always faced the *campo* rather than a canal, and because of its interior arcades, courtyards, and vast wings, which threatened to slowly encompass the entire neighborhood. Note the *palazzo's* own entrance *campiello,* sometimes used for outdoor performances, and the few small houses nearby that didn't get swallowed up as the *palazzo* grew. The *palazzo* now houses the Venice Conservatory of Music, as well as a banking house. Visitors are not generally welcome, but at times it's possible to see a bit of the interior during recitals, or, with luck, by sneaking in and asking about the school or concert programs when someone stops you.

From this side of the *campo,* look across to the:

⑩ Church of San Vidal (San Vitale)

This former church now houses an art gallery. Notice how the monumental facade, an imitation of Palladio's San Giorgio Maggiore, seems misplaced against a building with so little depth. Inside, Carpaccio's *San Vitale and Other Saints* survives from earlier times.

TAKE A BREAK
At the far end of the *campo,* you'll see the austere wall of the side of the Church of Santo Stefano; to the left, across the *calle* (street running alongside a canal) from the entrance to the church, you'll find the **Gelateria Paolin,** Campo San Stefano, San Marco 2962A (② **041-5225576**), one of the best ice-cream places in Venice, with flavors that are very rich and alive. You may not be in the mood to carry a cone or sherbet now, but we'll cross this *campo* a number of times, and, especially on a hot day, this is an option to keep in mind.

We'll leave the palaces and facades behind for a while and enter another world via the narrow Calle de Fruttarol, which starts between the side of the Church of San Vidal and the Palazzo Loredan. Follow this narrow passageway as it continues relatively straight (though it changes names), through a *sotoportego* (passageway beneath buildings) and over a canal (check the view each way as you cross the small bridge). Just after the end of the second *sotoportego,* turn left onto Calle dei Teatro, and then immediately onto the first right (Calle Malpiero), which goes through another *sotoportego.* At the end of the street, just before the intersection with Salizzada Malpiero, you'll find the:

⑪ Casanova plaque

It was on this street, once called Calle della Commedia, that Giovanni Giacomo Casanova (1725–98), the son of two actors in the nearby Teatro San Samuele, was born. The plaque conforms to the information in Casanova's autobiography, although no one can be certain in which house he was born or even if the events he recorded in his picaresque memoirs are in any way close to the truth. He became known as a libertine, spy, economist, philosopher, satirist, tax expert, and iconoclast, and we can only assume that Casanova's early years were spent planning how to escape to the glittering palaces and ballrooms only meters away from the world of his childhood.

At Salizzada Malpiero, look at the flower boxes that adorn the buildings to the right, but turn left, past the little-used Church of San Samuele, with its 12th-century campanile, and pass the *vaporetto* stop at Campo San Samuele, where you have a good view across the canal to:

⑫ Ca' Rezzonico

Look for the large white *palazzo* to the right of the Ca' Rezzonico *vaporetto* stop. Designed by the baroque master Baldassare Longhena in 1657, it was not completed until 1750; its top two floors were designed by Giorgio Massari. The Rezzonico family was legendary for its lavish entertainment; in 1758 they reached new heights of prestige when one of their members became Pope Clement XIII. He was the fifth Venetian to serve as pope.

In 1889, Robert Barrett Browning (known as "Pen"), the son of the poet Robert Browning, bought Ca' Rezzonico with the help of his wife, an American heiress, and together they refurbished the interior and built a chapel dedicated to Pen's mother, Elizabeth Barrett. They also installed a central heating system. Pen and his wife invited the 77-year-old Robert Browning, who had already spent much time in Venice, to join them in the *palazzo*, which the poet modestly described as "a quiet corner for my old age." Despite the heating system, Browning caught a chill and died there in December 1889. Ca' Rezzonico is now a museum of 18th-century Venetian art and furnishings (culled from many palaces) that gives you a sense of being in a still-functioning late-baroque *palazzo*. The attic houses a puppet theater and a period pharmacy.

In case you haven't already noticed the vast *palazzo* overpowering the far side of Campo San Samuele, you're facing Giorgio Massari's restrained, neoclassical:

⑬ Palazzo Grassi

Built between 1748 and 1772, this was the last of the great houses to be constructed on the Grand Canal; the Grassi family, latecomers to Venetian high society, didn't buy their way into patrician status until 1718. After the fall of the republic, the *palazzo* became a hotel for a time, and later a public bathhouse. In 1984 Fiat bought and refurbished the *palazzo* and converted it into a dazzling center for cultural and art exhibitions. The Palazzo Grassi's exhibits are beautifully mounted, often mobbed, and always worthwhile.

From Campo San Samuele, turn right onto Calle de le Carroze, and continue straight until it becomes the wider Salizzada San Samuele, which contains a number of interesting shops and galleries, some good for a quick glance, others worth further inspection.

At no. 3338 is the comfortable but nonpalatial:

⑭ House of Paolo Veronese

Veronese (1528–88) was the last great painter of the Venetian Renaissance and a master of the use of illusion in decorative art. Among Veronese's early triumphs are the lighthearted *trompe l'oeil* wall paintings of Villa Barbaro at Maser that create optical illusions of servants coming through nonexistent doorways, children peering through elaborate windows, and beautiful women gazing down from balconies. Venice adored his magic and showered him with commissions. For a Dominican friars' refectory, Veronese painted *The Last Supper* in the form of a lively and lavish Renaissance banqueting scene that some inside the church regarded as irreverent. Summoned before the Inquisition and ordered to change the painting, Veronese quickly complied by renaming the work *Banquet in the House of Levi*. Although (as his name indicates) Veronese was not a native Venetian, his work embodied the spirit of Venice at the height of its power—serenely joyful, poetic, and materially splendid.

Just past the house of Veronese, you might care to wander down the narrow:

⑮ Calle Mocenigo Ca' Nova

It doesn't look very interesting, but this was the land entrance to the Palazzo Mocenigo, a quadruple palace on the Grand Canal that was rented by British poet Lord Byron in 1817, 2 years after the final defeat of Napoleon. The more spectacular entrances would have been made directly from the Grand Canal—and not merely by gondola. At times the romantic Byron would swim from the Lido up the Grand Canal to his house, with members of the foreign community perched at various locations en route to admire his sagging but still heroic spirit and figure. The comings and goings at the rear entrance were interesting as well. Byron's household consisted of a wolf, a fox, and a number of dogs, cats, birds, and monkeys; it also included a mistress who was the wife of a Venetian draper. Later on another mistress was added, called La Fornarina ("the little oven") because she was the wife of a baker. The fiery La Fornarina, whom he described as "energetic as a python," attacked Byron with a knife and then threw herself into the Grand Canal after being banished from the *palazzo*.

Another important British poet, Percy Bysshe Shelley, would also have trod this alleyway. He and his wife, Mary (author of *Franken-stein*), visited Byron in 1818, accompanied by Mary Shelley's step-sister, Claire Clairmont, who was Byron's former mistress. The 19-month-old Clara Allegra, Byron's daughter by Claire Clairmont, had already been in residence for some time, under the care of La Fornarina. There's much more (when Byron finally decamped from the *palazzo*, he did so in the company of a new 19-year-old mistress, Countess Teresa Guiccioli), but perhaps this will be enough to entice you to detour down this alleyway with its walled gardens and hidden mysteries. Byron completed several cantos of *Don Juan* while in Venice; he died in 1824 at the age of 36.

The next part of this walk will explore the beauty and eccentricity of this hidden part of San Marco. Continue straight up Salizzada San Samuele, which narrows to become Ramo di Piscina, and ends at:

⓰ Piscina di San Samuele

The name *piscina* indicates that this was once a pool or sleeve of water leading into a canal that has long since been filled in with earth. In earlier times a piscina would have been used for bathing or for sheltering boats. Now it is a long, colorful courtyard.

Walk to the left. At the end of Piscina San Samuele, the way diverges into three possibilities. Take the small stairway with the iron banisters on the extreme right. Follow the narrow bridgeway to the first cross passageway, and turn left into the Corte Lucatello, which is a worthwhile dead end leading to a:

⓱ Palazzo land entrance

Now that private gondolas are history, this is the kind of daily route most modern-day *palazzo* dwellers must take, though not every *palazzo* is so pleasantly landscaped. Look through the gate into a secret garden, and beyond that, the *androne*, or water-level lobby. In this *palazzo*, you can see straight through the *androne* to the Grand Canal at the front of the building.

Retrace your steps, and walk a bit past the *sotoportego* on the left, then turn and look back. Roof gardens abound in this neighborhood—there's even one over the *sotoportego*. Go back and turn right through the *sotoportego*, which leads onto the canal-side Fondamenta Narisi. At the end you must turn left, and suddenly this traditional neighborhood has vanished. You're in:

⓲ Corte dell'Albero

This used to be a neighborhood of narrow canals and *calles.*

Walk a bit to the left and you'll see what has swallowed up much of this neighborhood, the massive:

⓳ Nardi Houses

The Veneto-Byzantine and Art Nouveau touches on this rare example of a 20th-century Venetian apartment building (built 1909–14) help it blend into the architectural fabric of the city. The building is interesting, but it reminds me how fortunate it is that large parts of Venice were not demolished to create more such complexes.

As you face the Nardi Houses, turn right and follow the *corte* (court) as it narrows and leads to the Grand Canal. Here you'll find a tiny *campiello* beside the Sant'Angelo *vaporetto* stop, and to the left, a rare walkway along the Grand Canal in front of the site of the former:

⑳ Teatro Sant'Angelo

We probably owe the existence of this small *fondamenta* (walkway) to the need for a landing spot to accommodate the many gondolas that once delivered the audience. The theater that once stood here produced many of Vivaldi's 40 operas.

Walk to your left, to the end of the *fondamenta*. The views from spots along the Grand Canal are always interesting. Directly across the Grand Canal, bordered by a *rio* (another word for canal), is the:

㉑ Palazzo Barbarigo della Terrazza

You can recognize this *palazzo* by its long side terrace with a white stone balustrade. Much of its famed art collection eventually came into the possession of Czar Nicolas II.

To the left of this *palazzo* is the large 15th-century:

㉒ Palazzo Pisani-Moretta

Note the elaborate Gothic windows. This house still remains in the hands of the descendants of the Pisani family and retains much of its original furnishing and interior decoration.

If you walk to the far right end of the *fondamenta*, beside the *vaporetto* stop, and look across the canal to the right, you'll notice a white three-story *palazzo* with triple-arched windows. This is the:

㉓ Palazzo Grimani

Built in about 1520, this is one of the first Renaissance houses in Venice.

The second Gothic house to the right beyond that, with two Gothic water entrances and two floors of six Gothic central windows adorning its *piani nobili* (main floors) is the 15th-century:

㉔ Palazzo Bernardo

If you look carefully, you can see that the two floors of central windows are out of line. Nonetheless, this is one of the most beautiful Gothic facades on the Grand Canal.

Retrace your steps to the Nardi Houses, turn left, and continue straight to the tiny, short *calle* at the far end of the *corte*. When you reach the canal, turn right onto Fondamenta de l'Albero, then take a left on the first bridge you come to, which leads to Ramo Michiel. The way jogs slightly to the left as it crosses the next *calle* to become Calle Pesaro. As you come to the next short bridge, look to the right across the *rio* and you'll see the canal facade of the Palazzo Fortuny. Continue straight along the side of the *palazzo*, then turn right into Campo San Benedetto, and at no. 3958 is the:

㉕ Palazzo Pesaro degli Orfei

Also called the Palazzo Fortuny, it was bought at the end of the 19th century by the Spanish-born couturier, fabric designer, and photographer Mariano Fortuny y Madrazo (1871–1949). The *palazzo* now houses a museum of Fortuny's varied works and is also a venue for temporary exhibitions. At the turn of the 20th century, Fortuny invented and patented a method of pleating silk ("Fortuny-pleated" skirts are still produced today), from which he created diaphanous gowns popularized by Isadora Duncan, Eleanora Duse, Sarah Bernhardt, and other romantic heroines of that age. The wide-ranging private collection of Fortuny is interesting but uneven; the studio and living quarters of this versatile genius, as well as the unrestored Gothic *palazzo* with its courtyard, ancient staircase, and wooden loggia, are all fascinating. During popular exhibits, the number of people allowed to enter the building must be limited because of the *palazzo's* fragile structure.

Exit the museum and enter Campo San Benedetto. From Campo San Benedetto, follow Calle a Fianco Ca' Pesaro to the right turn at the corner of the *palazzo;* at the *sotoportego,* turn left onto Rio Terrà de la Mandola until you reach the intersecting main thoroughfare, Calle dei Spezier, where you turn right. You'll quickly enter the bright, open:

㉖ Campo Sant'Angelo

Pause on this square to take in a view of the Chiesa di Santo Stefano, with the most oblique of the many leaning towers of Venice. The former convent of Santo Stefano fills one entire side of this square.

The first *palazzo* on the left side of the square is the:

㉗ Palazzo Duodo

This *palazzo* is privately owned and can't be visited, but you can admire its facade. Look for the numbers 3584 to identify this palace. It was once the Locando Tre Stelle, a historic inn that attracted many composers and writers in its 18th- and 19th-century heyday. The composer Cimarosa died at this inn in 1801.

Directly across, on the right side of the *campo,* is the:

㉘ Palazzo Gritti

This *palazzo* is unusual for its off-center doorway. Because they face onto dry land, these magnificent Gothic houses offer an unusual chance to study their carved stone ornamentation close up.

To the right, in the center of the *campo,* is the tiny 12th-century:

㉙ Oratorio dell'Annunziato

Here you'll find an *Annunciation* by Antonio Triva.

Walk straight across the *campo,* cross the Ponte dei Frati (enjoying views both ways), and continue straight. On your left, you'll come to the Gothic doorway of the:

30 Church of Santo Stefano

This church was built in the 14th and 15th centuries. The interior of the church is filled with rich patterning—gold and pale silver paneled squares on the ship's-keel ceiling, peach and maroon brickwork design on the upper walls, floral frescoes on the arches dividing the naves, delicately carved and painted beam work crossing the central nave, and a garden of red and white marble columns leading to the Gothic tracery of the apse. The space is lit by high windows recessed into the sides of the roof. In the sacristy you'll find three late works by Tintoretto: *The Washing of the Feet, The Agony in the Garden,* and *The Last Supper;* behind the altar you can see the elaborately carved 15th-century monks' choir. In the center of the nave is the tomb of Francesco Morosini, who was doge from 1688 to 1694. One of the republic's great leaders, he reversed Venice's sagging fortunes by briefly reconquering the Peloponnese in Greece (see no. 32, below). The far door in the left aisle leads into the cloister, once covered with frescoes by Pordenone.

Exit the church, and turn left toward the *campo.* Just as you enter the *campo,* turn right onto Calle de le Botteghe, take the first right, and climb the steps into:

31 Campiello Novo o dei Morti (New Campiello or Campiello of the Dead)

Today this spot is a pleasant discovery: a secluded plaza with gardens overhanging one wall and a terraced, vine-covered *locanda* (small hotel) at the right. The *campiello's* name, however, betrays a catastrophic history. The area was a mass grave for victims of the great plague of 1630, which accounts for its higher elevation. Until 1838 the site was closed to the public for health reasons.

Retrace your steps and enter Campo Santo Stefano. On the left side of the *campo,* just before it narrows, is the vast:

32 Palazzo Morosini

Palazzo Morosini has its own courtyard in the corner of the *campo.* This was the family palace of Francesco Morosini (1619–94), who, during the Turkish invasion of Crete in 1669, held off 17 sorties and 32 assaults before finally surrendering his besieged garrison to overwhelmingly superior forces. Morosini returned to Venice and was relieved of his command, but he refused to accept defeat. Fifteen years later, sailing into battle with his beloved cat at his side (in the true spirit of Venetian eccentricity), Morosini led the republic in the last successful military campaign of its history, the reconquest of the Peloponnese. Morosini is known to the rest of the world chiefly for lobbing a shell into the Parthenon, where the Turks were unfortunately storing gunpowder. Although the Parthenon had survived relatively intact until then, the explosion turned it into the ruin we know today. Morosini's bad luck with the Parthenon continued. Like Doge Enrico Dandolo, who had sent the *Triumphal Quadriga* back to Venice to adorn the Basilica of San Marco after the sack of Constantinople in 1204, Morosini envisioned sending home a spectacular trophy to mark his triumph. He chose the horses and chariot of the goddess Athena, which formed the western pediment of the Parthenon. In the attempt to dislodge the sculpture, however, it fell to the ground and was smashed beyond repair. Morosini was elected doge upon his return to Venice in 1688, and in 1694 he sailed off once more to fight the Turks. Again like Doge Enrico Dandolo, who had led a similar expedition in his old age 500 years earlier, Morosini died in the effort; within a few years his conquests were recaptured by the Turks. Although Venice never made a cult of its leaders, this last hero of the republic was gratefully revered. To commemorate Morosini's naval triumphs, a sculptured sea horse and various marine motifs adorn the main entrance of the *palazzo*. In 1894 the contents of the house were sold at auction. The embalmed body of his beloved cat is among the many Morosini possessions on display at the Museo Correr in Piazza San Marco.

One building to the left, as you face the Palazzo Morosini, is Calle dei Spezier, through which we'll exit the *campo*. The shops on this street bespeak the neighborhood's elegance. As you cross the small bridge, look left and you'll see that the apse of the Church of Santo Stefano has been built over the canal and that only low canal traffic can pass beneath it. A few feet beyond is the reserved, patrician:

❸ Campo San Maurizio

The *campo's* neoclassical church was rebuilt from 1806 to 1828. We're in the antique-gallery district of Venice, and this *campo* hosts occasional outdoor antiques markets; check with the Tourist Information Office if you're interested.

As you face the Church of San Maurizio, enter the narrow passageway to the right, which leads to a rabbit hole of twists and turns. Bear to the right, and take a right at Calle Lavezzera; at the *sotoportego* at the end of the *calle*, turn left onto Fondamenta de la Malvasia Vecchia, which ends at an angled bridge. Proceed straight into Campiello dei Caligari (the shoemakers' *campiello*), and exit through the ramp on the far right at the opposite side of the *campiello*. From this street, turn onto the first right, Fondamenta Cristoforo, which becomes a bridge. At the end of the bridge, a *sotoportego* takes you to the left. Turn right onto Calle de la Fenice. Turn left into the second *corte* you pass, the delightful, vine-trellised:

㉞ Campiello de la Fenice

At the left corner of the far end of the *campiello,* an interesting sequence of *sotoportegos* eventually leads back toward Campo Sant'Angelo. The building at the end of the *campiello* bears a plaque dedicated to the memory of those who died in the insurrection against Austria from 1848 to 1849. The Hotel La Fenice et des Artistes is on the left side of the *campiello.*

A right turn at the end of the *campiello,* and then the next right turn, will lead you to:

㉟ Campo San Fantin

On your right you'll see the remains of the legendary Fenice Theater, built in 1792 during the very last days of the republic and destroyed by fire in January 1996. (Controversy over its rebuilding is still going on.) Venice was the first city to have public performances of opera, and the jewel-like 1,500-seat oval interior of the Fenice saw the world premieres of Verdi's *Rigoletto, La Traviata,* and *Simon Boccanegra,* as well as Stravinsky's *Rake's Progress* (in 1951) and Benjamin Britten's *Turn of the Screw.* During the years of the Austrian occupation (and especially during productions of works by Verdi), the Fenice was a rallying point for patriotic fervor.

The **Church of San Fantin,** opposite the site of the theater, contains a beautiful Renaissance dome by Sansovino over its apse. At the head of the *campo* is the Venetian Athenium, formerly the Scuola della Buona Morte, a confraternity that comforted prisoners condemned to death.

As you face the Church of San Fantin, exit the *campo* via the street to the left of the church, Calle dei Fruttarol, which is home to a number of the city's most stylish and personal shops and galleries. As you cross the bridge, look to the right across the *rio* at the:

㊱ Mozart plaque

This plaque declares that "the city of Vivaldi and Goldoni" wished to record that the young Salzburger, Wolfgang Amadeus Mozart, festively sojourned during the Carnevale of 1771.

Beyond the bridge, the name of the *calle* changes to Frezzeria (street of the arrow makers).

TAKE A BREAK
We're almost at the end of the walk, but if you'd like to stop for a fast, inexpensive meal, **Le Chat Qui Rit**, Calle Frezzeria 1131 (*℡* **041-5229086**), a self-service cafeteria, is a good bet for soup or a quick bite. Follow Frezzeria until it makes a 90-degree turn; turn right and then immediately left. The restaurant is just on that corner. There are lots of rustic dining areas from which to choose, but they can be mobbed at mealtimes or when a tour group comes through.

To continue the tour, retrace your steps and take a right onto the upmarket Ramo Fusieri. Continue over the bridge, along the narrowing but busy *calle;* opposite no. 4460, turn right onto Calle de la Vida o de Locanda (Street of Life or of the Small Inn); continue until you turn left onto Calle de Contarini del Bovolo. On the left side of this narrow *calle,* you'll see the:

㊲ Palazzo Contarini del Bovolo

This *palazzo,* constructed in 1499, is known for its spiral-staircase tower and airy arcaded loggia. The large Contarini family built many palaces in Venice, each with its own identifying nickname—in this case, Bovolo comes from the Venetian word for "snail shell." Outdoor staircases were the rule in older palaces, but the Bovolo is unique. During the 19th century the palace changed hands a number of times and even served as a hotel for a time; it now houses an educational foundation. The ivy-covered garden has become a repository for architectural fragments and carved wellheads and is home to many local cats. The canal facade of this palace is unremarkable.

Retrace your steps to the intersection with Calle de la Vida, but at that point turn left. Then take the first right turn, which will lead you into the bustling:

㊳ Campo Manin

This *campo* was named for Daniele Manin, leader of the 1848-to-1849 insurrection against Austria (his house was on this plaza; looking from the statue of Manin, it's next to the left of the two bridges at the end of the *campo*).

The opposite end of the *campo* is graced by one of the city's few prominently placed modern buildings, the:

㊴ Cassa di Risparmio bank offices

Built in 1964, the offices were designed by noted architects Angelo Scattolin and Pier Luigi Nervi.

Exit Campo Manin by the left bridge as you face away from the statue of Manin. Continue straight on Calle de la Cortesia, a busy shopping street, which changes its name to Calle de la Mandola. Make a right turn onto Calle de la Verona, which will lead you back to Campo San Fantin. Continue straight across the *campo,* exit on Calle del Cafetier, and keep straight until this sequence of *calles* ends at Calle Larga XXII Marzo, a broad pedestrian street built in the 1870s and named for the date of the establishment of Manin's new republic in 1848. Turn left onto this important shopping *calle.* The dominant feature of this street, of course, is the:

⓯ Church of San Moisè

This church was founded in the 8th century. The current church building dates from 1632, with its facade designed by Alessandro Tremignon in 1668 and many sculptural decorations added by Heinrich Meyring in the 1680s to create a wildly roçoco presence. You either love this extravaganza or hate it. Inside, Meyring created an extraordinary sculptural altarpiece in the form of Moses receiving the Ten Commandments on Mount Sinai. Venice had an unusual tradition of naming some of its churches for Old Testament figures. Not quite like anything else in Venice, San Moisè might well be translated as "Holy Moses."

To the left of San Moisè is Salizada San Moisè, which will lead you back to Piazza San Marco and the end of this stroll.

8

Shopping

In a city that for centuries has thrived almost exclusively on tourism, there's certainly no lack of places to exercise your credit cards. On second thought, make that "exercise your *platinum* cards"—just as the hotel and restaurant prices in Venice are some of the highest in Italy, so are the price tags in most of its retail stores. However, there's a lot here to buy that's truly lovely and unique—and strolling and browsing just doesn't get much more enjoyable in any other city in the world.

1 The Shopping Scene

All the main shopping streets, even the side streets, are touristy and overrun. The greatest concentration of shops is around Piazza San Marco and around the Rialto. Prices are much higher at San Marco, but the quality of merchandise is also higher.

There are two major shopping strolls in Venice:

First, from **Piazza San Marco** you can stroll toward spacious **Campo Morosini.** You just follow one shop-lined street all the way to its end (though the name will change several times). Begin at Salizzada San Moisè, which becomes Calle Larga XXII Marzo, and then Calle delle Ostreghe, before it opens onto Campo Santa Maria Zobenigo. The street then narrows and changes to Calle Zaguri before widening once more into Campo San Maurizio, finally becoming Calle Piovan before reaching Campo Morosini. You can take a detour down Calle Vallaressa, between San Moisè and the Grand Canal, which is one of the major shopping arteries with some of the biggest designer names in the business.

The other great shopping stroll wanders from Piazza San Marco to the **Rialto** in a succession of streets collectively known as the **Mercerie.** It's virtually impossible to get lost because each street name is preceded by the word *merceria,* like Merceria dell'Orologio, which begins near the clock tower in Piazza San Marco. Many commercial places, mainly shops, line the Mercerie before it reaches the Rialto, which then explodes into one vast shopping emporium.

TAX REFUNDS As a member of the European Union, Italy imposes a **value-added tax (IVA)** on most goods and services sold

Venice Shopping

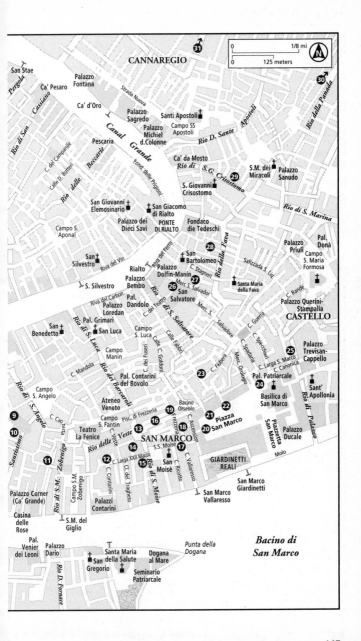

within its borders. If you're a resident of any country that's not a member of the E.U. and spend more than 155€ ($248) at any one store (regardless of how many individual items are involved), you're entitled to a refund of the IVA.

At the time of your purchase, be sure to get a receipt and an official IVA refund form from the vendor. When you leave Italy, find an Italian Customs agent at the airport (or at the point of your exit from the country if you're traveling by train, bus, or car). The agent will want to see the item you've bought, confirm that it's physically leaving Italy, and then stamp the IVA refund form.

In some cases, including leaving Italy via one of the larger airports, you can receive a cash refund directly on the spot. If the point of departure you've selected doesn't offer this (many highway and border crossings don't), you should mail the stamped form (keeping a photocopy for your records) back to the address indicated on your IVA refund form. Sooner or later, you'll receive a refund of the tax you paid at the time of your purchase. Reputable stores view this as a matter of ordinary paperwork and are very businesslike about it. Less honorable stores might lose your dossier or be unwilling to provide the forms you'll need. It pays to deal with established vendors, especially if you're making a large purchase. You can also request the refund be credited to the credit card with which you made the purchase.

SHOPPING HOURS   Most stores open at 9 or 10am, many closing for lunch around 1 or 1:30pm and reopening from 3 to 7:30pm. Many also close on Monday morning and reduce winter hours when business is slow.

2 Tips on Shopping for Glass & Lace

Venetian glass and Venetian lace are known throughout the world. However, there are so many shoddy imitations that selecting quality products of either craft requires a shrewd eye. Some of the glassware hawked isn't worth the cost of shipping it home. Yet other pieces represent some of the world's finest artistic and ornamental glass. Murano is the island where glass is made, and the women of Burano put in painstaking hours turning out lace. If you're interested in some little glass souvenir, perhaps an animal or a bird, you'll find such items sold in shops all over Venice.

SHOPPING FOR GLASS   Venice is crammed with glass shops: It's estimated there are at least 1,000 in San Marco alone. Unless you go to a top-quality dealer, you'll find most stores sell both shoddy and high-quality glassware, and often only the most trained eye can tell the difference. A lot of "Venetian glass" isn't from Venice at all but from the Czech Republic. (Of course, the Czech Republic has some of the finest glassmakers in Europe, so that may not be bad either.) Buying glass boils down to this: If you like an item, buy it. It may not be high quality, but then high quality can cost thousands.

If you're looking for an heirloom, stick to such award-winning houses as Pauly & Co. and Venini. Even buyers of glassware for distribution outlets in other parts of the world have been fooled by the vast array of glass in Venice. If even a buyer can be tricked, the layperson has only his or her own good instincts to follow.

SHOPPING FOR LACE   Most of the lace vendors are centered around Piazza San Marco. Although the price of Venetian lace is high, it's still reasonable considering the painstaking work that goes into it. A small handkerchief with a floral border can sell for as little as 3€ ($4.80); however, for large items like an heirloom-quality hand-worked tablecloth, the sky's the limit.

The catch is that a lot of imitation, shoddily made lace is also sold, and you have to check carefully to make sure you're getting the real thing. If you think you're getting a deal that's too good to be true, it's probably because what you're looking at really isn't Venetian lace but machine-made in who knows what country.

The name in Venetian lace is Jesurum, which has stood for quality since the 19th century. It has its own lace makers and, to guarantee its future, even has a school to teach apprentices how to make lace. Jesurum offers the most expensive, but also the highest quality, lace in Venice. At other places you take your chances. The lace shops are like the glassware outlets: They sell the shoddy, the machine-made, and the exquisite handmade pieces. Sometimes only the trained eye can tell the difference. Again, the best advice is to buy what you like if you think the price is reasonable. However, even if a piece is handmade, you can never be sure exactly *where* it was handmade—maybe China.

3 Shopping A to Z

ART

Imagina   This was the first cafe and gallery to open in the city of Venice. Shaped like a white cube, the building showcases a gallery that stays abreast of what's new and cutting-edge in the arts in Venice. The lounge bar changes its personality throughout the day. In the morning, it's a place where art patrons drop in for a cappuccino and a brioche, sitting back in designer armchairs and flipping through newspapers and fashion magazines. At lunch, the chef prepares tasty panini sandwiches and fresh salads. This is the time to check out the latest art exhibitions. The place is also a photography gallery. In the evening, the cafe takes on a party atmosphere, as more fashionable young Venetians and art lovers turn up to drink chilled *prosecco* (a type of sparkling wine) and, yes, talk about developing trends in modern art. Ponte dei Pugni, Dorsoduro. ℂ **041-2410625.** Vaporetto: Ca' Rezzonico or Accademia.

BOOKSTORES

Libreria San Pantalon   Known to Venetians as the bookshop with the cat in the window, this is the kind of store where you can browse for hours. It's known for its good selection of books on Italian music, especially opera, and it also carries beautiful arts and crafts books, gifts, games, children's books, and greeting cards. Dorsoduro 3950, Salizzada Pantalon. ℂ **041-5224436.** Vaporetto: San Tomà.

Libreria Sansovino   This store is centrally located to the north of Piazza San Marco. It carries books in English as well as volumes on art, literature, and history. Bacino Orseolo, San Marco 84. ℂ **041-5222623.** Vaporetto: Vallaresso.

BRASS OBJECTS

Valese Fonditore 𝄞𝄞   Founded in 1913, Valese Fonditore serves as a showcase for one of the most famous of the several foundries that make their headquarters in Venice. Brass copies of 18th-century chandeliers produced by this company grace many fine homes in the United States. Many visitors to Venice invest in these brass castings, which eventually become family heirlooms. If you're looking for a brass replica of the sea horses decorating the sides of gondolas, this shop stocks them in five or six styles and sizes. A pair of medium-size ones, each about 27 centimeters (11 in.) tall, begins at 150€ ($240). Calle Fiubera, San Marco 793. ℂ **041-5227282.** Vaporetto: Vallaresso.

CARNEVALE MASKS

Venetian masks, considered collectors' items, originated during Carnevale, which takes place the week before the beginning of Lent. In the old days, there was a good reason to wear masks during the riotous Carnevale—they helped wives and husbands be unfaithful to one another and priests break their vows of chastity. Things got so out of hand that Carnevale was banned in the late 18th century. But it came back, and the masks went on again.

You can find shops selling masks practically on every corner. As with glass and lace, however, quality varies. Many masks are great artistic expressions, while others are shoddy and cheap. The most sought-after mask is the *Portafortuna* (luck bringer), with its long nose and birdlike visage. *Orientale* masks evoke the heyday of the Serene Republic and its trade with the Far East. The *Bauta* was worn by men to assert their macho qualities, and the *Neutra* blends the facial characteristics of both sexes. The list of masks and their origins seems endless.

Mondonovo Here, talented artisans labor to produce copies of both traditional and more modern masks, each of which is one-of-a-kind and richly nuanced with references to Venetian lore and traditions. Prices range from 30€ ($48) for a fairly basic model to 1,830€ ($2,928) for something you might display on a wall as a piece of sculpture. Rio Terrà Canal, Dorsoduro 3063. ✆ 041-5287344. Vaporetto: Ca' Rezzonico.

EYEGLASSES

L'Ottico Fabbricatore ✪ Francesco Lincetto sells the chicest eyewear in Venice, maybe even in all of northern Italy. He is known in particular for his mod flexible-steel frames from IC! Berlin, as well as Lincetto's own line of Peggy Guggenheim–esque glasses made of buffalo horn. You'll never know what to expect, as the designs, including the materials used, are both daring and experimental. Lincetto also designed all the objects found in the store, including sunglasses, vases, Murano glass lamps, handbags, jewelry, and fashion accessories. Calle del Teatro 4773. ✆ 041-5225263. Vaporetto: Sacca Fisola.

FABRICS

Select outlets in Venice sell some of the greatest fabrics in the world.

Gaggio Rich This emporium offers unique items, the most stunning of which are velvets and artistic fabrics with filigree, all inspired by the deep colors and designs of fabled designer Mariano Fortuny. It's all very Venetian and very decadent. You can purchase these fabrics by the meter, or they can be fashioned into clothing, shawls, cushions, or whatever. San Stefano, San Marco 3451–3441. ✆ 041-5228574. Vaporetto: Accademia.

Norelene This legendary store features lustrous hand-printed silks, velvets, and cottons, plus wall hangings and clothing. Calle della Chiesa, Dorsoduro 681. ✆ 041-5237605. Vaporetto: Accademia.

Venetia Studium For years, Lino Lando worked to crack the secret of fabled designer Mariano Fortuny's *plissé* (finely pleated silk). Eventually he found the secret. The result can now be yours in his selection of silk accessories, scarves, Delphos gowns, and even silk lamps. There's also a newer shop at Mercerie, San Marco 723 (✆ 041-5229859). Calle Larga XXII Marco, San Marco 2403. ✆ 041-5229281. Vaporetto: Santa Maria del Giglio or San Marco.

Vittorio Trois Trois was selected to receive a priceless legacy. The great Mariano Fortuny revealed his exquisite printing techniques to a friend of Trois, the late Contessa Gozzi, and she passed them on to Trois, who made a business of them. Today, you can buy the same Fortuny patterns that stunned your grandparents on their visit to Venice decades ago. The radiant designs look like brocade and are sold by the yard. Campo San Maurizio, San Marco 2666. (*) 041-5222905. Vaporetto: Santa Maria del Giglio.

FASHION

Caberlotto We accidentally stumbled upon Caberlotto, with a stunning collection of classic apparel for both women and men, all in jewel-like colors. Head here to see the rich collection of Loro Piana shawls, cashmere sweaters, scarves, and other apparel. San Salvador, San Marco 5114. (*) 041-5229242. Vaporetto: San Marco.

La Coupole This is a large outlet for a stylish assortment of designers from throughout Europe. The most visible of several members of a citywide chain, it sells women's clothing from designers such as Versace Classic, Gianfranco Ferre, Calvin Klein, Alexander McQueen, and others. Calle Largo XXII Marzo, San Marco 2255. (*) 041-5231273. Vaporetto: San Marco.

FOOD PRODUCTS

Giacomo Rizzo For packaged food products, many from the surrounding Veneto, this is one of our favorite stores in Venice. On a recent visit, we counted 30 different types of pasta alone, with excellent selections in ravioli and tortellini. Sometimes the pasta is imaginatively shaped into Venetian symbols such as Carnevale hats or even a gondola. Flavors include zucchini, spinach, and beet. Other Italian specialties such as balsamic vinegar, all kinds of sauces, and refined olive oils are also sold. The location is northeast of the Rialto Bridge. Cannaregio 5778 (Calle San Giovanni Grisostomo). (*) 041-5222824. Vaporetto: Rialto.

GLASS

Domus On the island of Murano, home of the actual glassworks, Domus offers a good selection of designs by the island's top artisans, such as Carlo Moretti. The shop concentrates on smaller objects like jewelry, vases, bowls, bottles, and drinking glasses. Fondamenta dei Vetrai 82, Murano. (*) 041-739215. Vaporetto: 12 or 13 to Murano.

Galleria Marina Barovier (*)(*) This isn't just another store stocking the Murano-style glass trinkets found by the thousands throughout Venice—it's the repository for some of Italy's most creative modern glass sculptures. Since it was opened in the early 1980s by its namesake,

Marina Barovier, in the unlikely Venetian suburb of Mestre, it has grown in stature. Especially sought after are sculptures by master glassmakers Lino Tagliapietra and Dale Chihuly, whose chandeliers represent amusing and/or dramatic departures from traditional Venetian forms. Don't despair if you're on a budget; some simple items begin as low as 10€ ($16). Anything can be shipped. Salizzada San Samuele, San Marco 3216. ✆ 041-5236748. Vaporetto: San Samuele.

L'Isola   This is the shop of Carlo Moretti, one of the world's best-known contemporary artisans working in glass. You'll find all his signature designs in decanters, drinking glasses, vases, bowls, and paperweights. Campo San Moisè, San Marco 1468. ✆ 041-5231973. Vaporetto: Vallaresso.

Pauly & Co. ★★★   This is one of the oldest (founded in 1866) and largest purveyors of traditional Venetian glass, with a labyrinth of more than two dozen showrooms. Part of the premises is devoted to something akin to a museum, where past successes (now antiques) are displayed with pride. Antique items are only rarely offered for sale, but they can be copied and shipped to virtually anywhere, and chandeliers can be wired to work with the electricity back home. Ponte dei Consorzi, San Marco 4392. ✆ 041-5209899. Vaporetto: San Zaccaria.

Venini ★★★   Venini's art glass has caught the attention of collectors from all over the world. Many of its pieces, including extraordinary lamps, bottles, and vases, are works of art and represent the best of Venetian craftsmanship. Along with the previously recommended Pauly & Co., Venini represents the master craftspeople of Venetian glassmakers. Its best-known glass has a distinctive swirl pattern in several colors, called a *venature*. Venini is also known for the refined quality of its glass, some of which appears almost transparent. Much of it is very fragile, but the shop learned long ago how to ship it anywhere safely. To visit the furnace, call ✆ **041-2737211.** Piazzetta Leoncini, San Marco 314. ✆ 041-5224045. Vaporetto: San Zaccaria.

Vetri d'Arte   Here you can find moderately priced glass jewelry for souvenirs and gifts, as well as a selection of pricier crystal jewelry and porcelain bowls. Piazza San Marco, San Marco 140. ✆ 041-5200205. Vaporetto: Vallaresso.

GRAPHICS

Bac Art Studio   This studio sells paper goods, but it's mainly a graphics gallery, noted for its selection of engravings, posters, and lithographs of Venice at Carnevale time. Items for the most part are reasonably priced; care and selection obviously went into the gallery's choice of merchandise. Campo San Vio Dorsoduro 862. (C) **041-5228171**. Vaporetto: Accademia.

Petra Head here for that just-right, and light, souvenir. Osvaldo Bühm has a rich collection of photographic archives specializing in Venetian art as well as original engravings and maps, lithographs, watercolors, and Venetian masks. You can also see modern serigraphs by local artists and some fine handcrafted bronzes. San Marco 2424. (C) **041-5231815**. Vaporetto: Vallaresso.

HANDICRAFTS

Venetia Though not the friendliest shop in Venice, the small, well-stuffed Venetia is nonetheless a repository of some of the city's best crafts. Much of the merchandise is whimsical and creative, with a wide array of porcelain, Venetian dolls, pictures, frames, puppets, costume jewelry, and even music boxes. This is also one of the best places to find those famous Venetian masks used during Carnevale. Shop carefully, though—prices aren't always to our liking. San Marco 1232. (C) **041-5233851**. Vaporetto: San Marco.

JEWELRY

Artstudio Murano This store specializes in Murano glass jewelry, and does so exceedingly well. Collections include bracelets, earrings, long necklaces, pendant necklaces, and brooches—all made with authentic Murano glass or, in some cases, gold. Fondamenta Cavour 48. (C) **041-5274634**. Vaporetto: Museo.

Codognato For antique jewelry, there's no shop finer than Codognato. Some of the great heirloom jewelry of Europe is sent here when estates are settled. Calle Ascensione, San Marco 1295. (C) **041-5225042**. Vaporetto: San Marco.

Missiaglia ✸✸✸ Since 1846, Missiaglia has been the private supplier to rich Venetians and savvy shoppers from around the world seeking the best in gold and jewelry. Come here for that special classic piece. But, because the family keeps a sharp watch on the latest developments in international jewelry design, something a little more cutting-edge might also catch your eye. The specialty is colored precious and semiprecious gemstones set in white or yellow gold settings. Piazza San Marco, San Marco 125. (C) **041-5224464**. Vaporetto: Vallaresso.

LACE

Jesurum ✸✸✸ For serious purchases, Jesurum is the best place. This elegant shop, a center of noted lace makers and fashion creators, is located in a 12th-century *palazzo* (palace). You'll find Venetian handmade or machine-made lace and embroidery on table, bed, and bath linens, plus hand-printed swimsuits. Quality and originality are guaranteed; special orders are accepted. The exclusive linens are expensive, but the inventory is large enough to accommodate any kind of budget. Staff members insist that everything sold is made in or around Venice in traditional patterns. Cannaregio 3219–3121. ✆ **041-5242540.** Vaporetto: S. Marcuola.

LEATHER

Bottega Veneta Bottega Veneta is primarily known for its woven leather bags. These bags are sold elsewhere, too, but you'll get the best deals here at the company's flagship outlet. The shop also carries shoes for men and women, suitcases, belts, and an array of high-fashion accessories. Calle Vallaresso, San Marco 1337. ✆ **041-5202816.** Vaporetto: Vallaresso.

Furla Furla is a specialist in women's leather bags. Many of the leathers are stamped to look like alligator, lizard, or some other exotic creature. They come in a variety of colors, including what Austrians call "Maria Theresa ochre." Furla also displays a selection of costume jewelry and an array of belts, gloves, silk scarves, briefcases, and wallets. Merceria del Capitello, San Marco 4954. ✆ **041-5230611.** Vaporetto: Rialto.

Vogini Every kind of leather work is offered here, especially women's handbags, which are exclusive models. There are also handbags in petit-point embroideries and crocodile, as well as men's and women's shoes. Brand names include Armani, Moschino, Versace, and products designed and manufactured by Vogini itself. The travel department contains a large assortment of trunks, suitcases, and makeup cases. Calle dell'Ascensione, San Marco 1291, 1292, and 1301 (near Harry's Bar). ✆ **041-5222573.** Vaporetto: Vallaresso.

MARKETS

If you're looking for some bargain-basement buys, head not for any basement but to one of the little shops lining the **Rialto Bridge** (*vaporetto:* Rialto). The shops here branch out to encompass fruit and vegetable markets as well. The Rialto isn't the Ponte Vecchio in Florence, but for what it offers, it isn't bad, particularly if your euros are running short. You'll find a large assortment of merchandise, from angora sweaters to leather gloves. The quality is likely to vary widely, so keep your eyes open.

PAPER & STATIONERY

Florence remains the major center in Italy for artistic paper—especially marbleized paper. However, craftspeople in Venice still make marble paper by hand, sheet by sheet. The technique of marbling paper originated in Japan as early as A.D. 1000, spreading through Persia and finally reaching Europe in the 1400s. Except for France, marbling had largely disappeared with the coming of the Industrial Revolution, but it was revived in Venice in the 1970s. Each sheet of handmade marbleized paper is one of a kind.

Il Papiro ✿✿   If you've never considered paper and stationery a high art form, think again. Thinking of sending off a handwritten proposal of marriage? Pen it on something from Il Papiro, and it will certainly look a lot more impressive. In addition to absolutely gorgeous stationery, you'll find beautiful photo albums, address books, picture frames, diaries, and boxes covered in artfully printed paper. Campo San Maurizio, San Marco 2764. ✆ **041-5223055**. Vaporetto: San Maria del Giglio.

Piazzesi ✿✿✿   Stylish Piazzesi claims to be the oldest purveyor of writing paper in Italy (it opened in 1900). Some of its elegant lines of stationery require as many as 13 artisans to produce. Most of the production here is hand-blocked, marbleized, stenciled, and/or accented with dyes that are blown onto each sheet with a small breath-operated tube. Also look for papier-mâché masks and *commedia dell'arte*–style statues representing age-old professions like architects, carpenters, doctors, glassmakers, church officials, and notaries. We also like the whimsically decorated containers for CDs. Campiello della Feltrina, San Marco 2511. ✆ **041-5221202**. Vaporetto: Santa Maria del Giglio.

WINE

Bottiglieria Colonna   Come here for the best selection of wines from the Veneto, as well as from other winegrowing regions of Italy. Feast your eyes on the array of chianti, Brunelli, Varoli, and other wines. The selection from the north of Italy, obviously, is the strongest. Gift packages of six wines can be made up for you. Castello 5595 (Calle della Fava). ✆ **041-5285137**. Vaporetto: Rialto.

WOOD SCULPTURES

Livio de Marchi   This is a unique outlet in Venice. De Marchi and his staff can take almost any item, from cowboy boots to a Vespa to a woman's handbag, and sculpt it in wood in hyper-real detail. Even if you don't buy anything, just stop in to take a look at these stunning items sculpted from wood. San Samuele, San Marco 3157. ✆ **041-5285694**. Vaporetto: Vallaresso.

9

Venice After Dark

For such a fabled city, Venice's nightlife is pretty meager. Who wants to hit the clubs when strolling the city at night is more interesting than any spectacle staged indoors? Ducking into a cafe or bar for a brief interlude, however, is a nice way to break up your evening walk. Although it offers gambling and a few other diversions, Venice is pretty much an early-to-bed town. Most restaurants close at midnight.

The best guide to what's happening in Venice is *Un Ospite di Venezia,* a free pamphlet (part in English, part in Italian) distributed by the tourist office. It lists musical and theatrical presentations, along with art exhibitions and local special events.

Concerts are staged in at least 10 of Venice's historic churches. These include the Chiesa di Vivaldi, the Chiesa della Pietà, and the Chiesa Santa Maria Formosa. Many concerts are free; others charge an admission that ranges from 15€ to 25€ ($24–$40). For information about what's on, call ② **041-5298711.**

1 The Performing Arts

Teatro Goldoni ⑂ This theater, close to the Ponte di Rialto in the San Marco district, honors Carlo Goldoni (1707–93), the most prolific Italian playwright. The theater stages a changing repertoire of productions, often plays in Italian, and musical presentations as well. The box office is open Monday to Saturday from 10am to 1pm and 4:30 to 7pm. Corte Teatro, San Marco 4650-B. ② **041-2402011.** Vaporetto: Rialto.

Teatro La Fenice ⑂⑂⑂ In 1996, a dramatic fire left the fabled La Fenice, the city's main venue for performing arts, a blackened shell. Opera lovers around the world, including Luciano Pavarotti, mourned its loss. The Italian government pledged $12.5 million for its reconstruction. La Fenice reopened in 2004; the total cost of the restoration came to $90 million.

Tickets can be purchased directly at the theater box office open daily 10am to 6pm; at **Ve.La** box office at Piazzale Roma daily 8:30am to 6:30pm; and at Ferrovia La Scalzi daily 8:30am to 6:30pm. For further information, call Ve.La at ✆ **041-2424.** San Marco 1965, at Campo San Fantin 1965. ✆ **041-786511.** www.teatrolafenice.it. Vaporetto: Santa Maria del Giglio.

2 The Bar Scene

Want more in the way of nightlife? All right, but be warned: The Venetian bar owners may sock it to you when they present the bill.

Bacaro Lounge ✦   The Benetton family has taken a former cinema and hired Piero Lissoni, the Milanese minimalist, to redesign it as a chic lounge. Harry's Bar (see below) may be around the corner, but this place could be in a different city or century—it's a cool, contemporary spot for the fashionistas of Venice. Downstairs is a buzzing cocktail bar. A spectacular glass staircase takes you up to the main dining room, where main courses range from 15€ to 25€ ($24–$40). Bacaro also has a vast bookshop and multimedia center run by Mondadori. The drink of choice is *bucintoro,* a concoction made of crushed strawberries and champagne. Salizzada San Moise, San Marco 1345. ✆ **041-2960687.** Vaporetto: San Marco.

Bar ai Speci   This charming corner bar is only a short walk from St. Mark's. Its dozens of antique mirrors reflect the rows of champagne and Scotch bottles and the clustered groups of Biedermeier chairs. In the Hotel Panada, Calle dei Specchieri, San Marco 646. ✆ **041-5209088.** Vaporetto: Vallaresso.

Bar Ducale   Bar Ducale occupies a tiny corner of a building near a bridge over a narrow canal. Customers stand at the zinc bar facing the carved 19th-century Gothic-reproduction shelves. Mimosas are the specialty here, but tasty sandwiches are also offered. The ebullient owner learned his craft at Harry's Bar before going into business for himself. Today, his small establishment is usually mobbed every day of the week. It's ideal for an early evening cocktail as you stroll about. Calle delle Ostreghe, San Marco 2354. ✆ **041-5210002.** Vaporetto: Vallaresso.

Bar Salus   This is our favorite gathering spot for a hot night in Dorsoduro, Venice's Greenwich Village. Young people, both locals and visitors, predominate. The cafe has more outdoor seating than all its competitors. When the winds blow in from the Adriatic, you can retreat inside to comfortable booths in a spacious bar. Campo Santa Margherita, Dorsoduro 3112. ✆ **041-5285279.** Vaporetto: Academia.

Devil's Forest   Set a stone's throw from the Rialto Bridge, this Irish pub offers a good balance between the English- and Italian-speaking worlds. You'll find a comforting roster of beers and ales on tap here (Guinness, Harp, Kilkenny), along with platters of food that average between 8€ and 13€ ($13–$21). Don't expect bangers and mash—things are more Mediterranean, with an emphasis on sandwiches, pastas, and simple grills. Calle Stagneri, San Marco 5185. ✆ 041-5200623. Vaporetto: Rialto.

Do Leoni The interior is a rich blend of scarlet-and-gold carpeting with a lion motif, English pub–style furniture, and Louis XVI–style chairs. While sipping your cocktail, you'll enjoy a view of a 19th-century bronze statue, the lagoon, and the foot traffic along the Grand Canal. In the Londra Palace Hotel, Riva degli Schiavoni, Castello 4171. ✆ 041-5200533. Vaporetto: San Zaccaria.

Fiddler's Elbow Five minutes from the Rialto Bridge in the Cannaregio district, this Irish-style pub is run by the same people who operate equally popular Fiddler's Elbows in both Florence and Rome. Since its opening in 1992, it has become one of Venice's most popular watering holes, complete with satellite TV. In the summer, there's live outdoor music. Corte dei Pali, Cannaregio 3847. ✆ 041-5239930. Vaporetto: Ca' d'Oro.

Harry's Bar 🎦🎦 The single most famous of all of Hemingway's watering holes, Harry's Bar is known for concocting its own drinks and exporting them around the world. Fans say that Harry's makes the best Bellini (even Hemingway ordered a Bellini here once, though later he called it a drink for sissies and suggested it might be ideal for Fitzgerald). Harry's Bar locations are found everywhere from Munich to Los Angeles, but this is the original. (Except for a restaurant— Harry Cipriani in New York City—the other bars are unauthorized knockoffs.) In Venice, the bar is a local tradition and landmark. Celebrities frequent the place during the various film and art festivals. Calle Vallaresso, San Marco 1323. ✆ 041-5285777. Vaporetto: Vallaresso.

Inguanotto Venice's oldest pastry shop is a gelateria/pasticceria/bar. It's said to have virtually invented the spritzer, a combination of soda water, bitters, and white wine. Its drinks and cocktails are renowned, although enjoying a cappuccino can take the chill off a rainy day. Ponte del Lovo, San Marco 4819. ✆ 041-5208439. Vaporetto: San Marco.

Paradiso Perduto This likable tavern serves well-prepared seafood platters to locals who live close to Venice's train station, far from the congestion around St. Mark's Square. If you're interested in dining (the *frittura mista* of fish, served with polenta, is wonderful), main courses are quite cheap; dinner is served Thursday to Tuesday from 7 to 10:30pm. But the place is at its best after 11pm, when a mixture of soft recorded music and live piano music creates a backdrop for conversation until at least 2am. Fondamenta della Misericordia, Cannaregio 2540. ✆ **041-720581.** Vaporetto: San Marcuola.

3 Wine Bars/Taverns

Cantina do Mori Located at Il Mercato di Rialto, this is one of the most historic taverns of Venice, a tradition since 1462. The cellar stocks some 600 different types of wine, many available by the glass. Tasty food is also served; try the *grissini* (breadsticks) draped with prosciutto or fried dried cod. Delectable little triangular sandwiches—known as *tramezzini*—are a specialty. San Polo 429, Calle del Do Mori. ✆ **041-5225401.** Mon–Sat noon–3pm and 7–10pm. Vaporetto: Rialto.

Mascareta This wine bar, established in 1995, focuses on Italian wines, many from the Veneto region, with affordable vintages available by the glass. There's only room for 20 people, seated at cramped tables, but if you're hungry, you can order simple, cheap platters of snack-style food (prosciutto, cheese plates, and other dishes). Calle Lunga Santa Maria Formosa, Castello 5183. ✆ **041-5230744.** Vaporetto: Rialto.

Fueled by *Cicchetti*

Madrid has its *tasca* hopping, London has its pub-crawling, and Venice has its *cantina* or *cicchetti* crawl. Venetians thrive on small glasses of wine and bar snacks consumed in these little wine bars.

At **Enoteca do Colonne,** Cannaregio 1814C (✆ **041-5240453**), the owners turn out some of the best *tramezzini* (sandwiches) in Venice. Want to go native? Order the surprisingly delicious classic, *museto,* which is delectable until you learn that it is made mostly from the snout of a pig. Another delight is *nerveti,* or boiled veal tendons splashed with vinegar and fresh parsley.

The temperamental Francesco (when he's in a good mood) feeds his faithful habitués at **La Cantina,** Campo San Felice, Cannaregio 3689 (✆ **041-5228258**). Stop by to sample raw fish from the Adriatic, some of the best cured salami in Venice, and yummy cheese. Food critics rave about the crostini, especially tongue piled high under fresh horseradish shavings.

Vino Vino   Vino Vino attracts a varied clientele: It wouldn't be unusual to see a Venetian countess sipping *prosecco* (a type of sparkling wine) near a gondolier eating a meal here. This place is loved by everyone from snobs to young people to almost-broke visitors. It offers more than 350 Italian and imported wines by the bottle or glass. Popular Venetian dishes are also served, including pastas, beans, *baccalà* (codfish), and polenta. The two rooms are always jammed like a *vaporetto* (public motorboat) at rush hour, but there's takeout service if you can't find a table. Ponte della Veste, San Marco 2007/A. ℰ **041-2417688.** Vaporetto: Vallaresso.

4 The Cafe Scene

All of the cafes on Piazza San Marco offer a simply magical setting, several with full orchestras playing in the background. But you'll pay shockingly high prices (plus a hefty music charge) to enjoy a drink or a snack while you soak in this setting. Prepare yourself for it, and splurge on a beer, a cappuccino, or an ice cream anyway. It'll be the most memorable 15€ to 20€ ($24–$32)—yep, that's *per person*—you'll drop on your trip.

Caffè Chioggia   Chioggia has been flourishing here since the 1930s. Although it isn't the only cafe whose entrance opens onto the Piazza San Marco, it's the only one with a view of the Venetian lagoon (off to one side), and the only one offering live music that continues in one form or another throughout the day and evening. Starting around 8am and continuing, with reasonable breaks, until 1:30am, piano-bar music might begin the day, eventually terminating with a jazz trio. Light platters and sandwiches are served. Piazza San Marco, San Marco 8–11. ℰ **041-5285011.** Vaporetto: Vallaresso.

Caffè Florian 😸😸😸   This is Venice's most famous cafe. The Florian was built in 1720, and it remains romantic and elegant—a Venetian salon with plush red banquettes, intricate murals, and Art Nouveau lighting. It has hosted everyone from Casanova and Lord Byron to Goethe. You can even get an English tea from 3 to 6pm, with a selection of pastries, ice cream, and cakes. Piazza San Marco, San Marco 56–59. ℰ **041-5205641.** Vaporetto: Vallaresso.

Cips 😸 *(Finds)*   The hippest cafe in Venice today is funky little Cips, on Isola della Giudecca, run by the owners of Harry's Bar and the Cipriani hotel. Pronounced "chips" (as in potato), this cafe with its summer terrace frames one of the grandest views of Piazza San Marco. If you arrive between May and August, ask for a Bellini, made from *prosecco* and white-peach purée, or perhaps a Rossini, made from fresh strawberry juice and *prosecco*. Cips also serves terrific international and Venetian dishes, including the best bitter-chocolate gelato in town. In the Hotel Cipriani, Isola della Giudecca 10. (©) 041-5207744. Vaporetto: Zitelle.

Gran Caffè Lavena   This popular but intimate cafe under the arcades of Piazza San Marco was frequented by Wagner when he stayed in Venice. It has some of the most beautiful glass chandeliers in the city. The most interesting tables are near the window in front, though there's plenty of room at the stand-up bar as well. Piazza San Marco, San Marco 133–134. (©) 041-5224070. Vaporetto: Vallaresso.

Quadri 🏵🏵🏵   Quadri stands on the opposite side of the square from the Florian. It, too, is elegantly decorated in antique style. It should be—it was founded in 1638. Wagner used to drop in for a drink when he was in Venice working on *Tristan and Isolde*. Its prices are virtually the same as at the Florian, and it, too, imposes a surcharge on drinks ordered during concert periods. The bar was a favorite with the Austrians during their long-ago occupation (Venetian patriots went to Florian). Closed on Monday from November to March. Piazza San Marco, San Marco 120–124. (©) 041-5289299. Vaporetto: Vallaresso.

5 Nighttime Ice Cream & Pastries

Gelateria Paolin   For lots of visitors, strolling to the Gelateria Paolin and ordering some of the tastiest gelato in Venice is nightlife enough. That's the way many a Venetian spends a summer evening. This gelateria has stood on the corner of this busy, colorful square since the 1930s, making it the oldest ice-cream parlor in Venice. You can order your ice cream to eat at one of the sidewalk tables (which costs more) or get it to go. Many interesting flavors are offered; your best bet is one of the ice creams made with fresh fruit from the Veneto. Campo San Stefano, San Marco 2962A. (©) 041-5225576. Vaporetto: Santa Maria del Giglio.

Pasticceria Marchini   If you'd like to escape the throngs of visitors that overrun Venice in the early evening, head here, have a pastry and a coffee, and contemplate your plans for the night. This is where your Venetian friend (if you had one) would take you for the most delectable pastries served in the city. The small pastries are made according to old recipes—ask for the *bigna* or *cannolo*. Campo San Maurizio, San Marco 2769. (©) 041-5229109. Vaporetto: Accademia.

6 Casinos

Venice is home to two casinos. Regardless of where you happen to drop your euros, know that shorts and sneakers are forbidden. You must be at least 18 to enter. Both casinos offer slot machines, but more interesting are the roulette wheels, where minimum bets are 5€ ($8) and maximum wagers 200€ ($320).

Ca'Noghera ⟡ is the first American-style casino to open in the north of Italy, lying on the mainland opposite the Marco Polo airport. The casino, Vendramin-Calergi, is a glorious antique; in contrast Ca'Noghera is as modern as the 21st century. Expect the standard games of chance such as roulette, blackjack, and Caribbean-style poker, but also the latest electronic games. The Theater Arena hosts concerts, shows, and fashionable catwalks, and a restaurant serves first-class international specialties. The casino is open Sunday to Thursday 11am to 2:30am and Friday and Saturday 11am to 3am. A free shuttle service runs from the Piazzale Roma during casino hours. Dress here is informal. Via Paliaga 4-8. ℂ 041-2695888. Cover 10€ ($16). Vaporetto: Piazzale Roma.

Vendramin-Calergi Palace ⟡⟡ is Italy's most elegant casino. A frequent visitor, Gabriele D'Annunzio, called it "a sculpted cloud resting on water." Historically, the Renaissance *palazzo* (palace) was once a home to the doges and later a town mansion where Richard Wagner died in 1883. Opening onto the Grand Canal, the casino offers French roulette, blackjack, Caribbean poker, and chemin de fer. Gala dinners and even classical music concerts are occasionally offered in the garden in summer. Men must wear a jacket (available for rent on site). Hours are Sunday to Thursday 2:45pm to 2:30am, Friday and Saturday 2:45pm to 3am. A free shuttle from Piazzale Roma runs every 10 minutes during opening hours. Cannaregio 2040. ℂ 041-5297111. Cover 10€ ($16). Vaporetto: San Marcuolo.

7 A Dance Club

Il Piccolo Mondo   This pub, near the Accademia, is open during the day, but it comes alive with dance music and young crowds at night. It's open Thursday to Tuesday 10pm to 4am, but the action doesn't usually begin until after midnight. Calle Contarini Corfu 1056A. ℂ 041-5200371. Cover (including the 1st drink) 8€ ($13) Thurs–Fri, 10€ ($16) Sat; otherwise free. Vaporetto: Accademia.

8 Gay Clubs

Venice has little in the way of gay nightlife. A local count, a distinguished member of the Venetian homosexual community, said, "All bars in Venice are gay if you look in the right corner." There is one exception: **Bar Aurora,** Piazza San Marco 48 (℃ **041-52864050**), which has gay night 1 night every week, perhaps Thursday or Friday (call to confirm this). This small, cozy lounge bar has a view of St. Mark's. There is no cover charge, although occasional live music is presented. On any night of the week, we'd call it gay friendly. Attracting a crowd aged 18 to 40, it is open Wednesday to Sunday 8:30pm to 2am. Closed November 12 to November 30.

Appendix: Venice Fast Facts

AMERICAN EXPRESS The office is at Salizzada San Moisè, San Marco 1471 (© 041-5200844; *vaporetto:* San Marco). The staff can arrange city tours and mail handling. Hours are Monday to Friday 9am to 5:30pm, Saturday 9am to 12:30pm.

AREA CODES Dial **011** and then the country code for Italy **(39).** You then dial the area code for Venice **(041),** followed by the local number you want.

BABYSITTERS In lieu of a central booking agency, arrangements have to be made individually at various hotels. Obviously, the more advance notice you give, the better your chances of getting an English-speaking sitter.

BUSINESS HOURS Regular business hours for offices and shops are generally Monday to Friday 9am to 1pm and 3:30 to 7 or 7:30pm. From July to September, offices may not open in the afternoon until 4 or 4:30pm. Banks in Venice are open Monday to Friday 8:30am to 1:30 or 2pm, and then 3 to 4pm; they're closed all day Saturday, Sunday, and national holidays.

CONSULATES The **U.K. Consulate** is at Piazzale Donatori di Sangune 2, 30171 Venice-Mestre (© **041-5055990**).

The **United States, Canada,** and **Australia** have consulates in Milan, about 3 hours away by train. The U.S. Consulate is at Via Principe Amedeo 2-10, Milan (© **02-290351**). The Canadian Consulate is at Via Vittorio Pisani 19, Milan (© **02-67-581**). And the Australian Consulate is at Via Borgogna 2, Milan (© **02-777-04227**). Call ahead to confirm business hours before making the trip, as all of these consular offices tend to keep odd hours that frequently change.

CURRENCY EXCHANGE There are many banks in Venice where you can exchange money. You might try the **Banca Commerciale Italiana,** Via XXII Marzo, San Marco 2188 (© **041-5296811**; *vaporetto:* San Marco), or **Banco San Marco,** Calle Larga San Marco, San Marco 383 (© **041-5293711**; *vaporetto:* San Marco).

DENTISTS & DOCTORS Your best bet is to have your hotel set up an appointment with an English-speaking dentist or doctor. The American Express office and the British Consulate have lists as well. Also see "Hospitals," below.

DRINKING LAWS The legal drinking age in Italy is 16. In Venice with its canals, driving and drinking is rarely a problem unless you're piloting your own boat.

DRUG LAWS Penalties for violations are severe and could lead to either imprisonment or deportation. Selling drugs to minors is dealt with particularly harshly.

DRUGSTORES If you need a drugstore in the middle of the night, call ⓒ **192** for information on which one is open (pharmacies take turns staying open late). A well-recommended central one is **International Pharmacy,** Via XXII Marzo, San Marco 2067 (ⓒ **041-5222311;** *vaporetto:* San Marco).

ELECTRICITY The electricity in Italy varies considerably. It's usually alternating current (AC), varying from 42 to 50 cycles. The voltage can be anywhere from 115 to 220. Check the exact local current at the hotel where you're staying. We recommend getting a transformer if you're traveling with electrical appliances or gadgets. Note that plugs have prongs that are round, not flat; therefore, an adapter is also needed.

EMERGENCIES Call ⓒ **113** for the police, ⓒ **118** for an ambulance, or ⓒ **115** to report a fire.

HOLIDAYS Offices and shops in Italy are closed on January 1 (New Year's Day), Easter Monday, April 25 (Liberation Day), May 1 (Labor Day), August 15 (Assumption of the Virgin), November 1 (All Saints' Day), December 8 (Feast of the Immaculate Conception), December 25 (Christmas Day), and December 26 (Santo Stefano). Closings are also observed in Venice on April 25, the feast day honoring St. Mark, the city's patron.

HOSPITALS The **Ospedale Campo Santi Giovanni e Paolo,** Campo Santi Giovanni e Paolo in Castello (ⓒ **041-5294111;** *vaporetto:* San Toma), is staffed with English-speaking doctors 24 hours a day.

INSURANCE When traveling, any number of things could go wrong—lost luggage, trip cancellation, a medical emergency—so consider the following types of insurance.

Check your existing insurance policies and credit card coverage before you buy travel insurance. You may already be covered for lost luggage, canceled tickets, or medical expenses. The cost of travel insurance varies widely, depending on the cost and length of your trip, your age and health, and the type of trip you're taking, but expect to pay between 5% and 8% of the vacation itself. You can get estimates from various providers through **InsureMyTrip.com**. Enter your trip cost and dates, your age, and other information for prices from more than a dozen companies.

Medical Insurance   For travel overseas, most health plans (including Medicare and Medicaid) do not provide coverage, and the ones that do often require you to pay for services upfront and reimburse you only after you return home. Even if your plan does cover overseas treatment, most out-of-country hospitals make you pay your bills upfront, and send you a refund only after you've returned home and filed the necessary paperwork with your insurance company. As a safety net, you may want to buy travel medical insurance, particularly if you're traveling to a remote or high-risk area where emergency evacuation is a possible scenario. If you require additional medical insurance, try **MEDEX Assistance** (© 410/453-6300; www.medex assist.com) or **Travel Assistance International** (© 800/821-2828; www.travelassistance.com). For general information on services, call the company's **Worldwide Assistance Services, Inc.** (© 800/777-8710; www.worldwideassistance.com).

Lost Luggage Insurance   On international flights (including U.S. portions of international trips), baggage coverage is limited to approximately $9.07 per pound, up to approximately $635 per checked bag. If you plan to check items more valuable than the standard liability, see if your valuables are covered by your homeowner's policy and get baggage insurance as part of your comprehensive travel-insurance package. Don't buy insurance at the airport, as it's usually overpriced. Be sure to take any valuables or irreplaceable items with you in your carry-on luggage, as many valuables (including books, money, and electronics) aren't covered by airline policies.

If your luggage is lost, immediately file a lost-luggage claim at the airport, detailing the luggage contents. For most airlines, you must report delayed, damaged, or lost baggage within 4 hours of arrival. The airlines are required to deliver luggage, once found, directly to your house or destination free.

Trip Cancellation Insurance   Trip-cancellation insurance helps you get your money back if you have to back out of a trip, if you have to go home early, or if your travel supplier goes bankrupt. Allowed reasons for cancellation can range from sickness to natural disasters to the State Department declaring your destination unsafe for travel. For information, contact one of the following recommended insurers: **Access America** (© **800/284-8300;** www.access america.com), **AIG Travel Guard International** (© **800/826-4919;** www.travelguard.com), **Travel Insured International** (© **800/243-3174;** www.travelinsured.com), and **Travelex Insurance Services** (© **800/228-9792;** www.travelex-insurance.com).

INTERNET ACCESS It's hard nowadays to find a city that *doesn't* have a few cybercafes. Although there's no definitive directory for cybercafes—these are independent businesses, after all—two places to start looking are at **www.cybercaptive.com** and **www.cybercafe.com**. In Venice you can try such central locales as **Internet Point San Stefano,** Campo San Stefano, San Marco 2967 (© **041-8946122**), which costs 9€ ($14) per hour. Open daily 10:15am to 11pm.

LANGUAGE Italian, of course, is the official language of the land, but English is generally understood at most attractions such as museums and at most hotels and restaurants that cater to visitors. Even if few staff members at a restaurant, for example, speak English, one person almost always does and can be summoned.

LEGAL AID The consulate of your country is the place to turn for legal aid, although offices can't interfere in the Italian legal process. They can, however, inform you of your rights and provide a list of attorneys. You'll have to pay for the attorney out of your pocket—there's no free legal assistance. If you're arrested for a drug offense, about all the consulate will do is notify a lawyer about your case and perhaps inform your family.

LOST & FOUND Alert your credit card companies the minute you discover your wallet has been lost or stolen and file a report at the nearest police precinct. Your credit card company or insurer may require a police report number or record of the loss. Most credit card companies have an emergency toll-free number to call if your card is lot or stolen; they may be able to wire you a cash advance immediately or deliver an emergency credit card in a day or two. If you have lost your card, use the following numbers: **Visa** (© **800/819-014**); **Master Card** (© **800/870-866**); **Amex** (© **06-7228-0848**).

If you've lost all forms of photo ID, call your airline and explain; they might allow you to board the plane if you have a copy of your passport or birth certificate and a copy of the police report you've ed.

If you need emergency cash over the weekend when all banks and American Express offices are closed, you can have money wired to you via **Western Union** (© 800/325-6000; www.westernunion.com).

LUGGAGE STORAGE & LOCKERS   These services are available at the main rail station, **Stazione di Santa Lucia,** at Piazzale Roma (© 848-888088). The cost is 3.80€ ($6.10) for the first 5 hours and .60€ (95¢) per hour thereafter.

MAIL   Mail delivery in Italy is notoriously bad. Your family and friends back home might receive your postcards in 1 week, or it might take 2 weeks (or longer). Postcards, aerogrammes, and letters weighing up to 20 grams sent to the United States and Canada cost .85€ ($1.35); to the United Kingdom and Ireland, .65€ ($1.05); and to Australia and New Zealand, 1.05€ ($1.70). You can buy stamps at all post offices and at *tabacchi* (tobacco) stores.

MEASUREMENTS   See www.onlineconversion.com for details on converting metric measurements to nonmetric equivalents.

NEWSPAPERS & MAGAZINES   In major cities, it's possible to find the *International Herald Tribune* or *USA Today,* as well as other English-language newspapers and magazines, including *Time* and *Newsweek,* at hotels and news kiosks.

PASSPORTS   Allow plenty of time before your trip to apply for a passport; processing normally takes 3 weeks but can take longer during busy periods (especially spring). And keep in mind that if you need a passport in a hurry, you'll pay a higher processing fee.

For residents of Australia: You can pick up an application from your local post office or any branch of Passports Australia, but you must schedule an interview at the passport office to present your application materials. Call the **Australian Passport Information Service** at © 131-232, or visit the government website at www. passports.gov.au.

For residents of Canada: Passport applications are available at travel agencies throughout Canada or from the central **Passport Office,** Department of Foreign Affairs and International Trade, Gatineau, QC K1A 0G3 (© 800/567-6868; www.ppt.gc.ca).

For residents of Ireland: You can apply for a 10-year passport at the **Passport Office,** Setanta Centre, Molesworth Street, Dublin 2 (© 01/671-1633; www.irlgov.ie/iveagh). You can also apply at 1A South Mall, Cork (© 021/484-4700) or at most main post offices.

For residents of New Zealand: You can pick up a passport application at any New Zealand Passports Office or download it from the website. Contact the **Passports Office** (© **0800/225-050** in New Zealand or 04/474-8100, or log on to www.passports.govt.nz).

For residents of the United Kingdom: To pick up an application for a standard 10-year passport (5-year passport for children 15 and under), visit your nearest passport office, major post office, or travel agency, or contact the **United Kingdom Passport Service** (© **0870/521-0410** or search its website at www.ukpa.gov.uk).

For residents of the United States: Whether you're applying in person or by mail, you can download passport applications from the U.S. State Department website at **http://travel.state.gov**. To find your regional passport office, either check the U.S. State Department website or call the **National Passport Information Center** toll-free number (© **877/487-2778**) for automated information.

For Children: To obtain a passport, the child **must** be present, in person, with both parents at the place of issuance, *or* a notarized statement from the parents is required. Any questions parents or guardians have can be answered by calling the **National Passport Information Center** (© **877/487-2778**) Monday to Friday 8am to 8pm Eastern Standard Time.

If your passport is lost or stolen, go to your consulate as soon as possible for a replacement. See "Consulates," above.

POLICE   Dial © **133** for police emergency assistance in Italy.

POST OFFICE   The **main post office** is at Salizada Fondaco dei Tedeschi, San Marco 5554 (© **041-2717111**; *vaporetto:* Rialto), near the Rialto Bridge. It's open Monday to Saturday 8:15am to 6pm.

SAFETY   Violent crime is rare. But because of the overcrowding in *vaporetti* and even on the small narrow streets, it's easy to pick pockets. Purse snatchers are commonplace as well. Keep valuables locked in your hotel safe if one is provided.

TAXES   As a member of the European Union, Italy imposes a value-added tax (called IVA in Italy) on most goods and services. The tax that most affects visitors is the one imposed on hotel rates, which ranges from 10% in first- and second-class hotels to 19% in deluxe hotels.

Non-E.U. (European Union) citizens are entitled to a refund of the IVA if they spend more than 155€ ($248) at any one store, before tax. To claim your refund, request an invoice from the cashier at the store and take it to the Customs office *(dogana)* at the airport to have it stamped before leave. ***Note:*** If you're going to another E.U. country before flying home, have it stamped at the airport Customs office of the last E.U. country you'll be in (for example, if you're flying home via Britain, have your Italian invoices stamped in London). Once back home, mail the stamped invoice (keep a photocopy for your records) back to the original vendor within 90 days of the purchase. Reputable stores view this as a matter of ordinary paperwork and are businesslike about it. Less-honorable stores might lose your dossier. It pays to deal with established vendors on large purchases. You can also request that the refund be credited to the credit card with which you made the purchase; this is usually a faster procedure.

Many shops are now part of the "Tax Free for Tourists" network (look for the sticker in the window). Stores participating in this network issue a check along with your invoice at the time of purchase. After you have the invoice stamped at Customs, you can redeem the check for cash directly at the Tax Free booth in the airport (in Rome, it's past Customs; in Milan's airports, the booth is inside the duty-free shop) or mail it back in the envelope provided within 60 days.

TELEPHONE   A **local phone call** in Italy costs around .20€ (30¢). **Public phones** accept coins, precharged phone cards (*scheda* or *carta telefonica*), or both. You can buy a phone card at any *tabacchi* in increments of 2.50€ to 7.50€ ($4–$12). To make a call, pick up the receiver and insert .50€ (80¢) or your card (break off the corner first). Dial the number, and don't forget to take the card with you after you hang up. *Note:* Numbers in Italy range from four to eight digits in length. Even when you're calling within the same city, you must dial that city's area code—including the zero.

To call **from one city code to another,** dial the city code, complete with initial zero, and then the local number. To **dial direct internationally,** dial **00,** then the country code, the area code, and the local number. **Country codes** are as follows: the U.S. and Canada 1, the United Kingdom 44, Ireland 353, Australia 61, and New Zealand 64. Make international calls from a public phone if possible, as hotels almost invariably charge ridiculously inflated rates for direct dial—but bring plenty of *schede* (phone cards) to feed the phone. Direct-dial calls from the U.S. to Italy are much cheaper, so arrange for your friends or family to call you at your hotel, if possible.

International phone cards for calling overseas come in increments of 1€ to 7.50€ ($1.60–$12), and they're usually available at *tabacchi* and bars. Each *unita* is worth .10€ (15¢) of phone time; it costs 5 unita per minute to call within Europe or to the U.S. or Canada and 12 unita per minute to call Australia or New Zealand. You don't insert this card into the phone; merely dial **1740,** then *2 (star 2) for instructions in English when prompted.

To call toll-free **national telephone information** (in Italian), dial **12. International information** is also available, by dialing **176,** but costs .60€ (95¢) a shot.

To make **collect** or **calling-card calls,** drop in .10€ (15¢) or insert your card, dial one of the numbers below, and an American operator will shortly come on to assist you (as Italy has yet to discover the joys of the touch-tone phone, you'll have to wait for the operator to come on). The following calling card numbers work all over Italy: **AT&T** (© **172-1011**), **MCI** (© **172-1022**), and **Sprint** (© **172-1877**). To make collect calls to a country besides the United States, dial **170** (a free call) and practice your Italian counting in order to relay the number to the Italian operator. Tell him or her you want it *a crico del destinatario.*

Don't count on all Italian phones having touch-tone service! You may not be able to access your voice mail or answering machine if you call home from Italy.

TIME   Italy is 6 hours ahead of Eastern Standard Time in the U.S. Daylight saving time goes into effect in Italy from the end of March to the end of September.

TIPPING   In **hotels,** a service charge of 15% to 19% is already added to the bill. It's customary to tip the chambermaid .50€ (80¢) per day and the bellhop or porter 1.50€ to 2.50€ ($2.40–$4) for carrying your bags to your room. A concierge expects tips for extra services performed, such as procuring hard-to-find tickets.

In **restaurants** and **cafes,** 15% is usually added to your bill to cover most charges. If you're not sure whether this has been done, ask "*E incluso il servizio?*" (ay een-*cloo*-soh eel sair-*vee*-tsoh?). An additional tip isn't expected, but leave the equivalent of an extra couple of dollars if you're pleased with the service. Checkroom attendants expect .75€ ($1.20); washroom attendants should get .25€ to .35€ (40¢–55¢). *Note:* Restaurants are required by law to give customers official receipts.

TOILETS   These are available at Piazzale Roma and various other places, but aren't as plentiful as they should be. A truly spotless one is at the foot of the Accademia Bridge. Often you'll have to rely on the restrooms in cafes, though you should buy something, perhaps a coffee, as the toilets are for customers only. Most museums and galleries have public toilets. You can also use the public toilets at the Albergo Diumo, Via Ascensione, just behind Piazza San Marco. Remember, *signori* means men and *signore,* women.

Index

See also Accommodations and Restaurant indexes below.

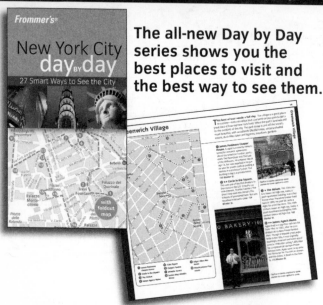

FROMMER'S® COMPLETE TRAVEL GUIDES

FROMMER'S® DAY BY DAY GUIDES

PAULINE FROMMER'S GUIDES: SEE MORE. SPEND LESS.

FROMMER'S® PORTABLE GUIDES

Acapulco, Ixtapa & Zihuatanejo
Amsterdam
Aruba, Bonaire & Curacao
Australia's Great Barrier Reef
Bahamas
Big Island of Hawaii
Boston
California Wine Country
Cancún
Cayman Islands
Charleston
Chicago
Dominican Republic

Florence
Las Vegas
Las Vegas for Non-Gamblers
London
Maui
Nantucket & Martha's Vineyard
New Orleans
New York City
Paris
Portland
Puerto Rico
Puerto Vallarta, Manzanillo &
    Guadalajara

Rio de Janeiro
San Diego
San Francisco
Savannah
St. Martin, Sint Maarten, Anguila &
    St. Bart's
Turks & Caicos
Vancouver
Venice
Virgin Islands
Washington, D.C.
Whistler

FROMMER'S® CRUISE GUIDES

Alaska Cruises & Ports of Call

Cruises & Ports of Call

European Cruises & Ports of Call

FROMMER'S® NATIONAL PARK GUIDES

Algonquin Provincial Park
Banff & Jasper
Grand Canyon

National Parks of the American West
Rocky Mountain
Yellowstone & Grand Teton

Yosemite and Sequoia & Kings
    Canyon
Zion & Bryce Canyon

FROMMER'S® WITH KIDS GUIDES

Chicago
Hawaii
Las Vegas
London

National Parks
New York City
San Francisco

Toronto
Walt Disney World® & Orlando
Washington, D.C.

FROMMER'S® PHRASEFINDER DICTIONARY GUIDES

Chinese
French

German
Italian

Japanese
Spanish

SUZY GERSHMAN'S BORN TO SHOP GUIDES

France
Hong Kong, Shanghai & Beijing
Italy

London
New York
Paris

San Francisco
Where to Buy the Best of Everything.

FROMMER'S® BEST-LOVED DRIVING TOURS

Britain
California
France
Germany

Ireland
Italy
New England
Northern Italy

Scotland
Spain
Tuscany & Umbria

THE UNOFFICIAL GUIDES®

Adventure Travel in Alaska
Beyond Disney
California with Kids
Central Italy
Chicago
Cruises
Disneyland®
England
Hawaii

Ireland
Las Vegas
London
Maui
Mexico's Best Beach Resorts
Mini Mickey
New Orleans
New York City
Paris

San Francisco
South Florida including Miami &
    the Keys
Walt Disney World®
Walt Disney World® for
    Grown-ups
Walt Disney World® with Kids
Washington, D.C.

SPECIAL-INTEREST TITLES

Athens Past & Present
Best Places to Raise Your Family
Cities Ranked & Rated
500 Places to Take Your Kids Before They Grow Up
Frommer's Best Day Trips from London
Frommer's Best RV & Tent Campgrounds in the U.S.A.

Frommer's Exploring America by RV
Frommer's NYC Free & Dirt Cheap
Frommer's Road Atlas Europe
Frommer's Road Atlas Ireland
Retirement Places Rated